# Solitude

John B. Hough

**Hamilton Books**
A member of
The Rowman & Littlefield Publishing Group
*Lanham • Boulder • New York • Toronto • Plymouth, UK*

Copyright © 2007 by
Hamilton Books
4501 Forbes Boulevard
Suite 200
Lanham, Maryland 20706
Hamilton Books Acquisitions Department (301) 459-3366

Estover Road
Plymouth PL6 7PY
United Kingdom

All rights reserved
Printed in the United States of America
British Library Cataloging in Publication Information Available

Library of Congress Control Number: 2007921286
ISBN-13: 978-0-7618-3720-6 (paperback : alk. paper)
ISBN-10: 0-7618-3720-5 (paperback : alk. paper)

∞™ The paper used in this publication meets the minimum
requirements of American National Standard for Information
Sciences—Permanence of Paper for Printed Library Materials,
ANSI Z39.48—1992

To Olga
My wife of fifty-five years
who, more than any one else,
has convinced me that love is possible.

# Contents

| | |
|---|---|
| Preface | vii |
| Acknowledgments | ix |
| Prologue | 1 |

**Part One**  The Novice Years

| | | |
|---|---|---|
| 1 | The Journey Begins | 9 |
| 2 | Hope and Despair | 35 |
| 3 | Lost in Dreams in the Present | 56 |

**Part Two**  Temporary Commitments

| | | |
|---|---|---|
| 4 | Turning Point | 75 |
| 5 | Contemplative Revelations | 91 |
| 6 | Beliefs in Transition | 110 |
| 7 | Community Ministry | 132 |

**Part Three**  Life Commitment

| | | |
|---|---|---|
| 8 | Thirsting for Solitude | 153 |
| 9 | Solitude at Last | 170 |
| 10 | Commitment | 191 |

| | |
|---|---|
| Epilogue | 209 |
| Sources Referenced | 211 |

# Preface

Would you pass up a seven-day trip with friends to tour Las Vegas casinos, nightclubs, and, of course, hotel shows, and instead take a one-week self-directed tour of English cathedrals and gardens alone or with a friend? If you would, then you may be one of those people for whom *Solitude* was written. If you were once told that you have an Enneagram Five or a Myers Briggs Introverted—Intuitional—Thinking personality type, then there's a fair chance that you will find *Solitude* enjoyable reading. If, in addition, you like thinking about matters of spirituality, religion and faith, then there is an excellent chance that you will want to read this book. Should you also happen to be one of those people who for some time has wanted to go on a spiritual quest or is already on one, then *Solitude* may already be on your bedside table.

If the profile I just described fits you, then you are more than likely already a member of a fairly small, loosely knit community of several million people who stretch around the world, who may or may not attend religious devotions on a regular basis and who are known as spiritual seekers.

Although a member of this unique community for some years, I have not always been able to find other seekers when I needed them. There were probably other members of that community near by but they seldom wore yellow tee shirts that advertised who they were. In fact, I have found that people who wear such tee shirts seldom are seekers; usually they have already found what they are looking for. In any event, I have been aware for sometime that spiritual companionship is not always that easy to find. It was this awareness along with the encouragement of my wife and daughter that finally convinced me to write *Solitude* and thus create an additional channel of communication among members of the community of spiritual seekers, even if it is at a distance, through the medium of a book.

One consequence of writing *Solitude* was that it required that I go public about aspects of my spiritual journey including parts that some may consider to be inappropriate for me to have revealed. I take no satisfaction in offending people, and hope I have not done so, but I could not have been frank and honest about my journey, my feelings, my values, and my beliefs without some of those personal revelations.

Writing a book can be a very humbling experience, and writing and getting *Solitude* published was no exception in my case. I quickly realized how many people during my life have had a marked influence on me, and how many of those people have been particularly influential during my spiritual quest. Some of these people have died and others have dropped off my radar screen, but I still remember them and I appreciate having known them. This is not to say that I have always had a completely harmonious relationship with all of them. In some cases we have had our moments of disagreement or even friction, but as I look back on the moments in which our lives crossed, I can easily say that I recognize and cherish their contribution to my spiritual life. In all cases I am a richer person for having known them. So, if you happen to recognize yourself in this book please be assured that I appreciate the part you have played.

Our move to solitude was greatly facilitated by our son-in-law Graham and his family who so unselfishly provided a place on their property for us to build our cabin. I appreciate Pam and Graham's untiring efforts to work with the builder to get the cabin constructed. They made that part of the process a lot easier, especially considering that otherwise, I would have tried to do it at a distance of over two hundred miles. Once the cabin was built and we moved in, their warm welcome continued and we became a real expression of community. Pam and Graham along with their children Kate, Thomas and Austin have renewed my hope for that time when communities of love will become the norm, and they did this even while they gave Olga and me free reign to pursue our life of solitude.

In the lives of most people who create something, a book in my case, there are usually a few who stand out as having played a special role beyond all others. In my case there were five: Susan, my first spiritual director, who taught me about faith when I had all but lost mine; Pam, my daughter, and her daughter Kate, who have, over the years convinced me that hope for the future is fully warranted; Olga, my wife, who taught me about love and to whom this book is dedicated; and Thomas Merton, who, though I never met him in person, has been for twenty years a constant companion and inspiration.

As is always the case, there are those who, in the creation of something, take the idea through to concrete realization. For this my thanks go to Johnny Dowell who took my handwritten scribble and turned it into the first draft of a manuscript, Bryan who took the manuscript and reformatted it electronically for submission and, of course, Patti Belcher, my editor who along with those in production and marketing have so skillfully guided *Solitude* to completion.

# Acknowledgments

Books and articles cited or quoted in the text under the usual doctrine of fair use are acknowledged in the notes or references cited.

Excerpts from other sources are reprinted with grateful acknowledgement by permission of the following institutions:

Excerpt from p. 34 from A TESTAMENT OF DEVOTION by THOMAS R. KELLY, Copyright © by Harper and Row Publishers, Inc. Renewed 1969 by Louis Lael Kelly Stabler, New introduction Copyright © 1992 by HarperCollins Publisher. Excerpt from pp. 104-105 from THE OTHER SIDE OF THE MOUNTAIN: THE JOURNALS OF THOMAS MERTON, VOLUME SEVEN 1967–1968 by THOMAS MERTON and EDITED BY PATRICK HART, Copyright © 1998 by The Merton Legacy Trust, by permission of HarperCollins Publishers. Excerpts from pp. 197, 218, 291, 321, 327, as submitted from TURNING TOWARD THE WORLD: THE JOURNALS OF THOMAS MERTON, VOLUME FOUR 1960–1963 by THOMAS MERTON and EDITED BY VICTOR A. KRAMER, Copyright ©1996 by The Merton Legacy Trust, by permission of HarperCollins Publishers.

Excerpt from "Chapter 25: Humility Against Despair" by Thomas Merton from NEW SEEDS OF CONTEMPLATION, Copyright © 1961 by The Abbey of Gethsemani, Inc. by permission of New Directions Corp. Excerpt from "Appendix VII, Marxism and Monastic Perspectives" by Thomas Merton, from THE ASIAN JOURNALS OF THOMAS MERTON, Copyright © 1975 by the Trustees of The Merton Legacy Trust, by permission of New Directions Publishing Corp. Excerpt from "Transcendent Experiences" by Thomas Merton, from ZEN AND THE BIRDS OF APPETITE, Copyright © 1968 by The Abbey of Gethsemani, Inc. by permission of New Directions Publishing Corp.

Excerpts from *Catherine of Siena: The Dialogue*, from Classics of Western Spirituality, Translation and Introduction by Suzanne Noffke, O.P., Copyright © 1980 by Paulist Press, Inc., New York/Mahwah, N.J.

Grateful acknowledgement is made to Bear & Co., a division of Inner Traditions, Rochester, Vt. for permission to quote from Blanche Marie Gallagher, MEDITATIONS WITH TEILHARD de CHARDIN, Copyright © 1988 by Blanche Marie Gallagher.

Excerpts from *Behold the Beauty of the Lord,* by Henri J. M. Nouwen. Copyright © 1987 by Ave Maria Press, P.O. Box 428 Notre Dame, Indiana, 46556, www.avemariapress.com.

Excerpts from p. 61 of Julian of Norwich, A LESSON OF LOVE: THE REVELATOINS OF JULIAN OF NORWICH. John-Julian, ed. and trans., Translation Copyright © 1988 by the Order of Julian of Norwich, The Walker Publishing Co.

# Prologue

Depending on who you were at the time, it was likely to have been either a time of anxiety or a time of cautious hope. Frankly, I wasn't sure what to make of it. But then what should I make of a time in which the past no longer predicted the future, leaving it to uncertain speculation, and the present had only that meaning that I gave to it? The year was 1968. In less than twelve months three bright lights that might have illuminated the path into the future were extinguished. Martin Luther King Jr. and Robert Kennedy were assassinated and Thomas Merton died an untimely, accidental death while on a trip to Asia to further open the windows of tolerance, both within the church and between the major religions of the world. The specter of an atomic cloud still hung over our heads. There was unrest in the cities. The United States was involved in a war in Viet Nam that it couldn't win; college students protested against the war, racism, and sexism. For those who saw these events as symptoms that pointed to inevitable change the winds blew fair for the future in spite of the chaos that brewed. For those who did not, the future looked bleak.

I turned forty, and the following year made a job change that took me to a large Midwest university with a great opportunity for advancement within my field. My friends, family and colleagues saw a bright future ahead for me. At least things seemed to point in that direction. I even saw it that way. But then I probably could not have seen it differently because I was caught in a thicket of denial and rationalization. I would not have admitted it at the time, but I had lost my orientation, and the seeds of discontent had been sown. It wasn't long before they germinated and grew vigorously. To the people around me, I needed nothing. But, I thought I needed a challenge. What I had been doing was not really working.

Intuitively I knew that I was not most comfortable when I was working with people. Twenty years earlier, I had considered a career in forestry and wildlife management. I fantasized about spending long hours of solitude in the woods, but I was told by others, mostly guidance counselors with scores from a vocational preference test in hand, that I was good with people and that I should seriously consider teaching.

So, I became a teacher, a good teacher, or so I was told. But several years of teaching teenagers convinced me that I really liked the idea of people better than intense personal contact with them. And so, I entered the world of ideas and became a college professor. One fortunate decision after another found me doing research, theory development and enough teaching to earn my keep. Yet the reality was that I was lost. I didn't know who I was, or why I was doing what I was doing, or if I wanted to do it for the rest of my life, except that what I was doing paid fairly well and was a position of status in the eyes of much of society.

It was at this time that I remembered my earlier interest in forestry, but I wasn't about to start all over again. However, I had moved to a university that had an excellent horticulture department and I reasoned that forestry and horticulture weren't all that different if I stuck to growing plants. So, a year later I arranged with my dean for a one third reduction in teaching and salary and registered to audit undergraduate courses in horticulture. In a little over two years I had the equivalent of an undergraduate education in horticulture, twenty acres of land, and a dual life as a college professor and nurseryman.

Surprisingly, I thrived on the dual career and the sixteen-hour workday that it took to make it go. But by the time I reached the age of fifty-five I was physically and emotionally exhausted. I suppose I could have gone on teaching until I was sixty-five or seventy but the nursery was different. In the beginning, it grew and promised to be an economic success, but by the end of the 1980's a new economic reality slowly became apparent. Labor, energy and land needed for continued growth of the nursery, or even just holding its own, became increasingly expensive. As the costs of growing plants skyrocketed in the Midwest, the large nurseries there moved to the Southeast and the Far West. There they could grow hundreds of acres of plants and market them at a lot less than I could produce and sell them.

At age sixty I took early retirement from teaching and a few years later I sold the nursery and moved south. I had put my faith in ideas, the small business dream, and in myself. All three had come up wanting and left me feeling a bit empty. I was ready for a radical change in the way that I looked at life.

I was aware of people who lived as contemplatives. I had read Merton's autobiography, *The Seven Story Mountain;* I had heard about Henri Nouwen's six-month sabbatical experience as a monk at the Abbey of the Genesee. *Walden* and *A Gift From the Sea* were a part of my reading some years earlier, and Marsha Sinetar's book *Ordinary People as Monks and Mystics* had just been published. I knew that not all people who lived a contemplative life were in religious orders. Indeed, many were people much like myself. They were married with a family, held a regular job and were dependent to some degree on the economic, social, and governmental institutions of the culture. Many were not even particularly religious, though all of those I knew about had a spiritual bent. Those who were not in enclosed religious orders and lived in the world, were known as secular contemplatives.

I soon realized that I didn't really know very much about what living as a secular contemplative involved. What I thought it meant turned out to be naïve, idealistic, and inappropriate for me. I thought that it meant something like being a part time monk without making any monastic commitments and having a lot more freedom. Somehow I got the idea that if I learned to do contemplative prayer, this would enable me to become socially transcendent and maybe even self transcendent, and so equipped I would be able to watch the rest of the world go by while I sat in blissful union with God watching and praying for them. That kind of detachment from social reality is definitely not what being a secular contemplative is all about. I learned that though it involved a certain detachment from the blatant violation of a person's privacy by unwanted agents of a materialistic, secular culture, it did not involve the rejection of social responsibility. In time I learned that the contemplative life often resulted in movement from the center of societal activity toward the margin of society, and that this move was usually associated with a decrease in dependence on the products and services of the culture. For me it was also associated with a transition from an other directed world to a world in which I became much less dependent on the collective values of social institutions, and what the members of those institutions thought, believed, and valued. I became much more in tune with thoughts and convictions that had their source within me.

From reading about Thomas Merton's theology of prayer I learned that the contemplative life is often associated with the growth of the true self, a more mature understanding of love, and a significant change in ones understanding of and relationship with God. Merton's theology of prayer[1] was richly grounded in the concept of the self. He recognized at least two aspects of the self: one he called the true self or sometimes the spiritual self, and the second he called the false self or sometimes the ego self. I found this way of thinking about the self to be very useful in helping me understand how my willingness to be transformed by God's love could be nurtured by contemplative prayer and how this transformation could affect me. Transformation of the self would not be achieved by a willfulness on my part to improve my quality of life. It would depend on a willingness to be loved by God, and a willingness to become God's love in the world.

As I became more and more deeply involved in the contemplative life, I slowly began to understand how central love was to the transformation of a contemplative, and how critical willingness was to the process of letting God do the transforming. I would find solitude on the margin of society but I would be close enough to people to have quality contact with them on a regular basis. I quickly realized that God was much bigger than the God I thought I knew, and much different than the God that man created to reign over an impersonal, materialistic culture in which shalls and shall-nots more often protect the social institutions of government, economics, religion, and education than they nurture the growth of individuals.

I learned that making a transition from the secular city to the contemplative community is no easy task. I had spent years building a false self that worked in the world. Success, stature, promotion, and recognition became characteristics of my false self, and my ego self developed effective ways of justifying and defending it. Of course I didn't see it that way until the possibility of an alternative perspective was seriously considered. But by that time my false self was robust and my ego self was skilled in warding off most challenges to it. Over the years I learned that if the false self remained dominant at the expense of the true self, then a healthy conception of love was often successfully stunted, because, a healthy conception of love for others is seen by the false self as a threat to its integrity. As the process of transformation of self takes place there is almost always conflict. The true and the false selves seldom coexist peacefully. I slowly became aware that a life dedicated to the decline in the dominance of the false self and the growth of the true self is what the contemplative takes on.

In time I learned that being a secular contemplative meant blending the contemplative life with an already existing secular life. This meant integrating a spiritual life into a life that was grounded in human aspiration, in human institutions, and a willful drive for competitive success. It meant mixing two seemingly paradoxical ways of life. In 1986, however, I had almost no idea of what was in store for me. I didn't know what a secular contemplative really was, or even if it was possible to mix these seemingly paradoxical orientations. I just announced to God and myself that I was going to be a secular contemplative.

At first nothing in my life changed very much. My dual career life in the nursery and at the university were overlaid with my conception of a contemplative way such as it was. But after I took early retirement from teaching, I realized that it was time to get a more formal preparation for what I was trying to do. To that end I applied for admission to the Group Leaders Program at the Shalem Institute, and two years later started a four-year extension course offered by the School of Theology at the University of the South. During this time the nursery was sold, and I moved south to the Florida Panhandle.

It wasn't long before the Mary/Martha issue raised its head, and for six years I tried to integrate the contemplative life with an active life of service. In the church I did this by leading programs on contemplative prayer, working with the Diocesan Commission on Spiritual Development, and participating in parish politics by serving on the vestry. In the community my service took the form of volunteer social work, but in time I had to accept the reality that I could not successfully integrate this busy life of service with the life of a contemplative. One of my problems was that I was involved in a very active ministry that was almost devoid of any extended periods of solitude. I had become frantically enmeshed once again in the active life. I might have thought that Martha had won out over Mary but I didn't; instead it became time to take stock and consider changing the balance in my life by moving toward a more intentionally contemplative life with much more solitude. And so in 2003 a move was made to the woods of Alabama where my wife and I have been living ever since.

During this period of trying to find out who my true self really was and developing a congruent relationship with God, I kept a spiritual journal that became a day-by-day record of what went on in my spiritual life. It became my story of a journey that is still in progress. In writing this book I have drawn from this journal, and I have added reflective commentary from a present perspective.

Keeping a spiritual journal served a number of purposes for me and still does. It was and is one of my most common forms of prayer. But when it came time to use it as the basis for a book, something that I had not originally considered, I was confronted by several challenges beyond making coherent sense out of several thousand pages of notes written while talking with God. A journal is always written in the present and read later as a record of the past. As a record of the past it inevitably lacks much of the physical, emotional and social context in which it was originally written. How much of the reality of the past that was once the present can ever be recreated? How much of the context that is necessary for understanding particular events of the past can ever be reconstructed? These are questions that passed through my mind as I used my journal materials as the basis for a story I wrote in the present. My approach was to let the journal stand largely on its own including its often casual and fragmentary style, and to insert reflective comments which came from a present perspective.

Another challenge I faced was telling the story in a way that would engage others as observers of my past without presuming that they ever could, or would, try to relive my life in theirs. If others can use this account of my spiritual journey to reflect light on their journey then it will have served its purpose.

I believe that one of the most important things that I learned from this process came not so much from trying to make sense out of the past, or in realizing how little of the future is ever really planned, but from seeing the past and the future as experienced in the present moment. It is here that we really live if at all.

## NOTE

1. John J. Higgins, *Thomas Merton on Prayer* (Garden City, NJ: Image Books, 1964), 48–70.

*Part I*

# THE NOVICE YEARS

*Chapter One*

# The Journey Begins

I've never been much of a traveler. Just the thought of taking a long trip could tire me out. I'd rather be there than coming or going or, better yet, I would rather be resting in the warm satisfaction of imagining what it would be like when I got there, than being there in all of its reality. It seems that I have always been that way until recently. Now, at last, I am finally convinced that whether it is being there, or coming or going, there is a lot more of living in the present than I ever dreamed of. But, it took me a long time to learn the truth. That wasn't something that I understood in 1986 as I packed the car in anticipation of a spiritual retreat and vacation that lay ahead. An eighteen-year journey was about to begin.

The Wednesday after Labor Day my wife, Olga, and I started out from Central Ohio to a barrier island off of the New Jersey Coast. The next day we registered at a motel in Ship Bottom, and settled into the process of renting a cottage on the beach for a few weeks. The place was practically deserted. Most of the summer vacationers had already left the island; the kids were back to school.

Forty years earlier, my family had vacationed on this island during the month of August. At that time the beach was mostly undeveloped. It was a quiet, uncommercial spot known for an historic lighthouse, fishing and solitude. During that summer vacation a friend and I frequently took long walks on the beach at night in search of girls, but our dating fantasies never turned out like we imagined, so instead, our attention occasionally turned to such heady topics as the universe and creation.

I remember one such night when, again, no girls appeared. I lay on the beach looking up at the meteor shower that seemed to be playing among the millions of stars that composed the August sky. The sand beneath me was still warm from the afternoon sun, and an ocean breeze blew gently from the water. With an ocean breeze, there would be no mosquitoes that night. There would only be the feel of the sand, the distant sound of the lap of the waves on the beach, and a powerful feeling of awareness of the Universe that surrounded me.

I remember looking up at the stars and thinking about such things as the speed of light and the great distances between heavenly bodies. I remember thinking for a fleeting moment that I knew what it all meant. But, of course I didn't. What it all meant was beyond my wildest teenage imagination. I was a fragile speck in a vast Universe, nothing more, and I sensed that there was too much beyond what I saw to ever comprehend it. Yet, somehow even then I knew that I was caught up in a moment of mystery and awe.

Now, forty years later, Olga and I had rented a cottage not more than several hundred yards from the very spot of that teenage experience. This time I had moments when I sensed that if I continued on the spiritual path that I had just begun, my life would be dramatically changed. I didn't know it, but taking the next step into the realm of faith would have important consequences. It would lead to a freefall that would last for as long as I was willing to experience a transformation of the self.

This transformation of the self would eventually be manifested by changes in four aspects of who I was: (1) my *false self*, that part of me that had been formed by me and by my culture, but was in conflict with who I had been created to be; (2) my *ego self,* that part of me that defended my false self from threatening charges of inauthenticity and inadequacy; (3) my *true self*, that part of me that was who I had been created to be; (4) my *spiritual self*, that part of me that would grow to become God's love in the world.

Transformation of the self was the process by which I would grow in love for others and for my true self, while my ego and false selves diminished. Contemplative prayer would be the rich soil in which my true and spiritual selves would grow. Contemplation, as a way of prayer, would assume faith, and the growth of faith. Transformation of the self would assume a willingness to see many of the values, beliefs, comforts, and prejudices of my false self die. In my case the ego self put up a stiff fight to defend my false self. After all, most people, and I among them, do not enjoy coming to the realization that they are living an inauthentic life that is inconsistent with the person they were really created to be. To put it bluntly, few of us take pleasure in coming to the realization that our addictions, and the enjoyable, comfortable, even exciting lives that we have been living are delusions, and we didn't know it. Yet one who follows the contemplative way must be willing to accept that possibility. In addition to watching our false self die, and our true self grow, we must be willing to accept long periods without apparent growth of the true self, and we must be willing to accept that if we do grow in authenticity, we may threaten or upset those around us who do not understand what is happening. With the real possibility of years of unpredictable change, frustration and even emotional pain ahead, why would I have ever chosen to follow the contemplative way? To a large degree I think that this was because I did not have a very clear idea of what lay ahead of me.

The reasons for adopting the contemplative life and the subsequent transformation of self differs for each person. For some it seems that they cannot do otherwise. It is a clear call. For some, their present life is so unacceptable that trying the contemplative way is worth the risk. Still others choose to follow the contemplative way because they believe that it will be consistent with who they think they really are. In my case I was not consciously aware of a call to contemplation. If I was aware of any reason at all for considering the contemplative life it was probably found in a naïve conception of what I thought it meant, coupled with a hope that it would be more meaningful than the life I was living. But beyond what I thought to be a choice, I believe that I was unwittingly drawn into it by a vortex of forces that surrounded me, and that I was unaware of at the time.

Regardless of my initial reasons for taking the contemplative way, as time passed I came to realize that in taking this step I had chosen a life that ultimately would lead toward a transformation of self. When I realized that transformation of self involves the death of the ego and false self, and the nurturing and growth of the true and spiritual self, I thought this would be exciting. But I soon realized that transformation of self was not a process that I could direct. I could not transform myself. I could only be willing to be transformed by forces that were beyond my power to control, and beyond my ability to understand. Being willing to be transformed by God requires faith. For me this was a step into an unknown realm filled with mystery. Indeed it was a very scary moment when I realized that willfulness is inconsistent with the contemplative way, and that willfulness must, in time, be replaced by willingness.

Fortunately, those who find that the contemplative way is not for them, have other choices within the active life. They can find fulfillment in a secular world where a healthy willingness can be mixed with compassion and love for others to make a life of service that is consistent with who they really are. But those who follow the contemplative life, and live that life for any length of time, are in for a different experience. In time they come to realize this, but mercifully that realization comes slowly. Those who follow the contemplative path ultimately come to understand that they are able to proceed, in part, because they are becoming the person who has been hidden within them all the time. This realization usually takes a while, but it is worth the wait. It is one of the really exciting fruits of contemplation. It sustained me over the many dry spots.

When I started life as a secular contemplative I really didn't know what was ahead for me. It was one surprise after another. Several years later my spiritual director said to me, "Jack, God had something in mind for you. He grabbed you by the collar and jerked you out of the line you were in. Then he said, 'Boy, you're in the wrong line. I have something different in mind for you.'"

When I began my spiritual journey my conception of God, love, and self were not a unity. They were three separate ideas. In my mind God, love, and self were three abstract concepts that had little to do with each other except in a linguistic construction such as, "God is love." But the concept of God as love had about as much personal meaning for me as the concept of zero-point energy or the Special Theory of Relativity.

What I thought about God at this time was pretty much summed up in the Creed, which I said about once a week without much thought except whether or not to bow a little when I said, "born of the Virgin Mary," and whether or not to cross myself when I said, "we look for the resurrection of the dead." God created the world but that was a long time ago and it was done and over with. I was supposed to love God "with all my heart, with all my mind and with all my soul," but I didn't have the faintest idea what that might mean. Jesus called God Abba, which meant daddy, but I preferred Father and never considered the possibility of mother. In short, I had reached mature adulthood and my conception of God was very much the same as it was when I was confirmed at the age of twelve. The God I worshiped was largely assumed and largely unconsidered.

My conception of love was not developed much further than my conception of God. Love was something I should do to God and to my neighbor and to myself. But I had no idea what it meant to love God. It was okay for God to love me if he wanted to, but God was for all practical purposes unknown to me, so how could I love him? This didn't bother me if I didn't think about it, so I didn't think about it. Loving my neighbor was just a little different. Most of my neighbors were decent people, but I hardly knew them. They were the guys next door who cut their grass, with whom I passed bland niceties over a cold beer, and from whom I borrowed a jumper cable on cold mornings. Their wives, of course, were different. Some of them were alluring, but they were to be known only at a distance. It was common knowledge that I was not to get too close to them physically, emotionally, or intellectually. I loved my parents, sometimes, and my wife and my daughter most of the time, but for different reasons. But I never really thought about that very much. Loving my daughter took on a whole new meaning after she grew up.

She became a friend. With the exception of my wife Olga, my friend Kelly and my daughter Pam I didn't love very many people. I liked some of them, but I certainly didn't love all the people I came in contact with daily. Many of them I barely tolerated. Love was something best not considered except for close family members. If I went beyond that, I might establish commitments and dependency relationships, and I thought that was best avoided.

The self was a different thing. I thought I knew who I was. I was a teacher, moderately comfortable, married, never really seriously in debt, introverted and responsible. I was also very careful to cover up that I was a person with lots of self doubt, that I often was very anxious about relating to people I didn't know, and that in spite of mood swings I was never ecstatically happy, not even at Christmas. I liked my ego and my false selves when I did well. They were an amazing part of my personality. They thrived on success, power, sensual gratification, material comfort and pride. They were what got me up and going every morning to face what was a challenging and often an absurd world. They created reasons why things didn't always go the way I wanted. They refused to let me believe that I wasn't always who I thought I was. Rationalization and denial were my ego self's closest friends, and when they deserted me and didn't come to my rescue, I employed power, anger, manipulation and deceit. The ego self is a work of art that if carefully developed, gets us through life in reasonable shape if we don't try to think about it too much.

The spiritual self and the true self are something else. When I was young, no one ever told me about my true or my spiritual self, and for most of my life I never knew they existed. It was usually the false self and the ego self that I was supposed to develop, only they weren't called that. I was a mature adult before anyone ever suggested to me that I had a spiritual self where God's love lived. I did not know that if ignored, my various selves would remain undernourished, unexercised and underdeveloped, but if let free they had great potential for shaping me into becoming a very different person. I did not know that my spiritual self had as much genetic potential as my ego self, it was just hidden and largely underdeveloped.

When I started my spiritual journey, I had only a vague plan or destination in mind. I found out later that this was normal. Each spiritual journey is different. For much of my life there were days when I thought I knew who God was and that we had a good relationship. But, most of the time I didn't care who God was, and I certainly didn't want to seek a relationship with someone I didn't even know or care about. But in 1986, I wanted very much to know who God was, and I wanted to have a fulfilling relationship with him. I was ready to develop a relationship, but I had little idea about where to start. From my reading I thought that the way to do this might be to put on a contemplative life-style.

This seemed to mean that in addition to leading an esoteric prayer life I should also keep a spiritual journal. And so I did keep a journal starting in the fall of 1986. This journal became the record of my spiritual journey and a spiritual life that is still being lived out. It began with a rather superficial understanding of God, self and love as they existed in my life at that time. It went on to contain an integrated conception of God, love and self that became associated with a challenge to many of my beliefs, but seldom challenged my faith.

Following a spiritual way presumes that there will be unknowns. It presumes that there will be questions. Those questions did a lot to shape my spiritual life and ultimately my relationship with God. My first journal entry in September of 1986 was filled with questions.

> September 9, 1986
> 
> Is it still possible to be a contemplative in today's world? Is it possible for me? Certainly I have considered these questions before, but not seriously. If my will becomes congruent with God's will, then it might be possible to live such a life, but until then I may be doing nothing but role-playing. How can I, through the practice of contemplative prayer, get to the point where God's will is my will if I don't even know what contemplative prayer is?

That was written while I was on my first of what would become a number of retreat vacations on Long Beach Island off the New Jersey coast. Here I hoped to have long hours away from the usual daily routine and interruptions, be able to read about contemplative prayer and spirituality, and pray the Office four times a day like I imagined a monk would.

> September 17, 1986
> 
> Just about none of the expectations that I had two weeks ago when I came here on retreat have turned out as I had hoped. I did most of the reading that I brought with me the first week we were here, and I didn't find it to be very informative or spiritually exciting. There have been few moments of enlightenment. I was going to do morning, noon, evening prayer and compline. I think I have done morning prayer perhaps four times, noon never, evening once or twice, and the same for compline. Contemplative prayer has been an equal disaster. I have a lot to learn.

Even though the vacation retreat in September of 1986 fell short of expectations, it did have some positive aspects. In my mind, Long Beach Island will always be the place where Thomas Merton introduced me to the ideas of the Christ within, and Christ as God's love. My introduction came in the form of a book that I bought on the island bookstore that was part of a Catholic church center run by Franciscans. That book was *Disputed Questions*. It contains a number of essays by Merton, including "The Power and Meaning of Love."

When I first read that essay in 1986 I was fascinated by it. The ideas were all new to me, and so I had little understanding of what Merton was talking about. It took years before it began to really sink in that the key to understanding and experiencing God lay in realizing that God really is love, and that the love that is God is not exclusively a property of God, but a potential property of all of God's creation. As we grow in understanding of what God's love is, seeing that love in others, being that love in our everyday lives, we grow closer and closer to becoming one with God. It was several years later when I realized that Christ could be understood as God's love in the world, that it all of a sudden dawned on me what Merton meant in "The Power and Meaning of Love" when he talked about Christ in the world and Christ in each and every person. At first, I intuitively understood that I had read something that was very significant, but I didn't know enough about what Merton meant to grasp its staggering implications. But those insights were to be the fruits of transformation and were several years into the future. I returned home from my Long Beach Island retreat to my life at the university and the nursery. The spiritual gains that many think they make during a retreat are often nullified by the experience of re-entry. The shock of re-entry into the busy secular life can be unsettling.

September 24, 1986
I have been back from my vacation retreat for three days and I have experienced a sense of hurried uneasiness. One day in the nursery getting caught up on things, two days at the university, one day going over back mail, getting ready for class, another day teaching and other regular duties. The whole thing has been so clearly a hectic re-entry to my old world that there has been no time during the day for contemplation.

My plan as of now will be to create a prayer discipline and daily schedule to follow as best I can.

| | |
|---|---|
| 6:00 | Get up—have coffee with Olga |
| 6:45 | Morning Prayer |
| 7:00 | Breakfast |
| 8:00 | Teach at the University, etc. |
| 11:30 | Meditation in my office |
| 12:00 | Teach, committee work, professional reading, etc. |
| 5:00 | Contemplation |
| 6:00 | Dinner |
| 7:00 | Relaxation, reading and study |
| 9:45 | Compline with Olga |
| 10:00 | Bed |

There will be some adjustments to make in my life and the lives of the people around me. I will need to share this schedule with Olga and ask her to honor my time for morning prayer and contemplation. She may wish to join me for compline. Students and faculty will need to respect my "I will return at 1:00 P.M." sign on my office door during lunch. It will not work perfectly and I must treat interruptions with charity.

Pam has loaned me *Sadhana: A Way to God* by Anthony de Mello. *Sadhana* is an eastern word that means discipline, technique, and spiritual exercise. At first I thought it would be a popularized theology of contemplation, but it's really a how to book on contemplation with prayer exercises. We will see, but at the moment, since I have no spiritual director, I'll approach it with an open mind and see how it works.

October 2, 1986

So far I have kept the discipline. This week I have been able to do meditation at lunch without distractions. Anthony de Mello's exercise, "Breath Communication With God," was a big step forward for me. My concentration was good and the half hour passed quickly. At least it did on Tuesday and Wednesday. Today at noon I went across the street to St. Stephen's for Eucharist. But, this evening before supper, I really had difficulty concentrating and I drifted into sleep. This sometimes happens when I am tired.

My journal reveals many thoughts and experiences that I had as a novice, but perhaps more than anything, it shows how inflexible I was in adhering to my daily discipline and schedule so as to manage my world and make room for my spiritual life. It took me a long time to realize that my inflexibility was an expression of my willfulness rather than an expression of my love for God. I failed to make a clear distinction between an appropriate spiritual discipline for a beginning secular contemplative and a discipline for a novice who is a member of a monastic community.

I frequently fell asleep while doing meditation. Sometimes I would dream, and at first I thought these might be prophetic dreams or visions. They were not. My experience with dreams will be described in later journal entries after I have begun to work with a spiritual director, but at this point the journal simply reports an experience with a dream that happened when I was using a meditation exercise of de Mello's called "A Place for Prayer," In doing this exercise, I was supposed to create a mental image of a place that was conducive to prayer so that I could return in fantasy to that place, and then imagine that I was present there while I was meditating.

October 17, 1986

Tonight after supper I was doing de Mello's exercise, "A Place For Prayer." I chose the interior of St. Stephen's Church because it has meant so much to me lately. I entered the church from the back and noticed the detail as I moved up the center aisle, through the sanctuary to the altar where I sat down on the steps that go up to the altar. Above me was a huge iron and stained glass cross. Jesus was there and we talked. I told him how much I needed him to guide me. Then suddenly I was among colonial brick buildings in a courtyard with trees all around, then I was on a city street with tall buildings, and at last I was walking down a long tree covered path that led to a cemetery with grave stones shaped like Celtic crosses. I walked back through the courtyard with the brick colonial buildings, and I was again in St. Stephen's Church below the cross where I sat down and talked with Jesus. Finally I was back in the room at home where I had started. I don't think that I had fallen asleep.

As a novice I attributed more meaning and importance to that experience than was warranted. At that point in my spiritual journey a spiritual director would have been helpful. A novice needs to know that this sort of thing happens frequently to some people and that it is more likely to have its explanation in human psychology than in spirituality or theology. Used as a metaphor, the experience might well be a point of departure for spiritual exploration. As a beginner, I was not ready to use that sort of experience productively without some guidance. Fortunately, in my case the experience was followed by a period of spiritual tranquility. I was not really bothered by it. Nor did I spend much time trying to make sense of it.

October 30, 1986
Often my contemplative prayer is just being quiet, especially if I am tired when I get home from work, and I sit for thirty-five or forty minutes while God and I rest. At other times it is just a fleeting moment of awareness such as one I recently had on campus. This autumn has been particularly beautiful. Among the falling leaves I saw people, some apparently happy, some not, each with a very human story that I would never know. As I walked along with a throng of students, I suddenly became aware that each step that we took was not a step toward nothing, but toward the Ultimate All that we are all a part of, and suddenly I felt as if I were one with all of these people who walked with me.

Momentary flashes of awareness and what appeared to be growth toward a contemplative spirituality were frequently followed by periods of despair or aimless wandering. The question was not if but when. A little over two weeks after the previous entry was written in my journal things were quite different.

November 16, 1986
Humility against despair! No one should ever think that contemplative prayer once a day is like a twenty-four hour trip that transforms the world into a rose garden of heavenly bliss. Nothing could be further from the truth. Faith and humility are conditions that make contemplative prayer possible. They guarantee

no success, but they help. If I never thought about myself, and I always believed that God was walking with me, then things might be different. But, there is much more of my false self still alive than I realize, and much less faith than I thought. This becomes so clear to me when I confront feelings of despair and doubt about the future. "Despair is the absolute extreme of self-love. It is reached when a man deliberately turns his back on all help from anyone else in order to taste the rotten luxury of knowing himself to be lost."[2] So wrote Thomas Merton in *New Seeds of Contemplation* and he should know.

November 18, 1986

Things have not been fun at all for the past week. It seems in retrospect that I have been pushing too hard in order to make things happen. It was not until last Friday that I realized that something was wrong. It was not until today that I began to get a better perspective on what I may be experiencing. The I between myself and God is resisting my giving myself to God. The words are there, but it doesn't feel natural. I sense that I am forcing myself on God and forcing God on myself. I have gotten off the trail and gotten lost already after only a few months. What would a spiritual director have said today if I had gone to him? How long dare I continue on this walk in the dark without one?

November 19, 1986

I awakened this morning full of feelings of frustration, defeat and anxiety. I really feel down. I can't even pray except in the most superficial way. It must have been obvious to Olga who said something like "When are you going to cheer up and show your positive side." I struck back in anger; I was hurt and I figured the best thing I can do today is separate myself from people so as not to have to deal with them and wait till I feel better. I really lashed out at her because I needed support not cheer leading. Now I realize how important a simple word of encouragement and support can be, and how significant failure to give support to others can be when they need it.

Though I didn't know it at the time, a lot of what I was experiencing, including the anger that I felt toward others and tried to keep under control so I wouldn't make a fool of myself, may have been associated with the onset of depression. Going through the process of getting out from under the control of the ego self is a long and painful process at best, and depression only heightens one's sense of inadequacy. I lost my ability to keep criticism, real or imagined, in perspective. My sense of reality became warped as I attempted to bend reality to protect my false self. I thought that the thing to do was to dig in and talk myself out of a bad mood. I would will myself to be a joyful person. What made things even more difficult at the time was that most people I knew didn't talk about depression, and they had very little understanding of how to relate positively to a depressed person. Without intending to do so they often made things worse. Call it intuition or a guardian angel looking over my shoulder, I somehow realized that it was time for me to see about getting a spiritual director to help me get back on the trail again.

November 20, 1986
I finally called Fr. Tom at St. Stephens and asked for an appointment to discuss spiritual direction. The appointment is set for next Wednesday morning. I hope to get a sense of what spiritual direction means for a layperson. Nothing is clear right now except that it seems like the right time to do something about this.

November 26, 1986
I met with Fr. Tom today and we talked about the provisions that are made by the Church for spiritual direction of lay people who want to remain in the secular world and feel drawn to contemplative prayer. He sized up the situation rather quickly and after saying that he would be unable to take on that responsibility at this time he recommended three people in the area, two priests and a layperson. He also recommended that I contact the monks at St. Gregory's Abbey in Three Rivers, Michigan, and suggested that a trip up there might be good for me. On the way out he introduced me to Susan B, a new person on the staff at St. Stephens. So, I guess it's time to pray.

November 31, 1986
The weekend has passed and I have come to the conclusion that I will get in touch with Susan about serving as my spiritual director.

December 3, 1986
Today I met with Susan. Most of the session was spent on what I would call assessment. Who am I? Where have I been? Where am I going? Further opportunities for support were mentioned, along with other spiritual directors who might be more appropriate, a workshop on spirituality that was going to be offered at St. Stephens this winter, and the desirability of spending several days on retreat in a supportive place like the Benedictine community at Three Rivers, etc. I felt that I had talked too much and that I was not always listening to myself or to her. I need to do better on that. Our next meeting is scheduled for December 16th. Tomorrow I am to pick up some reading materials, or an assessment inventory, or something that she will leave in the church office for me. Apparently I am to read these before our next session. If I had been listening better I would know more about it.

December 5, 1986
The whole thing is moving more quickly than I expected. Since Wednesday I have mapped out a strategy for doing the Steppingstones exercise that I picked up at the church yesterday. The exercise is based on something that is apparently in a book by Ira Progoff. It is in the library and is titled, *At a Journal Workshop*. In addition I also went to the west campus library and picked up some books by Merton including *Seasons of Celebration*. I read "Advent: Hope or Delusion,"

and I got the sense that my Advent this year is going to be tied to the Spiritual Steppingstones exercise.

The Spiritual Steppingstone exercise was intended to connect me with my past by meditating on moments in my spiritual life that might have been instrumental in leading me to the present, or might suggest some direction for the future. Normally the number of events chosen is limited to at least eight but not more than twelve. I came up with twelve.

As I look back on these past events I cannot see any obvious causal relationships between them and my spiritual development at that time. They seemed more like a list of random things that happened than a chain of events that led somewhere. Upon reflection I believe that the experience helped me to revisit moments in my past, and opened my perspective of who I was. At that time I believe that I saw myself through a rather limited vision of the future that I thought I would shape and be responsible for. I now think that the list may be more interesting because of what it did not include, and the almost complete lack of descriptions of what I was thinking or feeling at the time.

December 12, 1986
    Yesterday I was meditating on two quotations: "It is no longer I who live, but it is Christ who lives in me," and "If you meet the Buddha kill him." I was having some difficulty concentrating and was aware that I was forcing it, not just letting the experience be. When I was almost ready to conclude meditation a light appeared and illuminated a misty wooded area through which a brook was running. There was an arched wooden bridge across the brook. As I started to cross it, an oriental figure appeared on the other side and walked toward me. We met in the center of the bridge and the figure disappeared into me leaving me standing alone at the center of the bridge. The dimly lit woods were all around me. I felt peaceful but perplexed. What was this?

    Today I read *in Zen and the Birds of Appetite* by Merton:
       . . . it becomes overwhelmingly important for us to become detached from our everyday conception of our selves as potential subjects for special and unique experiences, or as candidates for realization, attainment and fulfillment. In other words this means that a spiritual guide worth his salt will conduct a ruthless campaign against all forms of delusion arising out of spiritual ambition and self-complacency which aim to establish the ego in spiritual glory. That is why St. John of the Cross is so hostile to visions, ecstasies, and all forms of "special experience." That is why the Zen masters say: "If you meet the Buddha, kill him."[3]

December 17, 1986
    Yesterday I had my second meeting with my spiritual director. The session was much more relaxed for me. Much of the time was spent in establishing

norms and expectations. Basically what this will mean is: (1) sessions are to be a dialogue, (2) sessions are to be used as a place for me to bring spiritual issues for discussion and direction, (3) if my spiritual journey begins to get off the track, then she will be more directive, (4) at present every two weeks seems to be an appropriate spacing for sessions, but this can be changed. The next session will be on December 30. I left my completed Spiritual Steppingstones exercise with her so that she could read it before our next session.

December 20, 1986

I had an experience yesterday that really got me thinking about people and the difficulties that we all seem to experience getting along with each other. Yesterday I went to let the cats out of the garage. As usual Mikie was first to the door with Bridget close behind. I opened the door and out they went. Almost at the same time I became aware of a red tailed hawk circling over the dogleg of the property that goes down the southeast side of the pond. The area is filled with juniper, pine, wild cherry and other shrub trees along the fencerow. Down near the pond there are thickets of willow. The cats stopped and quickly circled back to the garage. They were very content to be inside on a day they would normally want to be out. There was something going on out there that they just didn't want to get involved in. I came into the house and watched from the door. The hawk was a magnificent sight, a powerful bird of primitive beauty. Soon a stray cat that had been hanging around the nursery for some weeks came out of the willows near the edge of the pond and crossed the ice to the other side. The hawk flew low over the ice and I thought it was going to make a strike but it didn't. It just acted like an interceptor escorting an intruder well past the boundary of its territory. It made one last circle and returned to a hickory tree where it settled with a good view of the situation.

Clearly this was not a peaceable kingdom where the lion and the lamb lie down together. The strong and the beautiful had asserted its territorial rights and driven off an intruder—a motley, homeless cat. No blood had been shed, but a lot of anger and resentment had been expressed. I got the feeling that God was not bothered at all. It's the way things go in the world, nor did the hawk feel the least bit guilty. Anthropomorphism can be so seductive.

December 24, 1986

Advent has ended and the celebration of the Nativity begins at midnight. This Advent has been the most significant in my life. Spiritual direction has begun, and for the first time I understand the preparatory work of Advent. The journey is under way and I want Christ to be born into the world. That would be peace on earth.

January 2, 1987

Another session today with my spiritual director. This was a free flowing conversation that seemed to be devoted to finding out more about who I was. She revealed more about herself in what I suspect was an attempt to create a condition in which I would feel free to be more open. The conversation in part focused on my prayer life and I talked about several "visions" that I had in the past. She talked about the relationship between sleep and dreams and visions. Not the same thing, but related. Also she said, "You asked for it. If you asked him for bread would he give you a rock?" This was followed by a conversation in which she asked if I were concerned about the visions. I said, "No, if I were going to go over the brink I would have done so before this." That was all there was to it.

January 3, 1987

The work with my spiritual director is proceeding well, but not exactly as I had expected. I guess I thought more about a director being a strict father who would guide me with a firm hand. This, of course, has not been the way it worked out. First, no father figure, and in a real sense it is God who is doing the directing with Susan helping me to follow his lead.

January 11, 1987

I said something today that I don't regret saying but it certainly was not taken very well. I don't remember the exact words, but my comment was that I didn't believe that most people take their religion seriously. They turn to it in times of crisis, weddings, and funerals but between these times they put it off to the side. The reason that they don't take it seriously is that if they did, it would scare them to death with what it would demand of them. I really believe this, and I think that it applies to all of us. My comment was taken as if I didn't think it applied to me, and that I was showing spiritual pride. I may have come off that way, but again I felt put down. Perhaps the problem is that I express myself in the wrong way. Perhaps I should express myself in prayer and works of love for others and quit talking about it.

January 18, 1987

This is a cold, rainy day. Inside, there is comfortable warmth all around. The family is coming for dinner. Olga has been working all day in the kitchen. The table is set with daffodils in January. God is all around touching everything.

I know that there is great misery and injustice in the world right now. I know that, and I know that I am a party to it so long as I stand as a passive bystander. And right now I know that if God gives me such a beautiful day in the midst of it all I better enjoy it with him.

For the past week I have been expecting a spiritual eruption, something like geologists must experience when monitoring an active volcano. I don't know anything more, but things have happened. Lent is just a week away. Something is going to erupt out of this; I wonder what it will be? All of this is going on and yet my daily meditation is dry.

Around this time Pam and I went to a weekend workshop on prayer held at St. Patrick's in Dublin, Ohio. A young priest, Fr. S., was passing through Ohio from the Virginia Theological Seminary to the Episcopal University Center at the University of Arkansas. He was invited by the rector of St. Patrick's to do a two-day workshop on breath prayer. I had no idea what that was, so Pam and I attended the event. Over the two days, considerable time was devoted to Eastern Orthodox spirituality. In the 1980s a lot of people were finding aspects of Eastern Orthodox spirituality to be intriguing while others studied Yoga and Zen of the Far East. Still other people used breathing exercises, mantras and techniques for emptying the mind to prepare them for prayer. It is from the Eastern Orthodox tradition that the breath prayer, as taught by Fr. S., grew. He felt that to be an effective mantra, a breath prayer should be limited to something like eight syllables. An example would be: "Be with me Lord in prayer today." The first syllables are said as one inhales and the second four as one exhales. The prayer is repeated slowly over and over throughout the day, or as a centering preface to meditation.

February 2, 1987
Pam and I went to a weekend workshop on breath prayer at St. Patrick's. She thought it was great and apparently enjoyed it. I was struck by how much of a novice I really am if the comments by others at the workshop reflected their knowledge about and their involvement in prayer. The breath prayer that I developed was "Father teach me to love with joy." When we got home I shared my prayer and a lot of other ideas from the workshop with Olga and she said she would like to do breath prayer too. So, as of now the plan is to use our breath prayers as a centering prayer before compline.

February 6, 1987
Five minutes of breath prayer, interrupted by the phone that Olga answered. I was distracted but continued for several more minutes, but my wandering mind was quickly caught up in considering the case of a student at the university who is having problems with her dissertation. What should I do as a committee member, etc? I never returned to the breath prayer.

February 9, 1997
Ten minutes passed very quickly, all of this in spite of the fact that I had some difficulty concentrating on saying the breath prayer as a mantra. I wanted to think of examples and implications of loving with joy.

February 17, 1987
I felt quiet and at peace while saying my breath prayer before compline tonight. Most of the time was spent resting with God, not actively saying the prayer. I think I may have fallen asleep, but I am not sure.

February 28, 1987
Today was spent in quiet retreat, reading Ecclesiastes, meditation and rest. The reason for the retreat was that as of yesterday I was close to emotional and

physical exhaustion and perhaps I have even begun to slip back into that feeling that may be depression. I seem to have lost the excitement of faith and the relationship with God that had grasped me so tightly during the fall. Last night Olga and I had a talk before we went to bed. I told her about the desert nature of my spiritual life, my inability to turn the nursery over to John, and my problems facing retirement from the university. I can remember the way it was just a few short months ago when I felt both physically and emotionally well, I was happy to be with God in prayer and song. I liked people, people liked me and I looked forward to each day. But I now know what a desert is like. I know what it is like to be carried when I give up; I am ready to get back on track. I want to, more than anything in the world.

April 8, 1987

I have not been sleeping well, getting up any time from 2:00 on and not able to get back to sleep. On Monday night I woke up about 3:15 and got up at 4:00 and I read a bit in Ruther's *Sexism and God Talk*. Olga came out to know if I wanted to talk. I was feeling down about the nursery, the university and life in general. I told her that I didn't really want to talk about it—usually I would have. We made coffee about 5:00 and got up. At about 7:00 I lay down and fell asleep for almost two hours. After that, things seemed more positive. I am beginning to believe that God has something in mind for me, but do I want to suffer the pain that it will take?

At this time periodic experiences of aridity had become a way of life. The very center of my contemplative life was contemplative prayer, and I believed that it was through contemplation that the miracle of transformation of self would occur as my false self underwent the process of death and my true self was nurtured to fullness. The ego self is a powerful aspect of personality, and mine served well to protect my false self from diminishment in the secular world. But like most benevolent tyrants, in times of turmoil or challenge it assumes the face of power and willfulness. The spiritual self, which is God's love, uses its influence to transform the true self so that it becomes an expression of God's love in the world.

April 13, 1987

Learning to love with joy may mean loving in the most difficult of circumstances. Loving is not the warm feeling I get from being with God. Loving means compassion, sacrifice, and hope for others who may be most difficult to love.

At some point along the way I became aware that I had been using the terms meditation and contemplation indiscriminately. I thought that if I could straighten out the differences then I would be able to do better meditation, and do better contemplation, and thus improve my prayer. My concern with being able to make a clear distinction between meditation and contemplation probably came from a tacit assumption that I had held for some time. I believed that if I could name or define or characterize something, I would be in a better position to use or control it. As I reflect on this, it seems to have been a pretty willful approach to prayer. Nevertheless, I turned to books on prayer by people like Merton, Pennington, Edwards, Schideler, and Keating. I didn't learn much about praying but I did learn some things about contemplative and meditative prayer.

I found that meditation involved intentional or at least conscious thinking. In some cases the thinking might be fairly linear, but most often it was discursive. At times it may become free association thinking, presumably about something that is related to one's spiritual life, but the connection may not always be obvious. Thus, some discernment may need to be employed to control distractive thoughts that can actually interfere with prayer, and to encourage potentially useful divergent thoughts. Of course it doesn't always work out that way, and prayer sometimes becomes filled with daydreams or anxieties that are distracting. I learned that one of the distinguishing characteristics of meditation is that it is often accompanied by a sensory content that is filled with sights, sounds, smells and emotions, as one imagines themselves as a participant in a particular setting. Often scripture or other spiritual books act as a stimulus for imagining a setting. For example, most of the exercises in de Mello's *Sadhanna* are meditations. Because meditation places emphasis on conscious thinking, it is often referred to as mental prayer.

Contemplation, on the other hand, picks up where centering prayer or meditation leave off. Sometimes a mantra, a breath prayer or meditation can lead a person to the point where words or other formal symbols of communication are inadequate. The experience cannot be well expressed through words, but it can be sensed. We become aware of the presence of something in a natural or social setting that is beyond the capability of speech. Or we may have a spontaneous moment of the unawareness of self that last for seconds, minutes or even longer. We may become aware of the presence of something beyond the self. Or we may lose awareness of our self as a separate entity and sense that we are part of a void in the presence of God. There is often a tacit awareness that what is being experienced has not been willed or caused by the self. We do not will or cause a contemplative experience. A mantra, breath prayer, the prayer of the heart, or a meditation used as a centering prayer may lead us to contemplation, but it cannot cause us to have a contemplative experience. These differences between meditative and contemplative prayer certainly fit my prayer experiences.

May 3, 1987
    This evening I had the rare experience of having the entire house to myself and God for the evening. Olga had gone over to give Pam a knitting lesson and

put Kate to bed. I read the first chapter of the Gospel of John and a chapter of *Living in the Spirit*. Then I quieted myself and began to meditate on what I had read. After a while I realized that for some time (I don't know for how long) I had ceased to be aware of myself including any thoughts I might have had. I was unaware of thinking about God, but I remained aware of his presence. I had momentarily slipped from meditation into contemplation. I had broken free for a time from the control of my willful thoughts.

May 28, 1987

Last night was one of those extended moments of living hell. I awoke around 2:00 and didn't fall back to sleep until just before the alarm went off at 6:00. I can't remember the event being associated with any negative feelings about anything or anyone in particular, just things in general. I felt as if snakes were being torn from my flesh. When the alarm went off I was sore. It has been almost six months since I started spiritual direction. What is happening? Am I undergoing transformation? This past six months has been a particularly painful yet fruitful period for me as my false self has been challenged one time after another. It started in Advent, went through Christmas and Epiphany, Lent and now Easter is ending. Next Sunday begins the long season of Pentecost, and then into Advent again.

Occasionally I became aware that transformation of the self was going on. But most of the time I was not aware of the transforming experience as such. Life just proceeded day after day with nothing apparently happening. During these times I sometimes felt at peace and at other times I felt angry and frustrated or even unloved, but I didn't believe that these feelings were intentionally used by God to bring about transformation. On the other hand, I did believe at the time that such events as dreams and "midnight madness" might be used as metaphors for aspects of God's transforming work, but only as creative metaphors.

June 8, 1987

Last night I had another bout with "midnight madness". It was not directed at any specific issue, but seemed to come from a dream about various aspects of nursery operations. I lay awake for a while reflecting on what had happened in the dream and what was going on in the nursery. My thoughts seemed to center on what I saw as poor interpersonal relationships among key employees. All of this would be nothing more than just uncomfortable if it were nothing more, but it is. I see it as having a serious impact on the nursery and its future. The issues are human issues. They seem to lie in a lack of consideration of others, and failure to see Christ in others. The issues seem to be associated with multiple power plays and their effect on the financial bottom line. I raged. This time there were no snakes ripped from my muscle tissue, but I raged for almost an hour and finally fell back to sleep. This whole thing is having a real impact on my spiritual life and I can't seem to control it.

By this time the nursery had become a stone around my neck. At first it was a tunnel out of the stockade of midlife despair and boredom. The preparation, planning, and initial development of the nursery had been exciting. Seeing thousands of cuttings take root and grow to mature plants under my control and nurturing was fascinating. But by 1987 the real issues became business management: finance, personnel problems, inventory control and the logistics of preparing and shipping orders were not my strengths. I had pinned my hopes on my son-in-law, John, to cover those aspects of the business and the production manager to take care of the day-to-day horticultural aspects. This was my plan for a stable, though a little bit top heavy, management structure that would run the operation on a daily basis leaving me to retire from teaching and do what I wanted, which was to be a secular contemplative and to play to my strengths in the nursery, such as propagation. By 1987 I had so identified with this plan that I had invested an unrealistic hope in it. It became my vision of the future. My ego self became the defender of my faith in that future. Anything that challenged that future became a threat.

After a little over six months of procrastination I finally arranged for a retreat at St. Gregory's Abbey at Three Rivers, Michigan. I had been an Episcopalian all my life, and until Fr. Tom and Susan had mentioned the monastery as a good place for a retreat I not only did not know that St. Gregory's existed, I did not know that there were over forty different Anglican religious orders with about seventy different communities in Canada and the United States.

I asked John to go with me, hoping to provide an opportunity for us to get to know each other better on the drive up and back. I took a book of meditations on icons by Henri Nouwen. I had been working with Susan on darkness and light and good and evil in the world, and in the process of doing that had read *The Earth Sea Trilogy* by Ursula Le Guin and *A Swiftly Tilting Planet* by Madeline L'Engle. Susan had also recommended *Behold the Beauty of the Lord* by Henri Nouwen. I planned to use Nouwen's book to further my exploration of light, darkness and anger.

June 27, 1987
    I came here to meditate on light and darkness—good and evil. And as with so many other experiences I have had in the past six months it just didn't turn out as I expected. I ought to have known this was going to happen and avoided having such specific expectations. It took about twenty-four hours before the effects of the monastery environment set in and began to take hold. At first, the Liturgy of the Divine Office made no sense to me. I had read about it in books by Merton, but I was not really prepared for the experience.
    I have been reading back in my journal since I have been up here, and I have been struck by how much in the journal reflects an interest in light and darkness.

What I have been thinking while at St. Gregory's is nothing new, but it is refreshing to get a new perspective on it, and to find out that my interest has been shared by other people. It was Henri Nouwen who set me onto 1st John. "Fear is driven out by perfect love." I am beginning to think that what I thought was anger is really anxiety and fear of losing control. If my fear is ever driven out by perfect love then I would have nothing left to fear but God. Would I ever fear perfect love? Teach me to love you with joy, for he who loves you fears nothing that is of this earth. What broke this open for me was a meditation, "Living in the house of Love," in Nouwen's book *Behold the Beauty of the Lord*.

June 29, 1987

Back from St. Gregory's, followed by a typical day at the nursery, at home and at the university. I cannot be a secular contemplative with any integrity in this setting. I will have to accept the best of compromises, pray as much as I can, and learn to pray while driving, working, and eating.

June 30, 1987

It may be that after a long day, meditation is not the right thing to be doing. I need to reflect on this. In the afternoon I can usually do meditation with vespers at 5:00 P.M. But at night I am too tired to dredge up the energy to concentrate, and I often fall asleep.

July 4, 1987

"Fear is driven out by perfect love." I just finished using this piece of scripture to meditate on the humanity of Jesus. In one hour Olga and I will be spending at least three hours with John, Pam and Kate. It is inevitable that a conflict filled issue involving the nursery will come up in this time that is supposed to be social, Father, we are going to need your help. Make your presence felt among us.

August 20, 1987

I remain anxious about lack of fruitful contemplation concerning my retirement a year from now. Be still, have patience. Let God work. Let God guide you. Don't try to force yourself to come up with a plan of action. In time God will get around to you. Your part now is to die to that part of your false self that gets in your way of experiencing God. Now, begin working on that which separates you from God so that when God reveals himself to you, you will be ready for him.

The summer of 1987 was rather typical of summers in my life since I took on the dual life of teacher and nurseryman. There was never time to do either job well. Summer in the nursery was the time when we did most of the propagation, and sales were usually slow. It was hot and we often went for long periods without rain. Keeping the plants adequately watered was always a big issue. If a problem was going to happen in the nursery during the summer it was going to involve the irrigation or the mist propagation systems. It frequently happened. I found myself praying for small problems. Fortunately my work was lighter at the university during the summer, but still it demanded constant attention. I learned to dread the long hot summers. By 1987 it had become obvious that we were either going to have to do some controlled expansion and cut costs, or we were not going to be able to compete in the current market. This put additional pressure on John and on me. We did not always respond with cool confidence, and I am sure that we radiated a lack of confidence to the nursery staff.

My spiritual journey continued during this time and proceeded on a path that seemed as dry as central Ohio summers. Issues of good and evil, light and darkness dug in to return in the future. I continued with spiritual direction and meditative prayer in fits and starts, and I read the Daily Office regularly. The effects of the retreat at St. Gregory's had worn off and I was ready for another retreat vacation on Long Beach Island. The first part of September could not come soon enough.

September 8, 1987
Long Beach Island—We left Ohio on Thursday of last week and headed East with the intention of arriving at the island on Sunday after spending a couple of days with family and old friends along the way. In general, this happened as planned except that one of our visits was cut short after an episode that revealed the violence and lack of love that can characterize people, and the void of hope in which they can live. We left a day early and proceeded on to the island.

There is an expression that what goes around comes around, and that you meet yourself going and coming. For me, and for many others, I believe that this is true. It seems that once is not enough. It just doesn't stick. This was certainly the case as far as my understanding of the contemplative life and contemplative prayer was concerned. A rereading of Merton's views on contemplation and contemplative prayer nudged me enough to realize that for some time I had been drifting in understanding and in practice toward quietism. I was using the contemplative life and contemplative prayer to avoid my responsibility to love others. I was using the life of prayer as an end rather than as a means. If I ever understood it, I had forgotten that transformation depended on God's love and the love of others, to nurture growth of the spiritual self. How this happened I do not understand, but it happened. Fortunately, Long Beach Island had a positive effect on me. While I was there, I began to realize that I had some serious issues to face.

September 10, 1987
Over the last year I have made some progress toward finding God, but I have really missed the obvious. I thought that "The Power and Meaning of Love" had

turned me around but I suspect that I still miss the point. I still do not really understand what love is. Today I took the journey again into the depths of my spiritual self and found God where he has always been.

The real issue is not which is better, the expression of love in the active or the passive life. The real issue is that we love others. Both Mary and Martha really loved others. They just expressed their love in different ways. In my life I have failed to do that. I have always sought to love my false self above all else.

Each of us has, since the mythical Garden of Eden, been faced with the misuse of their capacity to be free. We have used our freedom to serve the false self first, and in doing so failed to love God first in other people.

September 15, 1987

It seems clear that either I will need to develop better concentration in the presence of noise and human interaction in close quarters here on the island, or in the future we will need to find a larger apartment on the beach. The television and Olga's need to talk with me when we are in the same room create real problems for reading and meditation. Two's company but three's a crowd, and that T.V. is a third party intruder. I am feeling a need for space, and time to be alone without demands. The need to resolve the struggle between the reflective and the active life remains.

While on Long Beach Island Olga and I took a day trip to again visit East Coast relatives and friends. The circumstances of the visit had the same effect on me that it had on the stopover coming here. It shocked me into a realization that I did not want, but ultimately it had a long-term positive effect on me. It raised once against the question of love and of responsibility to one's neighbor. It illustrated how broad a definition of neighbor can be, and indeed must be, if there is any chance of the world growing and maturing in love. The effect of this day of intense immersion with another very dysfunctional family situation took a number of years before it was translated into social action in my life, but the seeds were sown that day.

September 17, 1987

There is little sense in trying to deny my feelings or cover up the events of yesterday. We live in a world that is socially sick. Of course there is physical and mental illness and there is spiritual sickness, but on top of all of this sickness there is a fog of social sickness that feeds and grows on the physical, mental and spiritual sickness of the world.

No wonder the world lives on diversion: T.V., drugs, sexual flings, alcoholism, fast living of a hundred kinds that help us to deny how socially sick we are. Diversion deadens the pain for the moment, but does not cure. It is not that I became aware of this social plague yesterday for the first time. It is that I got deeply enough into it to see the death and despair of society so closely that I realized for the first time not just what is going on, but also what it is doing to me and those around me. I realized how it has infected us. The pebble causes a ripple that affects all—everything forever. It would take an army of Mother Teresas to gather the sick, wash them, feed them and begin to heal them. We do not have that army. At best we have a frail few, who are professionally trained and emotionally strong enough to tend the sick.

September 18, 1987
One day later and I am still shaken. I need to become better aware of my emotions and to develop greater ability to be sensitive to others around me. I need to be honest with myself. I need to be honest enough to hear what God says about this.

I was totally unprepared for this experience. It shook my conviction about following a path that would lead me to a contemplative life. I thought naively about creating an army of volunteers who would go into the communities and fight this social disease. Of course such an army already existed in the form of community social services, domestic violence services, alcohol and drug abuse programs, hospice support groups, psychological and family counseling that would at least try to contain the disease and slow its spread, but more needed to be done.

I had never considered a vocation of social work, and had no idea of where to start. The latent Mary/Martha conflict within me was ignited again, but by the time Olga and I got back from our retreat vacation, and I was involved once again at the university and in the nursery, the fire was stoked while I attended to other issues. I returned to a contemplative discipline as best I could, and resolved to redouble my efforts to bring love to the world.

September 25, 1987
Back from the vacation retreat. Met yesterday with Susan and started this morning with a discipline that reflects the back to basics plan that I considered before I left on vacation.

October 1, 1987
It has been a week since I started getting up at 4:30 to do Morning Office and meditation. I find it easy to get up at 4:30 for prayer, and my concentration has been good. I feel as if what I am doing is right. I have also been attending Eucharist on Wednesday mornings at 7:00. Olga thinks this is a bit much. At present I plan to continue and get some direction from Susan.

October 4, 1987
Something has been trying to come out but has just not made it to the bright light of awareness. I think that I made some headway in my last meeting with Susan. I said that I thought that I did not really know what love meant. In a meeting

with Cici on Friday about her being an aspirant for Holy Orders I realized how much joy and love she feels for people who she works with. I love the idea of people, but quite often not the reality of people. If I want to know what is meant by God's will for me it will certainly be found in that which is required of me in order that I may be united with others in love. The quiet life and the active life are both places for expressing God's love. Of course! But how do they work together?

October 18, 1987

Yesterday was a Quiet Day at Church, and several of us worked with Sr. Noreen, a Dominican nun from Columbus. It was a good day and from it came a bit more growth in being able to risk my faith and to trust God. I am becoming more and more aware of the need for a balance of quiet and action in my life. From my contemplative prayer comes the awareness that I must guide the love given me by God back through my life with my fellow man. To be in union with God is to experience God's love for others through my actions. But what is God's love like? The search continues.

October 23, 1987

I just read over the journal entries of the past few days and reflected on an emotional conversation with Olga on Wednesday in which she said that she "wanted an appointment with me." It was in this conversation that she suggested that I give up early morning prayer except on weekends because it was causing me to be tired, tense, irritable, short tempered, and that this was being directed toward her and others in the family, and further that it was bad for my emotional and physical health. Clearly, she thought the matter was serious.

This afternoon I happened to have a session with Susan and I presented the issue to her. She said that people who take on a spiritual journey open themselves to greater opportunities for failure and despair because of their covenant relationship with God. The thing to keep in mind is not how far I miss the mark. This will happen. The challenge is in how I respond to God. Susan's reaction was that as far as the early morning prayer routine is concerned it should be continued. Olga's reaction to it is common. Often friends, spouse, children, etc. feel distanced from a person who has chosen to take up with God in a serious way because of the attention that is obviously directed to God and not to them. But, it should not cause me to be unloving of myself or those around me. If the demands of the discipline are too great then I must look at my whole life and make necessary adjustments. I'm not a monk in a monastic community; I am trying to be a secular contemplative. There is a difference. In so far as Olga is concerned I must approach her, try to communicate my love for her and for God and help her to remember that I can't be in two places at the same time. I must negotiate an understanding with Olga so that the pilgrimage is maintained, so that others near me experience as much love from me as possible, so that my physical and mental health are not sacrificed. And when I fail, I must remember that I am not perfect, and that I should not try to be anyone other than a seeker who is trying to find God and be transformed into his love.

October 24, 1987

Last night Olga and I again discussed the issue of my prayer life, sleep, etc. We were in no disagreement on the desirability of prayer but rather on the matter of priorities. In this case I think that my highest priority, as perceived by her, is my spiritual life. For Olga it is my health and losing my relationship with her and the family.

We agreed that we would monitor my disposition and health, and that I would return to my prayer discipline so long as it was not detrimental to my health or family relationships. This morning I got up at 5:30 instead of 4:30.

By the end of October, I had been on my spiritual journey for a little over a year. I had experienced some satisfaction, some discomfort and some real despair. My relationship with Olga, with my spiritual director, and with God all played a critical role in helping me to keep on the path and get back on when I got lost. When I started a year earlier I had no idea how necessary it would be to recognize and accept the guidance of others. I am convinced that without the solicited and unsolicited feedback from Olga and Susan, and without the sometimes subtle and sometimes obvious markers left by God along the way I would have gotten hopelessly lost, given up and returned to where I started. No one, no matter how strong they think they are, should ever think that they can go it alone. Though I had little idea what was ahead for me, I had no thought of giving up. That thought would have been unthinkable.

At this point in my spiritual journey it was difficult for me to realize how much my willfulness and my ego self's protection of my false self were standing in my way. I was determined to succeed in being a secular contemplative, but this willful determination was not always the most helpful means to the desired end.

## NOTES

1. Thomas Merton, "The Power and Meaning of Love," in *Disputed Questions* (New York: Harcourt Brace Jovanovich, 1960), 123.

2. Thomas Merton, "Humility Against Despair," in *New Seeds of Contemplation* (New York: New Directions Books, 1972), 180.

3. Thomas Merton, *Zen and the Birds of Appetite* (New York: New Directions Books, 1968), 76–77.

*Chapter Two*

# Hope and Despair

My first year as a novice was intermittently filled with hope and despair. Some days I felt very encouraged. After all I had gotten started; I was able to find a spiritual director; I was following a prayer discipline; and things were happening in my spiritual life that were new and exciting. But the year also had its down side. There were dry periods in prayer; there were challenges to my beliefs; there were the uncomfortable times when my false self was confronted and challenged; and there was the ever-present potential for depression that, though I had at last named it, I could do little to control it. On balance I had reason to be encouraged. I was more or less living a contemplative life, if only at a surface level. But lurking beneath that surface was an issue that I had not yet seriously considered, and until I faced it squarely I ran the risk of going through the motions of living like a secular contemplative without a real understanding of what was involved. The issue had to do with the central reason for contemplative prayer. I was paying more attention to the externals of contemplative prayer than the essentials. I thought that I could become a contemplative by concentrating on such matters as posture and breathing during prayer, adhering to a strict prayer schedule, and mastering various types of contemplative prayer, rather than by developing an understanding of how contemplative prayer related to union with God or transformation of the self by God's love. In other words I did not yet comprehend that being one with God in creation, and being God's love in the world are the true ends of contemplative prayer.

    A better understanding of contemplative spirituality might have helped me to realize that the contemplative way is lived out as a willingness to experience God's creative energy and love in the world, and a willingness to share that energy and love with those around me. I might have realized that living the contemplative life becomes a life of prayer that is an expression of a willingness to let God transform the self so that the self can become an expression of God's creation and love, but I didn't. Somewhere I had gotten the idea that a disciplined prayer life was all that was called for. Thus it was perfectly appropriate for my spiritual director to point out that though I should have a prayer discipline that was appropriate for my life, that my life was quite different from the life of a monk who was part of a religious community, and that certainly my practices of prayers should not cause separation from those around me or unloving actions on my part as a result of striving for spiritual perfection. I needed a wife and a spiritual director to help me understand this. My journal shows that by the beginning of my second year I was starting to feel like a contemplative, but there was still a lot about contemplative prayer that I did not really understand such as the difference between willingness and willfulness in the practice of prayer.

And of course, I carried a preference with me for thinking my way to understanding rather than allowing myself, through faith and willingness, to let God take the lead.

October 30, 1987

A major difference between an active and a contemplative is that the active believes that "With God's help I can do it," while the contemplative believes that "God will use me as a part of the process if I am willing." The idea that God will do it by using me if I am willing gives new meaning to the statement by Paul in which he says, "I no longer live but it is Christ that lives within me." But I still believe that I must submit myself to a prayer discipline that gets me ready to do God's work in the world.

The issue might be framed as, "To think or not to think about my faith, religion, and God." If I don't think then what will I do, that's who I am?" I guess I will just experience the presence of God working in and through me, and let it go at that. I think that this has been Olga's position since the beginning and that is what Susan was saying to me at our last meeting. She had a lot of trouble with the active vs. contemplative distinction that I talked about. She kept asking me, "But what difference does it make?" And I kept saying that making a distinction and thinking about it helped me to understand God and how God works in the world. One thing is for sure and that is the distinction got a reaction from Susan, and it forced me to think about why it got such a reaction. It got me wondering if making the active vs. contemplative distinction really did help me to think about God.

November 22, 1987

In his August 12th entry of the *Genesee Diary*,[1] Henri Nowen asks his spiritual director some insightful questions that I can identify with. I too have often wondered who it is that I am really praying to when I pray. When I shared this with Olga she could not find it credible. She said, "I know exactly to whom I pray when I say Lord, and I have for a long time. It's a shame that some intellectuals feel the need to question such things rather than taking them on faith." I think that this is what Susan was saying to me about my interest in the difference between an active and a contemplative spirituality. Olga and Susan just accept on faith a lot of things that Henri Nouwen and I need to think about. But what am I to do? Am I to deny who I am, or shall I just accept who I am and enjoy the process?

What seems to be going on in my spiritual life at this time is that I am growing, but my growth is still very cognitive. I really thought I would be able to figure it all out, that I would be able to think my way to an understanding of who God is. I am beginning to question who God is for me. I am beginning to wonder why other people seem to be able to love and why I fall short. I am questioning whether or not I even know what love is in a spiritual sense. I am beginning to ask what love has to do with God and with the contemplative life. I am just beginning to become aware of my false self and my true self, but I have not yet seen the implications of the challenge of the false self by the true self. All manner of new ideas are entering my spiritual life that will come in conflict with an already existing system of beliefs that I have held for years in a largely unconsidered way. In time I will become aware that this is what is going on, that the old and the new quite often will be unable to coexist, that conflict will be inevitable. I will want to figure it out. I will want to resolve the cognitive dissonance that I am experiencing, and I will have to accept that thinking my way through this process will only take me so far, and that when I get to that point I will need to proceed on faith. I will need to accept that only faith will enable me to go through the death of the false self and the growth of the true self, not a regimen of discipline and hard work. All of this was stirring within me as I reached the second Advent of my journey.

November 28, 1987
Tomorrow is the first Sunday in Advent. Susan gave me a koan for Advent meditation—"Who is the Christ within you who is waiting to be born?" I am also to read my journal from last Advent before my next session with her.

December 5, 1987
My session with Susan on Thursday was very productive. I got the sense that she believes that I am making progress. Probably I have been making progress all along, but there comes a time when enough progress is made that it is noticed. I get the feeling that this is happening. I do feel changed in many ways. What has all of this to do with who I am becoming? And who is the Christ within me waiting to be born?
Tomorrow is the second Sunday in Advent. I am waiting, and in the meantime I ran into Henri Nouwen again. In his November 6th entry in his *Genesee Diary*

Nouwen talks with his spiritual director, John Eudes, about the exhaustion that he feels that is associated with conducting retreats. His spiritual director helps him to understand that it is his ego drive to want to prove to himself that he is worthy that causes the fatigue. This autumn quarter I have had fewer instances of feeling wiped out after class. Perhaps I am beginning to intuitively understand that feelings of worth are ultimately related to what God, and my true self think of me rather than what others think of me. In many respects I have done one of my best jobs of teaching this quarter.

December 12, 1987

Today I read the section on Student J's conversations with the Roshi in *The Three Pillars of Zen*. The Buddha is not Christ, but in too many ways to recount, the experiences of this woman (Student J) parallels my experience with my koan, "Who is the Christ in me who waits to be born?" Only she asks the question, "Who am I?"

December 14, 1987

In the last few days my reading has had a direct link to the pursuit of the question, "Who is the Christ within me who is waiting to be born?" In a sermon he gave recently titled "Asking The Question," Thomas Shaw says that we often do not ask such questions because we do not really want the answer. It seems that there is more than just a little of that in my prayer life. I am reminded that if I don't ask I might not receive, but if I ask for an elephant I better have a big living room. Am I waiting to become one who seeks knowledge of the source of all compassion, or am I waiting to become one who seeks to be compassionate?

December 18, 1987

What would I give for a penetrating view of God in me and in the world? I have had fleeting glimpses of light, union, and God's compassion for humankind and the world, but these glimpses have only given me a taste for the desire to see more of God. God must have been all over the place last night at the Partners in Prayer meeting at church, but I couldn't see him anywhere. I am always in my own line of vision. I always block my own sight.

December 28, 1987

Advent has come and gone and I have given no birth to Christ. There was no last minute flurry of spiritual enlightenment, no "Oh! Now I know who I am," or anything like that. It was a flat stretch of desert road and I walked the last few miles with little effort. I waited through the end of Advent and nothing happened. (I know that I don't really believe that "nothing happened" it's just that what I hoped for didn't happen.) I think that I am beginning to understand that the process of transformation by God is going on all the time in God's way. I just don't see it. I daily forget this by focusing on the "I" as if I could cause God to do anything. In short it seems that I have put too much emphasis on belief rather than on faith.

I still believed that I could think my way into union with God. In time I would get to the point where I could answer the question, "Who is the Christ within me who is waiting to be born?" by responding from faith and willingness and by saying, "The true self who has always been within me, the true self who God created me to be, love."

At this point in my journey, I could occasionally talk the talk, but I had not yet begun to walk the walk. I was still convinced that I needed to know the answer to the question in a logical or empirical sense. I had not yet realized that there is a big difference between "being who I am now" and "being who God created me to be."

January 6, 1988

How long will it take me to realize that I am standing in my own way, casting a shadow on my own true self? When will I really have faith that I am God's creation and that I am loved without condition? This is my third day back at the university following Christmas break and I already have distinguished myself by showing symptoms of anger, or stress or something that has caused me to blow things out of perspective. I have stood in my own line of vision again, covered reality with my own shadow, and let things get out of focus. On Monday I got angry with John for not being at the nursery at 8:00 given all the personnel problems we have. On Tuesday during a steering committee meeting at the university I became unreasonable and sarcastic, and at breakfast today I got upset with Olga for no good reason. I left the table and gastrointestinal pain took me to the bathroom three times. Before I left for the university an odd sound in the water softener caused, I thought, by the freezing of the discharge line, resulted in my getting water all over the garage and myself and getting furious with Olga again just because she was there. Stress, but stress caused by what? Nothing of any consequence has occurred in my life recently. It has been a walk over flat terrain in darkness. Easy going for a night person and yet I have despaired, gotten angry and lost my direction time and time again in the past two weeks. God where are you?

January 17, 1988

Olga and I started a twelve-week program of spiritual friendship developed by Dorothy Devers. It's called *Faithful Friendship*. We had our first session today.

January 30, 1988

After the meeting at church last night I gave our rector a copy of my letter of recommendation regarding Ceci's aspirant experience and I gave a copy to Ceci. I thought that she had shown great potential and I said so. Tonight Ceci called to thank me for the letter. However, most of the conversation was spent in her expressing disappointment, frustration and anger that our rector was going to block her aspirancy because she thought that Ceci was not strong enough to be a priest. I was furious. This whole issue of the priesthood, expectations, qualifications and assumptions is perplexing, and I think raises serious questions about the church and the process that is used to select people for Holy Orders. The focus seems to be on institutional image and not on helping people like Ceci develop their strengths and potential.

In a similar way the university was not created to be supportive of individuals in cases of promotion and tenure. Both the church and the university may, and in some cases do "grow people," but the good dean, the good priest, the good bishop or the good professor are not necessarily people who need to pay attention to compassion or developing human potential so long as what they do furthers institutional goals.

In retrospect I think that my anger with the church and the university during the winter of 1987–88 was exacerbated by a bout with depression. If this was the case, then this was not a good time for me to have gotten involved with university or church politics. But I did. At the university I found myself on a personnel committee considering matters of promotion and tenure. At church I found myself chairing an advisory committee for aspirants to Holy Orders. Both at the university and at church I took the same approach. I allowed myself to become personally involved. In both cases I took the position of an advocate, and in both situations I took the position of a prophet and framed the issue as being one of supporting the personal growth of the individual over the short term image of the institution. In both cases I ran head long into opposition that I interpreted as a personal challenge of my judgment and integrity. I saw both cases as involving people who had real potential and were capable of real growth if given a supportive, nurturing climate. I lost in both cases.

February 5, 1988
In my session with Susan yesterday we talked a bit about what had happened to me at the university and the church. Later she said that many demands of the parish priest require her to do things that are not congruent with who she is and she wondered if I were not experiencing something similar to this in my work. Later in the session I lashed out again at the church. I still had in mind the conflict between Ceci and the church. My anger and frustration over the matter had not been resolved in my heart. I did not identify the source of my anger as being specifically at my parish, but identified it more broadly as the Church. Susan asked me if I wanted to talk about what was bothering me about the Church. I dodged the question. The session ended with a discussion about contemplatives and prophets, and with her reminding me that it had taken me a year to believe that I was a contemplative and that now I was dealing with the other side of the coin, the prophet. She reminded me that contemplatives often have a prophetic side, for example, Merton did.

Perhaps the questions that I should have been dealing with are these: how is the love of God, neighbor and self, expressed in the contemplative and prophetic life, and the related question: how is this lived out without allowing the self to create idols of one's personal view of what is right and wrong in the world?

February 21, 1988

I met with Susan on Thursday. I felt good after the session, but I don't remember why. I remember her being supportive and encouraging and suggesting that I was getting better, or getting sane as Gerald May would say. This was mainly because I had gotten up and journaled when I became furious again early Tuesday morning after thinking about how I had been manipulated at church over the aspirant matter, and by John in the nursery when I agreed to sign for a $45,000 line of credit for the nursery, which given the financial situation, I had no business doing. Friday, I stayed home from school, got materials duplicated for church, and went to bank and signed for the line of credit. In the afternoon I wrote a letter to the Commission on Ordination saying that a process that gave the same person (such as the parish rector) a power of judgment that amounted to a veto and at the same time gave them responsibility for the support, nurturing and growth of aspirants would not work. It would not work because it intermittently encouraged: (1) subservient dependence on authority (2) aggressive counter dependence on authority (3) indifference and entropy caused by a lack of trust in the system.

I woke up at 5:00 this morning. I was not in panic as I was on Tuesday morning—just wakeful. This morning I felt sad even though it was a bright day, and I took a walk around the nursery. I guess it is just a down day even though I know that if I lose the moment it will never be again, and to do that seems foolish on such a clear, bright day. Spring is on its way. Next week will be the beginning of March.

Three things were going on simultaneously in my life at this time. First, I was experiencing constant itching particularly at night. I thought it might be an anxiety-stress reaction, but whatever the cause it was disrupting my sleep. Secondly, I believe that I was entering an active period of depression. And thirdly, I was probably experiencing the internal conflict that comes from having my beliefs and my integrity challenged at the nursery, at church and at the University.

New insights into self, God and love were being laid on top of an already existing set of personal, religious and social values and beliefs that I had held for years. Something within me began to send messages that I couldn't have it both ways. The new had to be rejected or modified to conform to the old, or the old had to be let go of or be rebuilt to conform to the new. The old conceptions of self, God and love were not going to give up without a fight. It is my contention that a lot of the anger that I felt at the time was an expression of this conflict that was going on within me.

If someone had asked me what I believed about God at that time, I would have said that the Nicene Creed pretty well summarized my position, and that what was true about Jesus or Christ could be found in scripture. This was why when I originally read what Merton had written in "The Power and Meaning of Love" it made no sense to me. I believed nothing that I could fall back on in order to understand what it meant to talk about Christ in ourselves and Christ in our fellow man. Seeing Christ in my brother meant nothing to me because Christ died and ascended to heaven. What was Christ doing in me or in my brother anyhow?

I believed that what was wrong with society could be fixed if we just put our mind to it. This was particularly true of moral perfection. I had not yet learned to accept that the rigidity of the society I lived in made effective human intervention much more difficult than I thought. I believed that society was not perfect but it could be fixed if we only had the will to apply knowledge, morals, and scientific know-how to handle the issues at hand. Moon shots today, the rest of the universe tomorrow, cancer today, a cure tomorrow, crime, corruption, cruelty today, a world of moral perfection tomorrow.

For sometime I had found the self to be something interesting to consider, but this did not mean that it had always been a beautiful thing to behold. In my way of thinking about the self, the ugly aspects of self could be taken care of by determination and or hard work, and sin could be handled by confession and absolution. That would take care of my moral problems. Determination was akin to will power, and being willful was normal, natural and desirable as long as it wasn't taken too far. Hard work, not cleanliness, was next to godliness. If one had a clear conscience, had a willfulness directed toward good purposes, and worked hard there would be no real problem with the self.

The existence of a false self largely shaped by society, and a true self created and shaped by God was something that I didn't really understand. The thought that my false self needed major repairs or needed to be ditched never occurred to me. My ego was under control. It was others who had some work to do. And, the thought that my spiritual self was God's love waiting to be developed within me and shared with others was as inconceivable as Christ being found within me and my brothers and sisters.

It is no wonder then that as my core beliefs and values began to be challenged by a new set of beliefs and values; my world was revealed not as I wanted to imagine it to be, but something a lot more earthy.

March 5, 1988

    I have been awake for almost an hour with severe itching. I finally got up and took a Prednisone pill. By this time I was wide awake and I began to feel anger creep over me, and the feelings that were at first directed toward the itching began to be directed toward my family doctor, John, and even my church rector. I began to experience those mixed feelings of anxiety, fear and anger that rendered me helpless to defend myself against myself. I decided to get up and journal rather than have these feelings overwhelm me.

March 10, 1988

It is 5:00 A.M. and I just lost it! I jumped out of bed, took my clothes, went to the bathroom, washed my face, brushed my teeth and got up. But why did I do this in rage? I did it because I was beside myself with itching. I have been itching since last August. I have itched mostly at home, and mostly at night and in the early morning. My sleep is constantly disturbed. Is it emotional or physical? What is the difference? I itch and I am getting to the point where I almost don't want to come home for another night of "torture." God where are you in all of this? I don't know, but you are in it somewhere. You know what is going on. O.K., I lost it. I jumped out of bed in rage and self-pity. I am, after all, a bit too human not to be human. Another day starts. There is no room left in what remains of this day for more self-serving pity.

March 11, 1988

I woke up this morning feeling rested and refreshed. What a wonderful feeling. It has been so long since I have felt this way. No itching, no feelings of depression, no anything but a desire to get up and start the day. Today, I go to see the people in the personnel office about retirement details. I have appointments with students, and then a faculty meeting. I will probably drop by the hospital to see if Kelly is still there.

Today I need to be concerned with love. There is more love to be spread around this world than the world can ever use up, and just one more drop of anxiety, anger, or fear may push the balance of this earth past the point of no return. I do not think that would happen. God would "clean things up" before he would let his whole creation go down the drain.

Later: When I got home I went into the nursery to inspect the irrigation renovations that involved installing gate valves on several major laterals. The men had not understood the system and had installed the valves in the wrong places. As I started to talk with John about the situation, I began to get worked up and felt a rush of anger, "If John had only walked the area with me this morning it would never had happened, etc." By the time I had said all I had to say I had effectively wounded his self-concept as an independent, competent manager. I would never have done that intentionally and only in retrospect did I see what I had done.

"I do not do what I want, but I do the very thing that I hate."
(*Romans* 7:15.)

God died for us, He hung on a cross and died for us, and all we are asked to do is to love one another. That seems like a pretty good deal and particularly when we realize that we continue to be loved even when we fail. What an amazing God! The trick is to be loving in good times and in bad. That's difficult enough for me to do when everything is going my way, but when things are not going so well, I find it almost impossible to love people who are a threat to my well designed world as I think it should be.

March 14, 1988

Why do sick people turn night into day? Is it because they finally get to the point where the day is so threatening or meaningless that they sleep it away and, then who are they faced with in the black of night but themselves who they can stand perhaps least of all?

I want to live. I don't want to die. My sickness now is not heart or vascular disease. My sickness now is losing heart. I have put myself in a box of my own making. Death is not the way out. There is only one way out and I seem to reject that way. I have come close to falling all the way to the bottom of the pit.

March 16, 1988

"Weeping may linger for the night, but joy comes with the morning. (*Psalm* 30:5)." Another night of itching starting at about 4:00, this time no anger. I just feel defeated.

March 19, 1988

Praise be. This is the first night's sleep without itching since last Saturday. The alarm clock awakened me, but I had slept for nine hours and I was rested. No itching, no disturbing dreams just a feeling of peace. And now to Morning Office as the sun rises into the pink and blue sky against which are silhouetted spruce on our property and the silos on Jim's farm across the road. The sun is now up and there is a heavy frost on the ground. The smell of coffee is in the air and I think of the great joy that this moment gives me.

March 21, 1988

Even though I was up at 1:45 this morning to take an itch pill, I feel better about myself. Why?—because I did not strike out in anger at anyone or anything. I accepted the condition as a state of being. I wonder what John Fandell or Madeleine L'Engle could do with the title, "The Midnight Itch?"

The itching persisted through March and April into May. That period covered the end of Lent and the Easter season. During that time I found myself dealing actively with a very central part of my belief system, the part that dealt with the death and resurrection of Jesus. It was also the time that led up to my retirement from teaching. I was entering the period in which I would no longer be a university professor, and I would have the time to become someone I had never truly been, a serious contemplative.

It was also the time that covered the terminal illness and death of Kelly, my closest friend and colleague. Kelly was a person whom I had known as a friend, fishing buddy and close professional colleague for over thirty years. In time, Kelly's death became a metaphor for considering the meaning of the death of Jesus. And from this experience came progress toward an enduring spirituality.

March 25, 1988
Today Susan and I discussed that part of the Creed that says that Jesus descended into hell and then three days later rose from the dead. I don't think I ever really understood what it means or what the implications are. I have just taken it literally, but I have had all kinds of problems with it. It is time to give this prayerful thought and meditation in the next few days.

March 28, 1988
I have been thinking that because Jesus was fully human, he was capable of experiencing all human conditions including doubt. As God, he knew God's full intentions but as man he was still capable of doubt. In the Garden he revealed his doubt, "Take this cup away from me." On the Cross he revealed his doubt, "My God why have you forsaken me?" And, as he died he entered into human death with doubt. Until the moment of his resurrection on Sunday his human spirit was tortured by the fear of trusting in what may have been nothing more than self-indulgence with the consequence of being separated from God for eternity. This was the hell he experienced. For now this is what descending into hell means to me, but there must be more to it then this.

By the end of March I had hit another spiritually dry part of the road. Issues relating to my early retirement from teaching and the nursery seemed to dominate my attention. I continued with meditation, Daily Office, the *Faithful Friendship* program with Olga and with spiritual direction, but nothing seemed to excite me. The source seemed to have dried up. Nothing bubbled up from inside.

Long periods of dryness seem to be a natural part of the rhythm of a spiritual journey. At times like this many people, and I have been among them, seek relief from their emptiness by finding excitement in the world of entertainment, exciting social experiences, or the use of substances to alter their perception of the world as being boring or painful. Advertising agencies know this well and are ready and willing to exploit human vulnerability and fill the void with products and services that will once again make life interesting. But the excitement of cultural stimulation sooner or later dries up leaving the answer to be found in more and bigger. The fun runs out before the time runs out and we are back to where we started—bored and empty walking a flat, dry road.

A working spirituality should help us to see that the spring has not dried up, that there is within us a source of purpose and reason for existence. There is within each of us a true self that if allowed to do so, can grow and prosper. But the true self will not be found by looking outward to society to find who we should be. It will be found by looking inward to discover what has always been there. It is real and it is good. It just needs to be uncaged and allowed to roam free and find its place in a very big world. That world would often wish that our true self would remain contained so that we would follow the way that the world would wish us to follow. Yes, we will go through dry periods on a spiritual journey, but an adequate spirituality should help us to see that dry and moist, hot and cold, up and down are part of the natural rhythm of life like winter and spring. We are born, we live and we die. We are a part of that rhythm of the universe whether we want to take part in it or not.

In my corner of the universe at that time, I was living through several significant death experiences. I was within a few months of early retirement from teaching and partial retirement from the nursery. This in turn would lead to a loss of an identity that I had lived with for over thirty years. My friend Kelly was in and out of the hospital and it was clear that he had only a short time to live. Incidentally, this was also the period of Lent and Easter in the liturgical cycle, the season for death and rebirth.

It was in this context that my spiritual director inserted a challenge that followed up on our discussion about Jesus dying and going to hell and then rising from the dead. In time that challenge would open my beliefs and bring me to a completely new way of looking at Lent, Easter and God. Her comment was that she was not at all sure that I believed in a bodily resurrection. At the time I took the challenge to be an empirical rather than a spiritual issue as my April 3, 1989 journal entry indicates.

April 3, 1988
Last Thursday, Susan said to me "I am not at all sure that you believe in a bodily resurrection." As a matter of fact, I am not certain about my beliefs. Yet today it seems that the evidence is in favor of a bodily resurrection of Jesus. The eyewitness accounts, the empty tomb, the burial clothes, the guards and the rock rolled away, the accounts of those who saw his nail wounds following that first Easter are empirical evidence to support a resurrection.

April 12, 1988
There are times when I think that my quest for God leads me to ideas that demand that they be lived out in my life before I can understand them, for example, the ideas of hell and resurrection. In recent weeks my life has been an exercise in understanding hell. Olga describes me as a person who has cut himself off from life by self-imposed sadness. She sees me as a person under the stress of two transitions: retirement from teaching, and giving up my central role in the nursery. I think she may be right. As a point of fact I could die to my conception of self as a professor and a nurseryman, both at the same time, and be reborn into someone else. Or, I could die to both selves and leave myself with no one to be, nothing to do, no place to go. That would be hell. And if I am frank and open with myself I do not know who or what I want to be, or what God wants of me.

April 19, 1988

I had a long conversation with Pam last night that gave me a deeper understanding of who I might become in the months and years ahead. I also had several conversations with John over the weekend as we drove to Spring Hill Nursery to get liner plants. In those conversations I said that I felt that I had not always been very clear or helpful in trying to determine a role for myself in the nursery when I retired nor had I always been consistent in giving John real responsibility. I still hoped that my life as a secular contemplative would enable me to become who I believed I had been created to be, but I am not at all sure what that will mean.

Today I thought of an idea that would enable me to be a serious contemplative and at the same time work in the nursery and be with the family as a member of community when I retire. I'll try to follow this plan for the next six to eight weeks, and see how it goes. Then when I finish up at the university this summer and start retirement, I will have some idea of whether it will work or not.

April 21, 1988

Yesterday, I tried to put my new plan into effect and there was both good and bad news. On the good news side I mostly followed the schedule in principle but on the bad news side I was the one who violated my own time for contemplation. This seemed to be the result of falling back on old, bad habits as much as anything else.

April 25, 1988

How goes the new plan and the discipline? They are being poorly kept. I can't compartmentalize my life this way and then stick to the schedule come what may. It won't work. This reminds me of a situation last year when I developed a prayer schedule and there were so many distractions that I started getting up at 4:30 in the morning to do prayer and I was so tired during the day that I got cranky and unreasonable. Am I repeating the same mistake again?

April 29, 1988

Yesterday I had a session with Susan and we talked about the plan I had developed. She suggested that the schedule and the discipline of the monks at Three Rivers was designed for an enclosed order of men who had a completely different life than I had, and that I should consider a more flexible approach that allowed the regular events of the day to enter and flow through my discipline. She did not think that I was crazy to consider a contemplative life, but she said that I still had to figure out a spiritual life that was right for me and for my circumstances.

April 30, 1988

I got a call from Kelly's wife. She said that Kelly had said, "I put it in God's hands but I think it is too late." He is in University Hospital again. From what I can understand he had a procedure for a colon blockage on Saturday, a catheterization and angioplasty procedure on Tuesday and then suffered a heart attack.

He asked his wife to call me before the angioplasty on Tuesday, but she never got around to it.

Jesus died and yet he lives. His resurrection does not have to have been a bodily resurrection for us to have faith and hope. If it was, O.K., if it wasn't, that's O.K. too. It really doesn't make much difference one way or the other. It's still the greatest story ever told because Christ lives. I hope Kelly didn't come to this too late. He may have come just in time, or perhaps he has known it all along. The dispute over the facts of the resurrection are not what is important. Kelly, like Christ, will continue to live because of the faith, hope and love he invested in the people who have known him.

May 1, 1988

What it comes down to is faith. The historical facts are suspect, and the search for historical truth leads us at best to legend and myth, the truth of which lies in the hearts of man. And when that myth is told in the language of poetry it becomes a very good story. It is unlikely that the search for the historical Jesus will lead us to an unchallenged narrative built on the life of the man. We feed on legend and myth; it nourishes our souls. Why not let it nourish?

May 4, 1988

Kelly died late Sunday afternoon. His wife called Sunday night about 10:00, and while she talked with me she asked if I would give the eulogy at the funeral service. I said I would.

May 5, 1988

Yesterday came as close to being a day lived in prayer as I can remember in the recent past. I accepted Susan's suggestion that I open the windows of my discipline and allow the Spirit of the events of the day to enter. I am not a cloistered monk in an enclosed community. I am a secular contemplative, and if I am I must live like one in the daily celebration of life in the secular world. Oh yes, I would have liked to have been aware of God all the time yesterday, but I was aware frequently enough to make yesterday a celebration of life.

May 16, 1988

I am not at all sure but perhaps the whole message that we are to hear about our life here on Earth is that it is a bumpy road with lots of ups and downs. We are controlled by things that we think we can control, and God lets us make our way through all of this waiting for us to turn to him. God wants us to love and trust him because loving and trusting are healthy.

Grief over Kelly's death, anxiety about my impending retirement from the university and from the nursery and an uncomfortable uncertainty about what I would do with my life when I did retire were constantly on my mind. Thinking about them just built up more anxiety that sapped the energy I should have been directing toward my spiritual life. I was indeed on a very uncomfortable stretch of road.

May 19, 1988

The diagnosis for the itching is scabies not a stress related allergy. I saw a dermatologist yesterday. O.K., but when I think of all the time since last August that I spent in misery I wonder why my family doctor didn't recommend the dermatologist earlier? I awakened this morning before the alarm. I was calm.

What is this world that I live in? On some days I think that it's a cruel, impersonal place, and on other days I think that it so wonderful that I could burst. Today it seems as if there is something about to happen, and that it will be one of those things that I will grow from. Perhaps it would be best to just let the day happen and go about doing those things that appear in front of me to be done. Perhaps it will be best if I just "do the day" instead of trying to make it into something more or less than it really wants to be.

May 20, 1988

I could have awakened this morning in panic, but I didn't. I awakened with a realization that when I allow the urges, sensations, feelings and forces of the world to act on me and diminish me while I stand by and let it happen, that this is not what God has in mind for me. It's O.K. to be willing to allow myself to be swept up by God and taken where God will take me, but it is not O.K. to be diminished by the forces of entropy in the world. Where did all of this come from? It came from a dream I had just before I awakened. In the dream I was doing my part in the big scheme of things to make sure that things turned out as I wanted them to. Doing my part and trusting others to do their part felt good.

It seems as if the task ahead of me is to help overcome entropy in the world, but to do this in a way that still allows time and energy to be me. This is a great deal different from spending myself in a frenzy of self inflicted activity and anxiety.

May 28, 1988

This has been a week with the Spirit. My life has been touched with that peace that passes understanding. Anger, anxiety and resentment have been given back to God for him to deal with. I have felt real joy. My whole body feels drunk with joy. Yes, joy. I found joy. I keep asking myself: "What am I doing when I feel the presence of God?" "Why does God want me to do this?" "Which of the talents given to me by God am I using?" In a few days Pam and I will be going to St. Gregory's Abbey for a short retreat. I look forward to it.

June 9, 1988

This morning I got up half an hour earlier to do the Office and meditate. This is the time between matins and lauds at St. Gregory's. While I was meditating it dawned on me that I really am spiritually in process, and that the process takes a lifetime. This is what being in process means, always approaching but never entering the inner room. I have my good days and I have my better days, and even really down days, but these down days are less frequent, less intense, and of shorter duration than they used to be. As I sit here at the table by the window writing in my journal this morning's sunrise is a classic example of God's work in full glory.

The summer passed much like each summer has since I took on a dual life as university professor and nurseryman. I met my classes, worked with students on their dissertations, did the ever-present committee work and professional reading. In the nursery things went much like they have for years. Propagation and irrigation assumed top priority and as usual there were problems with both. Sales fell during the hot summer season and we all lived in anticipation of autumn in hopes that the American Nurseryman's Association's slogan "Fall Is For Planting" would really catch on this time. The summer was much like many before it excepting for three things: it was my last quarter at the university; I was really trying to let go of the principal management role in the nursery and shift it to John; I was becoming increasingly aware that after almost two years on my spiritual journey things were beginning to happen. Slow transformation was taking place and I thought that my episodes of anxiety and anger were less severe and of shorter duration. My journal reveals that though there were spiritually dry periods, I seemed to be having greater trust in God and that I was having moments of peace that came with that trust. There had been no radical transformation, but there was evidence of change. I judged that change to be good.

July 15, 1988
Things are happening in me, and all around me. I sense that just over the hill is a more fertile area, one filled with potential for refreshment and growth. I want to see what is over the hill and what is ahead for me.

July 23, 1988
I didn't have any classes today and I was feeling anxious and very much on edge about the future, so instead of going to the university I went to Highbanks Park for the morning and the library for the afternoon. What happened between when I left and when I returned home was very important for me. I gave the whole thing to God in contemplative prayer. I did not just rehearse the problems to myself. I took a nap in the car, and did some reading. In short, I got away from the intensity of the immediate problem. It was a day of prayer and a realization that I could not willfully solve my own problems. I turned to God in a condition of indigence and gave my fears and disappointments to him. God wants me to do that. God wants me to come to him in despair as well as in joy. I slept through the night until 7:00. That is the longest night sleep that I have had in months.

July 29, 1988

I just came back from a direction session. We talked about how God works on me and how that feels (contrasted with how it feels when I take the initiative to improve myself spiritually). Susan asked me what God was working on with me now. I said that we were divesting myself of myself. She said that I will move into a state of divestment that is much more radical than at the moment. I will experience pain and those around me will experience pain as the old me dies. This is inevitable. She said that the historical Jesus was a model of self-divestment, but that at this point I was more into God and Spirit than Jesus.

As I think back over my journal entries for the last six months I am struck by how much my spiritual life was a roller coaster ride. Spiritual highs and lows seem to follow one after another in rapid succession. I had not realized yet that this giddy feeling of highs and lows was to become a common state of mind. It seems that, for me, it was an integral part of the process of transformation.

August 10, 1988

Yesterday morning I had another session with Susan that helped me to sort out my understandings and feelings about Jesus of Nazareth. I left the session realizing that ahead of me was the long, hard task of dealing with the bothersome Son of God. The young man who keeps telling me to be a loving person to my neighbor. I don't like that because I don't like some of my neighbors, and those that I do like are a never-ending demand on me. They won't go away and let me alone with God the Father. It seems like I must die and be born again. But Nicodemus and I are not quite sure why or how. As we discussed these things, Susan reminded me that Merton had his problems with people as well. He had to earn the right to be a hermit. He had to pay his dues. And then about the time that he was about to get solitude along came the Vietnam War, and the Civil Rights Movement, and one thing after another. Jesus would not let him alone. I left the sessions knowing that somewhere out there in the world, joy was a reasonable balance between an active life and a passive contemplative life and I would have to search for that balance again and again.

When I got home following the session with Susan, the path beneath my feet disappeared. I fell into another pit of despair. Once again it had to do with the nursery. The crew had not done what they should have done with ivy propagation. I traced the problem back to a lack of supervision, and then on to the impact on sales, the implication for the budget, the effect on my vacation starting in a few weeks and ultimately on the future of the nursery. I became furious. Damn the whole incompetent crew; they are as much a bother as Christ. But, of course Merton says that they are Christ. Why doesn't Christ just let me alone? The answer is clear. That is not what God has in mind.

## Chapter Two

August 11, 1988

Today I taught my last class. I feel a little hollow and a little sad, maybe even a little anxious but I am not sure that it is because I am no longer a teacher. Again, I remember Henri Nouwen:

> Hardly a day passes in our lives without our experience of inner or outer fears, anxieties, apprehensions and preoccupations. These dark powers have pervaded every part of our world to such a degree that we can never fully escape them. Still it is possible not to belong to these powers, not to build our dwelling place among them, but to choose the house of love as our home. This choice is made not just once and for all but by living a spiritual life, praying at all times and thus breathing God's breath. Through the spiritual life we gradually move from the house of fear to the house of love.[2]

I do try to choose but it is hard at times. It is hard tonight.

August 21, 1988

Something is going on in my spiritual life but I am not sure what. Perhaps if Olga and I can get away for a while I will be able to get it out into the open and be able to return to a renewed relationship with God that will be deeper and more intimate, more like what I have felt at times over the past year. Right now there is something wrong with our relationship.

It seems that I must reconcile my relationship with Jesus before I can straighten things out with God. I have ordered a book on the Gospel of John, *Journeying Within Transcendence*. The Gospel reading in the Office for the next four or more weeks is from John. Perhaps the Jesus of John will merge with the Christ of Merton in the "Power and Meaning of Love" when I get down to the island.

September 1, 1988

Yesterday was my last day at the university. Today is my first day of early retirement. But, who was I today? I have the feeling that the person who is inside me waiting to be born is still there, hidden from my view. But would I recognize my true self, if I met myself? Perhaps this is where faith comes in. A step into the twilight of faith may involve believing that God will protect me from believing that my false self is really my true self if I just leave it up to Him.

September 10, 1988

We have arrived on Long Beach Island. This morning I got up at 4:00 refreshed. I tried to go back to sleep but I was awake. In no time I had unpacked *The Phenomenon of Man* and was reading the introduction by Julian Huxley. One of the joys of life ahead of me is to live life fully when I feel the desire to. This morning I felt that desire and I enjoyed it.

September 13, 1988

Waiting for something to happen and being satisfied with the simplicity of eating, sleeping, reading, fishing, walking on the beach.

Since Friday, I have had an awareness that keeps slipping in and out of my consciousness. It has to do with myself as a teacher who was, from beginning to end, excited when I taught well. I was excited by how much the students learned. I was a good teacher—the university said I was a "distinguished teacher." But, I think that I missed seeing the joy in students when they learned what they wanted to learn. For all these years I thought that distinguished teaching was teaching something well that I wanted students to learn.

September 14, 1988

It is so quiet. I experience no anxiety, no fear, no anger just peaceful quiet. The nursery, the whole world seems to exist only in some distant dream. There is here, there is now, there is quiet, peaceful quiet.

September 15, 1988

Life is not a problem to be solved let alone a problem to be lived. My life is a moment in eternity for my true self to be lived out in a way that is consistent with who my true self is. God only asks that I spend my moment in eternity being my true self, the true self that is within me. I cannot find it in the world around me.

Yesterday I wrote about life here being quiet and peaceful. Could it be that my true self has been given a moment of space, and that I have been given permission not to be occupied with the "shoulds" of the world around me? There will be time enough to deal with the world's "shoulds." Rejoice in the gift of the moment, another hour, another day, another week here on retreat.

September 22, 1988

Today Olga and I started the self-directed retreat that we had planned based on the Gospel of John. We read the Prologue and Diarmuid McGann's commentary on the Prologue then did fifteen minutes of meditation.

September 25, 1988

The reading in our study of John today was titled "From Secular to Sacred." Without knowing it I have been drawn back once again, not to Jesus, but to the notion of Christ within me that I met two years ago in this very place. Today I see myself as a place where two selves live, the false self, and the true self. I see the two selves in a continued state of tension. Will Barrett in *The Second Coming* experienced this struggle, and only when he accepted his condition of a living death could he confront life and celebrate the life that was in him all the time. He had to recognize the despair of the false self and choose to do battle with it in order for the true self, the Christ within him, to live and thrive.

It is strange how here on the island I keep coming back again and again to the truths embedded in Merton's essay, "The Power and Meaning of Love." The words fascinate me and haunt this place as much as they did two years ago.

The struggle between my false self and my true self had been going on for two years during which time God's love had been laying bare the defenses of my false self, and my ego self had been losing its controlling influence. Its position of dominance was slowly being replaced with the love of the true self. My journal is a record of this process, and as I read back over it I realize in retrospect, how much of a two step forward and one step backward process this had been. Transformation is not a straight line, forward-moving process. As I read through my journal I am constantly surprised by how often I had new insights only to remember later that I had a similar insight into a similar situation just a month or two or even a year earlier—an insight that apparently had not made a lasting mark on me. One of the most frequently occurring examples had been the awareness that God is the love that is the spiritual self. Perhaps the two most obvious ways to see God in human beings are in the unfathomable complexity of their creation and in their capacity to be love in the world. But time and time again I would lose my focus on the obvious, and then have to discover it all over again.

It was almost as if I still wanted to believe that Christ really did live within me wanting to be love, but that I was unwilling to resist the urge to satisfy my false self in situation after situation rather than allowing my true self to become dominant.

Another theme that kept coming up in my journals was my inability to make a clear distinction between the historical Jesus and the Christ. I did not understand yet that the spiritual self of Jesus was the same Christ that was my spiritual self and the spiritual self of all people. I had not yet come to realize that Jesus could only be God in the sense that his spiritual self was God's love, and that his true self became dominant over his false self. Thus when I think that Jesus is in some way nagging me, it is really my true self, wanting to grow. When Jesus continued to live after his death, it was God's love that lived. It was the Christ that lived. God, Jesus, Christ, and my spiritual self shared the same common reality, but I had not yet come to grips with that reality. I had not yet realized that we are all one. We are all Love growing in the world.

But at the end of the second year of my spiritual journey I still saw God, Love, Jesus, Christ and the spiritual Self as being separate and different things rather than being all part of the same whole. This fracturing of reality continued to make it impossible for me to understand what Merton meant when he talked of the Christ in me and in all people. So long as I held this fractured view of reality, Merton's words would remain just a fascinating idea. They would just be talk, not a way of being.

I would continue to talk the words without understanding what they really meant. I wanted to have faith in an integrated whole that is God, but my false self supported by my ego self kept structuring reality for its own purposes. I wanted to be God's love, but I didn't know how. I still failed to realize that the first step was to be willing. I think that this is what I was experiencing in the fall of 1988. This is what I was sensing, but not seeing, when I said that I was standing in my own field of vision. The more I sensed this, the more my interior conflict grew. That's where I was.

## NOTES

1. Henri Nouwen, *The Genesee Diary* (Garden City, NJ: Image Books, 1981), 107.
2. Henri Nouwen, *Behold the Beauty of the Lord* (Notre Dame, IN: Ave Maria Press, 1987), 19.

*Chapter Three*

# Lost in Dreams in the Present

Something was different. Something had happened, but I couldn't put my finger on it. Was it the personal feelings of loss that I had experienced last year? Was I tiring of the journey? Had I taken a wrong turn somewhere along the way? I didn't feel totally lost because my spiritual guide was still walking with me, and certainly she would not let me stray too far from the trail. But, as I reflect back on this phase of my journey, perhaps the one thing that comes to mind is that I felt as if I were floating, and that I was unsure about where I was going and what the future held.

Previously I might have thought that I could regain my orientation by visualizing the future, focusing on what I wanted it to look like, and then setting out to make it happen. I would not have spent much time experiencing the present moment, letting it reveal whatever it had to say, and letting it instruct me. I didn't use up a lot of time living in the present. Mostly I thought of it as a stop on my way out of the past on my way to the future.

But around this point in my life I began to think about time a little differently. Nothing radical, but I began to feel the stirring of change. I would come to attribute this feeling to the slow process of transformation that was taking place. Certainly my beliefs were changing, or at least being challenged. If some of my beliefs were changing, why not my beliefs about time: the past, the present and the future? My conception of time slowly became more present oriented. I began to see each new day as a step into a present that yesterday I would have called the future, or see each new day as a step into a present that tomorrow I would call the past. This led me to realize that all that I ever really experienced was the present. When I remembered something that had happened, the memory of it, accurate or not, became a part of my present. When I thought about the future, which might or might not ever happen, the thought always occurred in the present. The result was that the time I actually spent in the present attending to what was going on around me at the moment was crowded out by my recollections of what had gone on, or my predictions and fantasies about what I wanted to happen or thought would happen. This, of course, limited the time that I had to live in the actual present, thus limiting what I experienced – what I heard, saw, felt, and even thought. It limited the richness of my life, and limited my opportunity for spiritual growth and understanding. If I really wanted to get the maximum advantage from living in the present I would need to spend less time thinking about the past and fantasizing about the future, and more time attending to what was going on around me at the time.

As a person on a spiritual journey, I, like so many before me, sought to understand the relationships between my self and the ground or purpose of my existence. My encounter with these relationships was largely attributable to the experience I had with God through contemplative prayer. This approach to prayer, and thus the type of experience that I had with God, ultimately shaped, my faith and my beliefs. And it was contemplative prayer that became my way to the Master of the Universe and the Ground of My Being in the present. Living in the present in a universe in which all is related made a big difference in how I viewed things.

During the first two years of my spiritual journey I had begun the process of deconstructing my beliefs. By the third year my belief system was coming apart fairly rapidly and I had no plan for putting it back together. I wasn't sure who God was, even though by then I had developed a real interest in knowing. I had no coherent theology, either borrowed or self-made that I could use in developing my spirituality. My spiritual journey was being sustained by grace and by people to whom I could turn for help such as Merton, and my spiritual director. Even so, I had begun to lose my sense of direction. In an attempt to get back on track I followed one star after another in an effort to find my way until my true self could begin to develop its new identity, my belief system could be reconstructed, and I had gained the faith that God and I could work this out together. During this time I was slowly developing a spirituality that would guide me from one day to the next.

In retrospect, I am convinced that it was inevitable that I would go through the process of deconstructing my belief system, and that my false self would gradually lose its dominance as it was challenged by my true self. I continued on my spiritual way much like I had before retirement except that I had more time to spend in reading and prayer. At this time, prayer meant Ignation meditation, intercessory prayer, the Daily Office, and contemplation when it occurred. In time, I would find myself working with the ideas of Catherine of Siena and dialogical prayer, and this in turn would lead me to establishing a dialog with God about spiritual and theological issues in the hope that this would lead me to knowing.

Other than my early retirement from teaching and my decision to cut back on my involvement in the nursery, much of the next two years of my life was largely unplanned. I would have said that things just seemed to happen. As I look back on this, I now realize how important this was for me because much of my life up to this point had been shaped by conscious, willful decisions designed to influence my future. This lead to a way of life that was alien to risk taking, but was comfortable for my false self. Yet my contemplative's faith in transformation of the self by God required taking a step beyond the known. I might have considered a direct assault on my false self that, in many ways, had become so comfortable to live with, but to have consciously encouraged a fight between my false and true selves would have been expecting a lot, and it would have been a very willful approach. That was why taking a step into the unknown became so critical to my spiritual and personal growth. Taking that step implied a willingness that would be guided by faith. This was comparable to being led blindfolded up several steps to a platform and then having someone say to me "Now turn around and just step backward. I will catch you." I wasn't quite ready to do that even though I said I wanted to. That would happen in its own time as a result of the transformation process.

November of 1988 found me retired and adrift with a spiritual navigation system that wasn't working very well. If no big storm came up I would be OK for a while. I still had an engine and a rudder. I just didn't know which way to go. At first this felt freeing, but in time it was obvious that it was foolhardy. Without a spirituality to guide me, the loss of a spiritual director could be serious.

One of the directions that I took for a while led me to an interest in contemplative communities. My only direct experience with a contemplative community had been limited to time spent at St. Gregory's Abbey as a retreatant. After reading *The Bell* by Iris Murdoch, I became interested in the contemplative community of Little Gidding developed by Nicholas Ferrar. This led me to visit a contemplative community in Columbus, Ohio that was composed of Carmelite nuns and lay people from the Columbus area. In time this led me to an interest in developing an ecumenical community in central Ohio.

November 6, 1988

The last entry in my journal was made two weeks ago. What has happened since then? Much work –too much – done in the nursery, including a trip to Michigan for liner plants combined with a visit to St. Gregory's on the way back. During these two weeks I have kept up the Daily Office, though at times I was just going through the motions. This morning I thought back to the conversation that Olga and I had after we left the abbey. We had used some of the driving time on the way back to talk about developing our spiritual life with others. The conversation was a surprise to me. I did not expect that the side trip to the Abbey would have such an effect on Olga. As we discussed the topic, there was something in our conversation that echoed presumption and separatism almost to the point of elitism. We both became aware of this, and we were both a little taken aback by our tone. The issue focused on kindling an interest in a lay contemplative community within the church. We were both aware that we didn't know what we meant by that, but we saw it as a major project that would take several years to get started. We saw it involving at least Episcopalians, Lutherans, and Catholics. I plan to take this idea to Susan at our next meeting and see what she thinks.

November 10, 1988

Several evenings ago I talked with Pam about how the community at Carmel met her spiritual needs and the needs of others. It was a conversation with mixed results.

Today, I had a meeting with Susan. It was a lively meeting with a lot of give and take. I came home with a deeper insight into several aspects of the community idea: 1) the likelihood of the Episcopal Church supporting a lay contemplative community effort was not good, 2) the way to proceed at first should involve lay people, 3) then the clergy could be brought in later after we had something more clearly formulated. Susan said, "Don't look for the priests of the Church to do it for you. What you propose is too radical and they are most likely to see it as a threat to the status quo that they have taken a vow to support. But if such a community were formed then they could associate with it like they do at Carmel. Along the way you might get a reaction from the Benedictines at three Rivers or The Cowley Fathers in Cambridge, Massachusetts." Another thing she said was, "Pray on it hard."

November 19, 1988

Today, Pam and Ceci and I met to discuss the idea of a community. The session lasted for over an hour and a half. The issues we talked about were largely ecclesiastical and of little interest from my perspective. Spirituality is the issue for me. We agreed to meet again to continue exploring possibilities. I left with Ceci's words ringing in my ears, "Without ecclesiastical sanctions there can be no sustained community."

November 20, 1988

Yesterday, I had a real feeling of alienation while I was at church, and I was definitely bothered by it. This is the Body of Christ and yet I felt little comfort in it. Superficial exchange of the peace and small talk at coffee hour were strained and forced. I did not find anyone with whom I would feel comfortable as a spiritual friend.

I also felt quite uncomfortable in the meeting on Saturday with Ceci and Pam. It has opened up old wounds that never really healed. This whole idea is no good. It can not lead in any way that I can see to furthering God's love in the world unless people, both lay people and clergy, are willing to face the situation in honesty; unless they are willing to sit down and talk it out with God as a participant.

November 22, 1988
As I reflect on the idea of a spiritual community, I realize that all my life I have had a very small circle of friends, and that I work with people better one at a time rather than in a group. Perhaps there is something in this that I should consider as I think about a community. Certainly what is considered should not be like Pam's experience with Carmel. It's too large and too social.

In time my interest in a contemplative community in Central Ohio faded, and it never amounted to anything other than a diversion from the main path.

December 3, 1988
Almost a week of Advent has passed, and Olga and I have started a program of Advent meditations that we are using along with compline. It is appropriate for the season but not really exciting, and it doesn't seem to be going anywhere. I also had a disappointing meeting at church about Partners in Prayer. Beyond this, the past week has been work in the nursery, including a heated meeting with John about staffing issues and their implications for the budget.

Personnel matters were but one example of interpersonal conflict that I frequently faced in my venture into the world of small business. I met similar interpersonal issues in my work with personnel committees at the university, and my involvement with the aspirant committee in the case of Ceci's desire to become an Episcopal priest. I had a tendency to want my own way.

The issue often took the form of identifying with and championing the cause of an individual who was in conflict with a social institution. In my case the social institutions were the business world, the university and the Church. In all cases there was a social institution and its norms and expectations that I saw as being used primarily to protect itself. I saw individuals who were in conflict with those norms as needing an advocate. At times I had a tendency to escalate advocacy into becoming a social activist and to uncritically presume that I had a unique insight into the underdog, when in fact I might have been acting out of willfulness and the needs of my false self. I had not gotten to the point where I could see these matters from the perspective of the true self. I did not ask the question, "What would be the loving thing for me to do at this time that would facilitate the growth of the person?" I presumed I knew.

December 6, 1988
I am not at peace. Yesterday, I began to twitch, I felt that old pressure building up, and my inability to cope with it returning. I feel an overwhelming desire

to get out from under the pressure of the nursery. In short, the situation seems to be caving in on me. I see myself as a grim willful person slogging along daily out of what I consider to be my duty. Lord help me, I despair.

Later: This morning's despair has become evening's peace. My life was positive today. My life was directed today. My life had purpose today. Tonight as I listen to the Advent service at St. John's, Cambridge, I seem to know that the lost sheep hidden in me is Christ waiting to be born.

December 7, 1988

Today, I met Thelma Hall through *Too Deep for Words: Rediscovering Lectio Divina* and this may be the key to Bible study at church. You are near, very near, and I feel your presence. You are within me where you have always been. I need to be more willing to listen.

December 10, 1988

I was not sent into the world to do your work. I was sent to be a contemplative in an active world, but how can I do that? Isn't my love for you fulfilled through my love of others? I need some help in working through this. I can't be both Mary and Martha.

Christmas came and went, and I began to believe that there would be no Christ born of me, and then I realized that was not so. There would be a birth, but the child had not yet come to term. Ahead of me was the growth of a whole new person. The process of birth and growth was not going to be without pain, but it would happen. If I could just let my false self die, my true self would emerge. This would require the long painful diminishment of the false self, and faith that the true self would grow into a robust person. I had no sense of how long this would take, how much faith would be required, or the intensity of the conflict that lay ahead, but I was aware that something significant was going on.

My journal entries at this time reveal that a conflict was brewing. Later I would characterize this dispute as a conflict between my willfulness and willingness. The resolution of this conflict would be aided by my ability to discern when to take a willful stance and when to take a stance of willingness.

In the process of pursuing this aspect of discernment, I became interested in the role of dreams as one approach to discernment and decided to bring this to spiritual direction. I stayed on this path for several months, but in time I left it behind as a main theme of my spiritual development just as I had left behind my exploration of developing a contemplative community.

January 1, 1989

It occurred to me this morning after awakening from a vivid dream, vivid at the time but not now, that I would like to delve into the spiritual meaning of my dreams. Perhaps this will be a way of sensitizing myself to the world of the spirit from which I have been so separated for most of my life. I am ready for the use of dreams in discernment, and I am ready to tell this to Susan at our next meeting.

January 2, 1989
Each time I awakened last night following a dream I tried to recall the content of the dream and asked myself, "What does this dream say?" In other words I tried to attend to the dream as a message being "spoken," and tried to attend to what was being "said." It's now mid morning and I am unable to remember any of the dreams.

From my reading, I found that the use of dream content in spiritual direction is fairly common, but that does not mean that there have been recent breakthroughs in either applied pastoral theology or psychiatry that allow us to now deal with this subject with greater clarity or certainty. That people have dreams is accepted without much dispute. Many people, sooner or later, experience dreams about matters that have loomed large in their life. Many people experience some dreams concerning matters that they cannot recall ever happening in their life. Many people at one time or another experience dreams that are reasonable, coherent and make about as much sense as every day conscious experiences. And some people sooner or later experience dreams that make sense only if they are understood as being filled with meaning cloaked as metaphors and filled with symbolism of the most complex nature.

One point of view about dreams is that they are a normal process of expressing an existing, subconscious reality that is generally not available unless approached through a disciplined and informed process that is grounded in the theoretical work of people such as C.G. Jung. Others prefer an approach to understanding the dream phenomenon from the perspective of recent work that explains dreams as the random firing of large neurons in the brain during certain cycles of sleep and attempts by the brain to make sense out of the random events. Dreams can also be seen as being a common type of human experience that occurs during sleep, and like most experience may have meaning if we wish to pay attention to it, and delve into what it has to "say" to us.

When I first became interested in dream analysis I saw dreams as a typical human phenomenon that I experience on a regular basis and like all experience, might contain potential content for spiritual growth and discernment. I still hold a similar position modified only by the belief that my dreams are most likely to hold the potential for stimulating significant growth when I am on the verge of having some kind of cognitive breakthrough and need additional experiential input to trigger that cognitive change. In these cases dreams seem to function as a piece of the whole that triggers something that I would describe as an insight.

January 5, 1989

I can remember two dreams that I had just before dawn this morning. One had no particular meaning for me beyond what it portrayed. The other seemed to be using a rather unusual situation as a symbolic way of describing me as compulsively seeking approval.

The first dream had to do with a light aircraft that had landed on a highway and could not take off because of electrical wires across the road. The airplane had to be taken to a place where it had overhead clearance before it could take off.

The second dream involved something that Olga was involved in. She had noticed that Equal "capsules" varied in content from the equivalent sweetness of one to two teaspoons of sugar. She had written the Equal Company and they had sent her a coupon for a box of fifty capsules. However, the box that she had originally bought contained 200 capsules. We had used the defective capsules already, so I was emptying out Equal from some of the capsules in another box we had just bought to send back to the company for a refund for 200 capsules. I was doing this for her because I didn't want her, and by implication me, to look bad in the company's eyes, because the capsules that we just bought were not defective. If this dream had any meaning, it represented a desire on my part to conform in little matters that for all I knew made no real difference. But there I was trying to look good to people I don't even know. Equal isn't even marketed in capsule form! Why capsules in the dream?


January 8, 1989

In my last session with Susan I said that, "I was becoming aware that I was not a very loving person." I have had problems working out a valid loving relationship with some people in the past. This had almost led to disastrous consequences by both spiritual standards and by the standards of the culture. I now believe that my capacity to love is far from fully developed. I now know why Will Barrett and Allie in *The Second Coming* represent a positive, growing relationship, whereas other relationships that seem similar can be very destructive.

I sense a new dimension in my relationship with Susan. I have had some erotic fantasies and dreams about her, and I am concerned about this. I know that it's inappropriate but I still have these dreams. Sanford in *The Kingdom Within* says that what I am experiencing is common and indeed can be directed to something positive, if it is worked out in a non-destructive way. I think I have some understanding of this, but I am unable to deal with it except by repression of my feelings, thoughts and fantasies. I don't know how to channel this into something positive in a spiritually meaningful way. Is this what is interfering with my ability to understand the spiritual side of love?

These fantasies and dreams never got out of hand, and I believe that one reason for that was that I was ready for a more mature relationship with women and a deeper understanding of love. And because I was ready, I was able to see these dreams for what they were and recognize the symbolism that they contained. This experience represented an important point in my spiritual life that led to a much richer understanding of the positive elements in human relationships that can grow from the development and expression of the spiritual self as a manifestation of God's love. Expressing God's love is a whole lot more than erotic and possessive feelings worked out in a kind and well-meaning relationship.

Though these dream experiences sometimes served as a catalyst for insights at the time, it often took several years for those insights to be worked out more broadly in my life. For example, I believe that my dreams about Susan led to a much more constructive relationship with women on a spiritual and intellectual level, that continues to enrich my life.

January 15, 1989

I have been awake for an hour and it seems natural to get up and write in my journal. The past week has been far more significant than I expected it to be. Something seems to have crept up on me and grasped me in its hands and said, "I am with you and I have been bound to you for eternity. I am always with you, and don't you forget that. Now that you have let me find you, things will not be the same."

The events of the past week came and went with a quiet recognition of God's presence. There was work in the nursery. There was the meeting with John in which he recognized the importance of hiring a sales person as an investment in the future of the nursery. There was the continued awareness that next week is John's appointment with his doctor for his six month cancer check-up. There were the arrangements to get a place in Florida for a month this winter. There was the session with Susan in which I said I was ready to start dream analysis as a part of my spiritual direction. Starting now I am to write down a few words about the dream immediately upon awakening. This will stimulate recall when I get up in the morning, and then I am to describe the dream with as much detail as I can. I am to let the dream work on me. I am not to work on the dream. We will follow this procedure for a month and then see where it goes from there.

All of these things that are going on seem to be what Walker Percy describes as an awareness that "something is going to happen," and that whatever it is will be important. I don't know what it is, but I am allowing it to work on me rather than working on it. Just let it happen.

January 24, 1989

Last night I had one of those dreams that if I had not written down a few key words at the time I would have probably forgotten it. It was a noisy dream—lots of activity and change of scene, etc. It took place at St. Stephen's Church on a Sunday evening. There were lots of people there involved in many activities. There were several priests and one was a woman, but not Susan, and I wondered who she was. Then I saw Susan; she was dressed in a habit of the Order of Julian of Norwich. Some of the people there were all upset because someone had spilled wine on an altar napkin. They were concerned with what the bishop would think or say. Susan seemed not to be at all concerned.

Another dream involved being at a conference with Pam. The opening address had been given but we had not met in discussion groups yet, and I was trying to find lunch for us. I finally saw a tray of sandwiches and some fruit salad and I asked Pam which she wanted. She said the fruit salad. I went to get a salad for Pam and a sandwich for myself. A kindly looking old man came along and took the last sandwich out of my hand. I returned with the fruit salad for Pam. I felt a bit put upon, but I was calm about it. When I awakened this morning and recalled the experience, I did not feel pleased at being a "suffering servant."

February 3, 1989

I had several complex dreams last night, but in only one case did I write down key words to help me remember it. This dream had to do with the funeral of a previous member of our church. Several of us were sitting around a table at a Bible study group at church, and during the conversation I made it clear that I would not be able to attend the funeral because I would be out of town. The focus of the conversation did not seem to be on whether or not people were going to attend, but whether or not they should attend. It was suggested that even if I were going to be out of town I should find a way to attend. The conversation continued about what people should or should not do. Then for some reason I became keenly aware that what I want for myself and what others want for me are often not the same thing, and just as often I suspect not what God wants.

February found Olga and me on the Florida Panhandle. We rented a beachfront condo owned by an old law school friend of John's. In the 1980's the Beach was not a very active vacation resort during the winter months. November through March was the season for winter visitors, mostly from the north-central United States and Canada who wanted to avoid the congestion and high prices of South Florida. These people created their own social circle and one either joined them or there was not much to do. This made it a particularly good place for solitude, especially for an introvert such as myself. In the twelve years we were on the Beach we were always on the edge of the winter visitor crowd. The church we attended had an active winter visitor ministry, but this was as close to joining the winter visitor culture as we got. This meant that there was a lot of solitary time for walking the beach, and this became the activity of choice.

February 8, 1989

Today is Ash Wednesday and Olga and I went to church at St. Thomas. There must have been at least fifty people there for imposition of ashes. My estimate is that the church holds a hundred and twenty people.

After only two days it has become clear that we're going to have to make something out of this place, because there's not much to do here in the winter except to sit on the deck of the condo and look at the Gulf. The view is spectacular. As I sit here I can see up and down the beach for several miles and out to the horizon, and not be aware that there is another person in the world. Though the fishing is not much now, it seems to have potential, and there's lots of opportunity for reading, prayer, study, rest, good food, exercise, shopping at the few stores that are open, and time for Olga and for me to be together undisturbed by anything.

February 10, 1989

I have always wanted to have a mountain top experience with God. This trip to Florida has not been a mountain top experience. Indeed it has been marked by a comfortable flatness. I fear becoming bored. The high spots of the day are morning prayer, nap and walking the beach. Since we left home, I have had nothing but an occasional, casual conversation with anyone. I haven't even had a good talk with God. I do not have the feeling that something is going to happen as I have on so many prior occasions like this. My dreams are not memorable and I can't even get motivated to write anything down about them.

For some time I had been aware that Olga had a claustrophobic reaction to tight and enclosed spaces like elevators and airplanes. But I was not aware that she also had occasional anxiety attacks associated with my absence, or anticipation of my absence. I became aware of this one night in Florida.

February 13, 1989

Tonight I wanted to go out and get a Valentine card (I forgot to get one earlier in the day) and as I put on my coat Olga expressed real anxiety about the thought of me going out and leaving her alone. We talked about her problem for over an hour and it became clear that it is real and that it is getting worse.

February 21, 1989

I think I am beginning to understand that peace does not necessarily come from having pious thoughts or even from behaving in an outwardly loving way. Peace comes from knowing that regardless of who or what I am, I am loved, and that in time, after enough dying of my false self, I will be able to return that love in a genuine way. First, however, I must die to that self, and this includes dying to things and relationships. It's one thing to willfully and violently sever cherished ties that enslave the true self, but there is a gentler way that allows those ties to remain a part of us but be assigned to the past, by affirming that a free true self is of greater value than possessing things or people and being possessed by them. This kind of poverty, which is the absence of a need to possess people or things, brings an inner peace. Perhaps it is this kind of poverty, that I am beginning to understand and even appreciate. Yet, I still want to control people and events in my life. Why can't I just accept things and people as they are, including myself?

February 22, 1989

I had a dream last night that dealt with the nursery. The usual people were present in the dream. We were discussing the design of an over-wintering structure for plants and the procedures for building it. The work crews were working well and the social climate was positive. It was already past 5:00 P.M. and people were working willingly without concern for overtime. I was in control of things.

February 27, 1989

This morning Olga and I had another conversation about her anxiety and her feelings of being cut off from home and abandoned. The main thrust of our conversation involved a long statement by Olga about how unloved she felt by me at times, and how this lack of love was manifested by me as a lack of caring, and indifference. She said that this was a mystery to her because it was so inconsistent with the message that I had put on her birthday card:

"I love you more and more as the you that is your true self unfolds and prepares to fly beyond the sun. Help me to support you as you fly a little more each day toward who you are to be. Help me to support you on those days when you fall and hurt. May you only fall and not despair of flying beyond the sun."

Olga said that my behavior belied my words. We talked about what it meant to love, and concluded that our conceptions of love were quite different. To Olga love is giving of self, of time and possessions to others. Love is the Golden Rule. To me love is supporting others as they grow and become what God created them to be. We talked about how a person who held the perspective that Olga held might fail to see love in my behavior, and how a person like myself could give the wrong message through my behavior. If Olga gives love by giving herself, her time and her possessions to others, and I just talk about love as supporting the growth of others, does that make me self serving and uncaring? If so then we are both in for rough weather ahead.

March 1, 1989

Last night I had a strange dream. Olga and I had gone to a store to buy a sofa. We selected one and gave them a check as a deposit. Later we went back to pick up the sofa and got a run around from the salesman who finally got the sales manager. The sofa, it seems, was not ready to be picked up. He proceeded to explain how an employee had been seduced by one of the other employees and that this somehow explained why the sofa was not ready. I pointed out that he had a personnel problem but that I failed to see what this had to do with my sofa, etc. This was never answered. They returned part of the down payment. In the end, it occurred to me that everyone involved had been diminished by the manager, who told the story about the employee with a drinking problem who had been seduced. I don't know where that one is going, but I'll let it work on me.

March 10, 1989

We are back in Ohio from Florida. This week of re-entry has been so different from the past month on the beach. I have gotten back into the routine of the nursery, and have had a direction session with Susan.

March 13, 1989

Yesterday Olga and I attended a quiet day at church led by Sister Noreen. Privately after the session Olga told Sister Noreen about the Valentine card episode and revealed an ending that I knew nothing about. When we got home Olga told me about sharing the event of the night of February 13th with Sister Noreen. She also told her about what happened when she went to bed that night and prayed that God would bring her peace to replace her fear and anxiety. She felt at peace almost immediately and reached out and touched Him. Reassured of his love and presence she slept soundly.

I clearly remember praying for Olga that night when I went to bed, and I remember feeling assured that she would not feel alone and anxious because God would be near her. I remember questioning how I knew that this was God, and how I knew that he would be with Olga. Now I know that it was faith in God that made it possible for me to ask him to protect Olga from her fears. I prayed that he would stay close to her while we were in Florida. But, I never knew of Olga's experience that night until she told me about it following the quiet day.

The two experiences with Olga, the first in Panama City Beach on the night before Valentine's Day, and the second, following the quiet day with Sister Noreen, combined to reveal a conception of God, and a faith that up to that point I did not know that I had. On that night I was aware of God's presence as I prayed that his love would be present for Olga, but it was a month later that I became aware that Olga also had prayed for God's presence that night, and that she had felt him near. We had shared a common experience. The experience was set in the context of two very different conceptions of what constituted love. Today, I think that we still hold different conceptions of love. Hers is characterized by a giving of self that involves doing something for another. Mine is characterized by providing another with the freedom and support to grow toward what God created them to be. I really have no idea how God would define love. I say that God is ineffable, and as such cannot be known in any objective sense. And for me this is true. Yet, at the same time I have known God in relationships that have been characterized by love and compassion. I have sensed God's presence and God's love flow through me, and I have been able to share that love with others in supporting them. I felt that the events of the past month had been real evidence of spiritual growth and insight. So, needless to say, I was taken aback when Susan said to me in March that she thought that my spiritual life had become lackadaisical and that I should give it more serious attention.

March 22, 1989

I had a difficult session with my spiritual director today in which she said that she thought that my spiritual life was becoming superficial and that I needed to dig deeper into its meaning. I am to do this by selecting a theme from my journal and working with it. I don't recall being aware of a slacking off of interest, but apparently Susan has noticed something that has caused her to challenge my spiritual conviction.

March 27, 1989

It was a week ago that Susan suggested that I draw a theme from topics that I had identified in my journals. In addition to my recent interest in dreams, I have for several months wondered if I have a calling to be a spiritual director sometime in the future. I have usually suppressed those thoughts because I think that they are premature to consider, but on Saturday I got some material that Sister Noreen sent me about programs at the Shalem Institute for Spiritual Formation. They offer a number of programs including spiritual direction. Now I must ask if this is what I should be doing? Am I ready? Am I ready for Shalem?

April 4, 1989

I had my regularly scheduled session with Susan yesterday. It was a good session. Two weeks ago she said that she thought that I was coasting and not being serious about my spiritual life. I have meditated on that a lot over the past two weeks, and during that time the envelope from Sister Noreen came. I told Susan about the materials and we talked about whether I had a calling to do spiritual direction. We also talked about dream analysis and the record I have been keeping of my dreams. I have done nothing more with this other than to record my dreams and accept them as experiences that might contain material for insights into my spiritual life. Some interesting insights have come out of them, but I don't feel pressed to do much more at this time. I will pray on this and see what happens.

We did, however, spend some time exploring the issue of sexuality and transference in a spiritual direction relationship. What I did not say, because it didn't seem appropriate, was that my experience with dreams about Susan was potentially valuable for me because I would be much better prepared to deal with issues such as sexuality and transference in a positive way in the future when I was a spiritual director.

April 8, 1989

I just read Chapter Eight of *In Search of* Spirit.[1] There's a lot in that chapter that is applicable to my prayer life. If I am honest with myself, I have to admit that sometimes I really don't feel like praying. I would rather be doing something else I want to do, but I pray because it is part of the discipline of prayer. I know that this might sound silly and hypocritical to lots of people, but when I think about it, prayer is much like the rest of life. We can't always do what pleases us, and there are lots of times in life when being faithful to those that we are devoted to is what's called for. So, yes, to be honest I guess that in many ways I have just been going through the motions. I practice contemplative prayer in hope of knowing God better. But, to do this seven days a week, fifty-two weeks a year gets "old" at times, especially when lethargy leads to a lack of real interest in anything. This past week seems as if it has been very flat. Rainy days make things seem very dull, and a stretch of such days can begin to wear on a person. Some people even get depressed at times like this.

April 19, 1989

If I were to summarize how I feel I would say angry (but I don't know about what), rushed, anxious, separated from God (but I don't know how or why it started). I am about to hit bottom (but I feel as if I have much further to fall). Catch me Lord for I am falling again. In my last session with Susan, I remember her saying, "Jack, God does not want you to be good, he wants you to be obedient." To obey God is to answer, "Here I am Lord" when he calls.

April 21, 1989

A letter for more information about Shalem and a request for an application remain on my desk. This year in the nursery was to be a trial year to see if I could still contribute but have John be in charge. Already I look forward to getting away this winter and going to Florida. Why am I holding back from sending the letter to Shalem? Is it because I am afraid that I will not be able to do the required work? Or, am I afraid that making a commitment would be a price too great to pay for foregoing pleasures of wintering in Florida? Or, do I doubt that I really have the commitment or calling for a spiritual development ministry?

April 23, 1989

I have such a deep longing to pull away from the world and spend time alone with God. Again, I am torn between loving God through loving my neighbor and loving God as I meditate on his glorious creation. He must be so sad when he considers what we have done to his creation and to each other.

April 24, 1989

Last night Olga suggested that I try to return to a 12:00 to 3:00 period away from the nursery. My first reaction was, what will happen to the nursery? What will John think? But, I followed her suggestion and I could not have been more pleased. I did noon Office, had lunch, took a nap, exercised for a half hour and continued my study of the Psalms. The three hours went by like a moment, and when I returned to the nursery all was well. This has been a day of work, prayer and study, the type of day that I once envisioned a secular contemplative living.

April 29, 1989

I still spend too much time centering on my past and thinking about the future, and not enough time living in the present. A lot of the time I think that I am too busy, that I have too much to do. Yesterday I started meditating on parts of *Bread in the Wilderness*, but I didn't stay with it. I had to busy myself with locating maps and doing other things in preparation for another trip to Grand Haven to get liner plants and a stop at the Abbey at Three Rivers. I was "too busy" thinking about tomorrow to spend time with God in the present with prayer.

May 2, 1989

Yesterday, driving home from Grand Haven I stopped near home to fill the tank with gasoline and standing there at the pump, seemingly without warning, the bottom fell out of everything. I had no energy; I twitched uncontrollably; I lost all will to do anything. I spent a wakeful night with dreams about my typical anxieties. This morning I could hardy put one foot in front of the other. I felt widely separated from God. At midmorning I went to Columbus for a session with Susan. She was the most direct she has ever been with me. "Stop making excuses for why you can't sustain a twenty-four hour a day spiritual high. Live life as it is with constant ups and downs. Admit that your life is that way and will always be. Send your letter to Shalem. Make a decision."

At first I don't think that Susan was aware that I had, seemingly without warning, slipped into a serious episode of depression. This time it lasted, with a few days of reprieve here and there, for the next five months. In the weeks before the depression erupted I may have acted like I was going through a period of spiritual apathy, and for a while Susan seems to have thought the same thing. Had it just been spiritual lassitude though, I believe that I would have worked that out, and I am confident that I would have profited from the experience, but the depressive episode disrupted that sequence of things for a while.

Depression and spiritual apathy can occur simultaneously, but they need not do so, and, of course, it is a lot easier to deal with them one at a time. But when they do occur at the same time it is sometimes difficult to sort out which is which. John of The Cross provides some guidelines as have later authorities such as Gerald May, but at the time I was not familiar enough with their thinking to make use of it. Fortunately, I believe that Susan was. For the past month and a half she had been helping me confront what she may have thought was spiritual apathy. She had made comments about coasting and needing to do something to regain focus and momentum. She also had been working with me to overcome my unrealistic conception of spiritual perfection, accept myself for who I am, stop trying to manipulate God, and make a decision about Shalem. I was a novice and I thought that I was just experiencing some typical travails of the beginner. But she soon realized that the major issue at the moment was not spiritual apathy but depression, and she quickly focused on that in the weeks ahead.

## NOTE

1. Mary McDermott Schideler, *In Search of the Spirit* (New York: Balantine Books, 1985), 193–213.

*Part II*

# TEMPORARY COMMITMENTS

*Chapter Four*

# Turning Point

I didn't have a very clear understanding of what was happening to me. This is not to say that I was completely naïve about depression, spiritual apathy, or the dark night of the soul, but I didn't have an adequate integration of knowledge and personal experience. I didn't understand how each was being expressed within me, or how each was related to the other. I was a typical novice. In addition, my depression clouded and distorted my clarity about how all of this influenced what was going on in my life.

On the other hand, I believe that my spiritual director quickly discerned that whether or not I was experiencing spiritual apathy or the dark night of the soul, I most certainly was experiencing depression. It took her little time to recommend that I see my family doctor about it. In 1989 depression was even less well understood than it is today. At that time there were theories about the cause and treatment of depression, but just because the knowledge was theoretical this did not mean that the depression was not real. As any one who has gone through depression can attest, it is very real. As far as I know, modern depression is similar to what John of the Cross called melancholia back in the sixteenth century. So, it is not just a modern condition caused by dysfunctional consequences of our postmodern society. Fortunately it is, in many cases, a treatable disease and both medication and several types of therapy, including cognitive therapy, have proved to be very effective. Depression is frequently accompanied by anxiety, something that many people experience when their beliefs and values are challenged during the process of transformation. Depression is of interest to people who work in the area of spiritual development because it often mimics some of the symptoms of spiritual apathy and the dark night of the soul.

Spiritual apathy is primarily associated with a loss of spiritual interests, a decrease in motivation to do what it takes to pursue a spiritual journey, and a cooling of spiritual fervor that may be recognized as lukewarm feelings toward spiritual matters. It is like what happens to a person who gets bored with a hobby and loses interest in it. Spiritual apathy primarily affects the spiritual life, not the whole person.

Depression on the other hand is more generalized. When I was depressed I lost interest not only in religion but in such things as food, sex, entertainment, work, and human relationships. I had difficulty making decisions, and I frequently avoided activities in my daily life that I normally would have participated in. I often had generalized or specific feelings of hostility when people around me expected me to get socially involved. My withdrawal from, or avoidance of many things deepened and broadened, and I became over sensitive to imagined or actual criticism.

Depression and the dark night of the soul can occur together, they appear to be related, and they frequently mimic each other. It usually takes a trained and skilled person to tell the difference. If there is any real question as to whether it is depression, or the simultaneous occurrence of depression with the dark night of the soul, there is no reason to put off seeking help.

I believe that I was experiencing the dark night of the soul around the same time that I had the depressive episode. Because of the depression, however, it would have been difficult for me to tell the difference, but as I look on it from a later time perspective, the dark night was a much more instructive experience than the depression. It was an integral part of the process of transformation that I was undergoing. When I was experiencing the dark night of the soul and not depression, I was aware that my beliefs were changing. I was aware that my false self was being challenged by my true self, and I was often aware of who the victor was. But most important, I was aware that my true self was growing. Slowly but certainly I was becoming an expression of God's love in the world. I knew when my true self won a conflict, and I was aware when my ego self or my false self won. I was uncomfortable when the false self and the ego self took the day of battle because I was aware that their victory was a failure for love. I felt guilt when I realized that I had made a decision in favor of self-pride, self-convenience, or self-satisfaction at the expense of love for others. The dark night was uncomfortable at many times over the years and it was typically so when my beliefs and values were in flux leaving me uncertain and adrift, but even though the trail was filled with failure and disappointment there were moments of consolation that became more frequent, more exciting and cumulative as time passed. I continued to grow in God's love, and to regret those days when I didn't. I seldom despaired during the dark night of the soul. When I despaired it was related to depression, and I frequently despaired. When I was experiencing the dark night of the soul, I knew, though sometimes darkly, that all would be well.

May 3, 1989

Today, I came close to hitting bottom. I lost focus and concentration. John hovered over me in the nursery and helped me make decisions that I was not able to make. Olga asked me not to be in the nursery tomorrow or Friday.

May 4, 1989

I did not go into the nursery today. I spent the morning at Highbanks Metro Park where I took a long walk on the Overlook Trail. When I got back to the car, it being Ascension, I read, "The Blue Balloon" the chapter on the Ascension in *The Irrational Season*. Then I went home, had lunch and took a nap.

May 7, 1989

Last night Olga and I had a talk about the future of the nursery and about my doing something different from what I am currently doing. What I am doing in the nursery seems to be placing too much emotional stress on me and it spills over into unhealthy interpersonal relationships with family and employees. From Olga's perspective the conversation was unsatisfactory because we didn't arrive at a specific plan of action that I could take. From my perspective it was a successful talk because it got me thinking and confronted me with the realization of how serious Olga thought the situation was. It also helped me to accept, at least for the moment, that my approach to the nursery and the people in it was unhealthy. As was typical for me, I came up with twelve ways of looking at the problem. This was clearly an unmanageable number to do anything with, but I felt that there was some merit in each. Then I went about trying to fit each of the twelve perspectives into my spiritual life. This didn't work very well.

May 8, 1989

I woke up at 3:00 this morning and couldn't get back to sleep. I kept thinking about the conversation with Olga, and the fact that I had again slipped into depression. Then I thought about Kelly's death last year. It was exactly one year ago last Monday.

May 9, 1989

More information about the Shalem Institute came in the mail today including an application for admission. I have some doubt about whether that will be possible now. Were the events of the last couple of weeks an example of God getting my attention? If so, what does he want?

May 13, 1989

I had my regular session with Susan today. I told her of the past two weeks and the depths to which I had fallen and risen during that time. I told her about the association with the anniversary of Kelly's death. I told her about the list of twelve perspectives for looking at my behavior. She said that she thought that I should see my physician for help right now. She also strongly suggested that I accept what God has in store for me rather than trying so hard to make God make things happen.

May 18, 1989
I went to see my doctor today and he put me on Norpramin for my depression. He said that he could refer me to a psychologist but that I should try the medicine for a while.

June 1, 1989
It has been two weeks since I first went to see my doctor. At that time I started with the medication he prescribed, I have seen Susan, and have had two meetings with the family about the business. It is quiet clear that I am not capable of doing what I once did, and it is quite clear that the nursery is not doing very well again this year. Sales are down, and staff is about to be laid off again. I doubt that we can stay in business very much longer unless things turn around next year. I am finally beginning to see the nursery as an idol that I worship, but at the same time it is a failure for John, for me and for all of us. If John gets sick again we are certainly in rough water.

Yesterday was the first good day I have had since I started taking the medicine. Perhaps it has begun to kick in. I have my wife, I have my life, I have reasonable economic security, and I have God. But right now I am dealing mostly with survival. Help me.

June 5, 1989
Another day of the empty feeling of hollow despair, and the weakness that has made it difficult to work or think or even pray. The lack of reason and purpose for life has lead to loss of hope. I am unable to make even simple decisions without great effort. Sadness constantly covers me so that I feel that I could cry at any moment. I fear being tested by even simple requests and expectations of those closest to me. These feelings and Susan's concern took me to my family doctor in May. In addition I have been experiencing anger, anxiety, and distrust of others.

During this whole time, spontaneous prayer or contemplative prayer has been impossible. It is the Daily Office that I turn to. It is the petitions and intercessions, those I pray and those prayed for me that kept me in contact with God.

June 18, 1989
I have made no entry since June 5th. In large measure this is because I have had nothing to say to God except that I still feel hollow. In spite of my struggle with myself, and my separation from God I continue to move toward an understanding of what has been happening to me. When I do things out of a concern for others and not just out of a concern for myself, I feel better. And when I do,

I take some comfort in considering the words of Nicholas Herman (Brother Lawrence) when he said, "...Our sanctification [does] not depend upon changing our works, but in doing that for God's sake which we commonly do for our own."[1]

July 30, 1989

It is overcast and rainy, but for the moment the sun has broken through. The depression continues, and I have not gone into the nursery for the last few days. I have said almost nothing to God in my journal for the past six weeks. As I sit here this morning I have difficulty remembering much of what has happened over the past month and a half.

My session with Susan this past week was strange. It ended by being a sort of declaration of independence. I shared a bit with her about Merton's last public appearance before his death and what he said on that occasion, "If you forget everything else that has been said, I would suggest you remember this for the future: From now on, everybody stands on his own feet."[2]

This is about where I am. Right now it's Olga and God and me. Susan has been an ever-present support but Susan will be leaving. "Where do you go from the top of a thirty foot pole. . ."[3] is equivalent to saying where do you go when you lose your spiritual director. What with her vacation, then a six week sabbatical, then my planned trip to Long Beach Island in September and October, it will be the middle of fall before we can meet again, and then Olga and I leave for Florida in December and stay through February. By the time we get back from Florida, Susan will probably be getting ready to move to a new position on the West Coast.

August 9, 1989

I was restless last night, and yesterday Olga became aware that something was wrong. "Did anything happen in the nursery?" she asked, and I knew what she meant. I awakened at 3:00 this morning and lay there in anger and anxiety. Things are not going well in the nursery. Then I felt guilty about going to Long Beach Island next month and leaving everyone in the lurch should they needed me. I was caught in the clutches of despair again and the only positive thing I could think of was how good it will be when I die and I can end this life.

August 13, 1989

In *The Power of Myth*,[4] Joseph Campbell reminds us that those who created our myths also experienced despair, and that they, like us, were often called out from deep despair by the voice of hope. Somehow, now as then, light still penetrates the dark night and leads us out of our deepest shadows. I should remember this.

I was unable to entertain the thought of going to church this morning. My feelings of resentment had returned. Instead I did exercise #10 in *Sadhana: A Way to God*. This is an exercise on release from resentment. In that exercise I was asked to identify specific things that I wanted to forgive that others had done that upset me, but I could not. I was unable to come up with one specific thing that anyone at church had done. My resentment was generalized. I began to wonder if the problem perhaps was not theirs but mine. When I finished the exercise things hadn't changed, and I didn't feel well.

September finally arrived and it was time for our yearly retreat to Long Beach Island. One topic always seemed to surface when I spent time on the island – loving God through loving others. The trip in 1986 introduced me to Merton's "The Power and Meaning of Love." The next year brought intense awareness of the lack of love in the world and raised a question in my mind as to whether this lack of love caused a social disease or if the social disease caused a lack of love. At that time my mind turned to thoughts of a trained army of volunteer social workers to combat this social epidemic. And in 1989 my focus seemed to be on loving God through service to the needy.

In all these cases, I limited myself to talking about love and not doing anything else to address it in my life. In other words love remained an abstract issue for thought, but not an issue for action. But, the door had been opened so that I could see the love of God in a new light. In the past all that I had accomplished was to stimulate unobtainable ideals that set me up for failure (and consequently depression) by convincing myself that I was not a loving, and thus, adequate person. It would take some time for me to face this directly both in terms of my depression and a realistic conception of love in my life. But, at this time I still had not been able to see that this was related to giving my self to others. This was still too much of a threat to my false self for that to happen.

> September 14, 1989
> It has been just a little over a month since my last journal entry. Olga and I have been on Long Beach Island for a week. I have been reading, *Feeling Good: The New Mood Therapy* by David Burns, a psychiatrist at the University of Pennsylvania Medical School. I am not sure what I think of his cognitive approach to dealing with depression, but along with the medicine I have been taking it can't hurt.
> Olga and I have started a study of the parables in the synoptic Gospels to see if there is anything there that would help to clarify what appear to be two very different perspectives on loving God through loving neighbor. The first is to set out each day looking for needy people to serve and then serving them by acting out God's love. The other is to set out each day to do whatever it is I do, and if I happen to meet people in need along the way to show God's love for them by serving their needs.
> In any event it feels good to be journaling again and talking with God about things.

### October 1, 1989

I continue to read and study David Burns' book on cognitive therapy and I have no difficulty in applying it to myself. Finding examples of negative criticism is easy. Today, I was reflecting on two prior incidents in which I felt guilty about my failure to love others by serving the needy. Both incidents involved church sermons which contained examples of people who gave up their careers to spend full time serving homeless people. I remember leaving church both times thinking that if I didn't go out of my way to help the needy that very day I would have failed in my responsibility to love others.

Fortunately my work with Burn's book has helped me to realize that I am not always self serving at the expense of others and that has helped me to realize that my negative self-criticism, and my feelings that I am being judged by others as unloving are related to the distortion of reality caused by the depression.

Today at Holy Innocents the sermon involved a rich Frenchman who gave up his life of wealthy living and came to the United States to live in the Bowery and serve the indigent. I heard this story free of cognitive distortion. I am not a wealthy Frenchman who has devoted his life to helping the needy in the Bowery. I am who I am. If I meet needy people on the road I travel and fail to minister to them, then I have to answer for that. But God is not going to make an example out of me in church on Sunday morning.

### October 2, 1989

This has been another day free of thoughts of self-criticism and another day free of symptoms of depression. I can do nothing more than give thanks. I don't want to analyze it. I just want to live it and enjoy it.

### October 5, 1989

Today was almost symptom free until an incident came up at the Hand Store involving a coat that Olga wanted me to buy. It would please her if I did. It would disappoint her, if I didn't. I'm always disappointing her in things like this.

Cognitive distortion involving what my inner reality saw kicked in. I experienced cognitive distortion involving should statements, overgeneralization, magnification, the fortune telling error and emotional reasoning. But I was able to put an end to my automatic thoughts of self-criticism, and I was able to generate a rational response. My response was to say, "Hold it! I don't have to criticize myself. I am no less worthy because I didn't want to jump to buy a new coat." I let external stimuli cause me to have negative thoughts about myself. Later Olga initiated a conversation about the incident, and I think that now we both better understand how I am drawn into depression, and how I can take charge of my life and not be drawn into a depressed state by others or my own thoughts. In the end, the incident turned out to be a positive one. The previous four days I had reported as symptom free days, but there had been nothing in those days that had triggered negative thoughts about myself. Today was a mild test of the strength and the stability of my healing and it came out just fine.

October 9, 1989
   Our stay on Long Beach Island is about to end. I will be pleased to return home to whatever is there, and to see if I can live day after day free of depression when I return home.

I don't want to give the impression that reading David Burns' book and practicing his principles of cognitive therapy caused an immediate and full recovery from my depression. It did not. Nor did Norpramin successfully treat my depression chemically. It didn't. But I continued to integrate cognitive therapy principles into my daily life, and as more sophisticated drugs became available, both behavioral and drug therapy along with the process of transformation played important roles in my successful fight with depression. I would mark the fall of 1989 as the turning point in that battle. As my journal shows the years ahead of me would be characterized by the usual ups and downs, but the trend would be upward.

For some time journaling had been a form of prayer that took on some of the functions of the Psalms. My spiritual journal became a written record of what I was thinking and wanted God to "hear." In bad times entries often took on the form of an individual lament. In good times they functioned like psalms of trust or thanksgiving or praise. When I quoted others in my journal, I did so because of the wisdom that I thought was expressed by those people. God was almost always implicit as the person to whom I was talking, though occasionally God as the listener was explicit, such as "God, help me I am sinking again." I did not have a particular image of God in mind when I journaled, though I did believe that he was aware of my prayers, undistorted by the defense mechanisms of my ego self.

As I read back over my journals it became obvious to me that short or even long periods of time occurred in which there were no entries. I believe that there were several reasons for this. One could have been that I had nothing to say to God; or perhaps I didn't want to talk with him for any number of reasons; or maybe I was using a different form of prayer at that time. But I have noticed that the lack of entries was often related to periods of depression. Some days or weeks or even months I just didn't have the interest or the desire or the energy to write in my journal. Perhaps I tired of the lament as a form of prayer. But, in December I was recovering from my most recent bout with depression. Things were looking up, and I wanted to use my journal to record a second stepping stone exercise.

December 13, 1989
   Wow, I am journaling again. So much time has passed since my last entry. In that time I did another Stepping Stone exercise as a part of spiritual direction. It was done over a month ago using a tape recorder. I then transcribed it to my journal.

## Turning Point

It was almost three years ago that I did my first stepping stone exercise. At that time I was just beginning spiritual direction. I don't remember all of the ground rules that I used at that time, but the outcome of this second attempt is quite different from the first as I remember it. The current effort is much more holistic. Indeed it is much more like a series of connecting trails that wonder through a maze than it is a series of small flat stones of a path leading to a destination. This time the trail takes me back to the beginning, thus suggesting that I am seeing life in the round rather than as a straight line from one point to another. Stones of the original process dot the trails, although there are four trails on which none of the original stones are present.

While on the first trail I sense that I have existed from before the beginning. I see the preconscious existence of a self in the form of energy floating in cosmic time. Before I was born, the elemental nature of my physical being was, and always had been.

On the second trail, life is breathed into preconscious energy and living matter is created. I am conceived, born and live my early years as an infant. During this time I believe that the subconscious formation of a self was begun.

The third trail traverses the distance between early childhood and the late teen years. Symbolically I see it as a foreboding period that begins with a promise that didn't materialize but hints of a promise for potential fulfillment in the future. This is a period of the development of the conscious self. I want to call it a negative conception of self but there is something in me that reists that. It was what it was, and there are moments of it that I cherish today.

The fourth trail begins with leaving home for the first time in my life to do my military service. This includes my first real full time job after my time in the service and goes to my sophomore year in college. I experience the acceptance of those around me and I begin to see myself as a person who could succeed. It was a time of coming of age.

The fifth trail spans the period from my junior year in college to the campus riots of the spring of 1970. During this time I marry, start a family, get three degrees, hold four teaching jobs (each one considered better than the last). I was an anxious, terrified, success by cultural standards at age 40.

The sixth trail leads me through an arid land of infrequent oases. I start the nursery as a response to my mid-life crisis, and I learn to survive in part by always facing the sun so I cannot see my shadow. I suffer from doubt, self inflicted defeat, and I retreat deeper and deeper into the desert to avoid the eyes of others. I might have withdrawn to the desert to find my bearing as Anthony did, but I didn't. I fled to the desert to escape the world.

The seventh trail is the one on which an Angel of the Lord appeared one day and started out with me on a spiritual journey. I began spiritual direction. I retired from teaching never having found, to my satisfaction, the ideal teacher within me. Though I didn't know it at the time, this period of my life was to be a preparation for a new challenge.

I now walk on the eighth trail of my life journey. I started without a map. I have drawn a map as I go. I started without a specific end in view. I will know what I seek as I find it along the way. I will return to where I began, free energy in the cosmos.

Those familiar with the Stepping Stones exercise described in *At a Journal Workshop* will recognize that the product of the exercise that is included in the December 13, 1989 entry deviates somewhat from the format proposed by Progoff. This second attempt at the process focuses on periods of time rather than single events. When I did it, it seemed like a reasonable approach to take. In any event, it served the purpose of seeing myself holistically at that moment in my life.

February 26, 1990

We are packing to go home from Florida. From the few entries in my journal since October of last year one might speculate that my spiritual life has dried up. Nothing could be further from the truth. We went home for Christmas and stayed a few weeks longer to be with the kids. Since we have gotten back to Florida, I have begun serious walks and talks with God. The beach is a great place for this. The conversations with God have been exciting and it seems as if they have taken the place of journaling. I have never been more at peace. My depression seems to be in remission. I think I am getting a better handle on knowing God and myself.

March 8, 1990

We are home, and though God lives in the surf with all its power, he also lives in Ohio. The Sunday after we got back, Olga and I went to our home church, and in no time I was back where I had been. By Tuesday morning at 4:00 I had fussed myself into a fit about it. Later in the day Olga and I talked about options. The one that seems most realistic is to face up to the fact that I just can't cut it at our parish without getting angry and separating myself from God. "O.K. I have to accept the reality that I separate myself from God by my own feelings. I have to fight this Sunday after Sunday. Better to find a place like St. Thomas where I can feel at peace with God. In time perhaps I will be able to heal, but for now it isn't working out." As Olga and I talked about the church situation she helped me to understand the heavy emphasis that I put on accepting the responsibility for my actions and their consequences. This sounds like an admirable trait, but in fact it is an "I am in control; I will take the high road and I am proud of it" attitude. Its pride protected by the ego self.

I talked with Susan about this and she agreed that I had failed to provide for God to take the initiative. It was always my responsibility to find him. I had left out of my theology a God who was in control.

October 11, 1990

The bottom has really fallen out of my use of the journal as a central part of my spiritual life. The last entry was in March. In any event since then a lot has happened.

Olga and I did visit other churches in the area in search of a more compatible community with which to worship. We ended up staying where we were.

Susan left to go to the West Coast to take a job there. I lost my temper in the nursery on several occasions and went off to St. Gregory's for a retreat. This was one of the most gratifying things I have done in some time.

I decided after all to apply to the Shalem Institute Group Leader's Program, not the Spiritual Direction Program, and to ask the Epiphany Foundation for a $1000 grant to help with tuition.

I made my peace with my rector at church and now feel a genuine sense of healing. I even considered having her as my spiritual director when Susan left. I have no way of knowing where this will lead, but for now it's O.K. I am healing, but I don't know how much stress to put on the fracture.

I have started with a new spiritual director, and I had my first session with him before we left for Florida. Two future meetings have already been scheduled for when we come back to Ohio for Christmas. The first session was very positive and as supportive as I could have hoped for. During this session he reflected on my prayer life and suggested that I was using a type of prayer called dialogical prayer. He suggested that I formalize this in my journal work. Before we left for Florida, I got a copy of *The Dialogue* by Catherine of Siena and took it with me. It's tough going for a 20th Century person such as myself, but I have some sense now of the depth and intensity of her mysticism and her spirituality of love. In *The Dialogue* she says, ". . . through this union of the divine nature with the human, God was made human and humanity was made God."[5] I was struck by this and finally put it out as a subject for mediation as I sat on the porch with the surf breaking just a few yards away. A day later I took it up as a topic of conversation with God on a beach walk.

October 16, 1990

Recently I have been aware that my approach to contemplation has not been very fruitful. In the past when this has happened I tried to push it. The result usually was tension, and so this time I just let it be and gave it back to God to deal with in his time.

This morning when I awoke I lay in bed for quite a while and was washed over by a calm awareness of the need to pay more attention to the purpose and direction of my life. From my wondering mind came the awareness that I have been doing some things just to fill in time rather than to celebrate just being. I also became aware that I have not seriously considered my motives for applying to Shalem. It must be more than filling in time. It must be a test of vocation.

October 20, 2990

I just came back from a four-mile walk on the beach. The tide was out and thus the footing was flat and firm. The walk was a "walk and talk with God" in the tradition of dialogical prayer. Good prayer time. We're still talking about that quote from *The Dialogue*.

At this time, talking with God did not mean that I heard his voice speaking to me. It did not mean that I carried on a verbal dialogue with God as I would with another person. What happened was much closer to thinking a thought, and then testing the validity of that thought against my beliefs and my experience of how God worked in my life, and then perhaps revising the thought depending on how the thought fit with my experience and beliefs. In order to carry out this give and take between my thoughts, my experience, and my conception of how God worked in my life, I needed a belief system and a theology. I needed a conception of who God was and how he functioned. But, my beliefs and theology were still going through reconstruction and they were far less than a sure guide. Nonetheless it proved to be a stimulating time of prayer. Even though we did not really have a conversation, it often seemed as if we were.

November 2, 1990
I started Evelyn Underhill's *Mysticism* today. So far it is very readable. About sundown I went out on the porch and watched the end of the sunset. A scientist could have told me all that I ever wanted or needed to know about what was happening, and would have spoiled it on the spot. A philosopher could have analyzed the aesthetic experience in any number of classic ways and each would have dismembered the experience. A painter could have preserved a slice of the moment of brilliant reality but something would have been lost. I stood and stared in awe and became a part of the event. Any attempt to capture it would have been like capturing a rare life giving gas in a birdcage and climbing into the cage to inhale it.

Changing spiritual directors resulted in a change in approach to spiritual direction. Susan's style had led me to focus on a self-discovery, personal and emotional issues, and an ineffable God who could be known only through a faith relationship. This approach stimulated the recessive side of my personality and helped me to grow in areas that I had largely avoided for most of my life. Michael's approach was more cognitive. I soon found myself interested in such ideas such as the incarnate nature of God, and how to see him manifested in people and the world around me. In Susan's approach, the ability to communicate with others about my experience of God was less important than building a faith relationship that sustained meaning and purpose in my life. In the more cognitive approach taken by Michael, my ability to communicate with both myself and with others about God took on greater importance. I hoped that dialogical prayer would help me clarify my relationship with God and learn how to communicate the experience of God to others in a society in which so many people saw him, if not dead, at least on his death bed, and had lost the ability or taste for talking about him.

In my reading I came upon two authors who expressed concern over God's disfavor in society at the time. In their novels and short stories they addressed their concern in a number of ways. Flannery O'Connor said that a moral sense had been bred out of large segments of the population. She compared the current culture to a society of wingless chickens, selectively bred for more white meat. Walker Percy said that the old ways of talking about God had been devalued like faceless coins worn thin. My need to learn about God from others, and to communicate with others about the experience of the Almighty, led me to a book by Peter Hawkins, *The Language of Grace*. In this work Hawkins pointed to Flannery O'Connor, Walker Percy and Iris Murdoch as authors who were particularly interested in communicating the experience of the Holy One through fictional characters. The difficulty they experienced as authors was how to communicate the experience of the Ineffable One to a generation of people who had all but lost a moral sense of God and all but lost a desire or inclination to see him in the everyday events of their daily lives. This generation, they said, hardly ever thought, let alone talked about God.

November 4, 1990
 If I were interested in a language of grace, who would I be, what would I be interested in? It seems that the language of grace might enable me to talk to others about the transforming action of the Divine for people who have lost a sense of God. But there is also the language of grace created and used by authors. Flannery O'Connor seems to sense a need to develop new methods of indirection, new strategies of communication that might open the reader to dimensions of life that have become remote if not inaccessible. Walker Percy has said that our current symbol system has lost its value. It seems that people like O'Connor and Percy think that we are going to have to develop a language of grace ourselves. God isn't going to do it for us. It seems that they want to create a new language (a language of grace) that enables people to talk about the experience of the Almighty.
 I wonder if soul has something to do with this? What is the quality of music that has soul? Is it a quality that expresses something about what it is like to experience the ultimate? Soul music or soul language might lead us to love and then lead us to the Source of Life.

November 8, 1990
 I am now able to talk about the state of my mental health, and my anger with others who confront my ego self. We have been down in Florida for over six weeks. During this time I have had one episode of self-anger and only a couple of episodes of anger toward others who aroused my ego self. Other than this I have not had symptoms of depression.
 Something has happened and I am conscious of it. I lie in bed or sit in prayer, read or do any number of things with an overwhelming sense of peace and joy. I wonder if this is permanent or if not, how long it will last.

November 9, 1990

On a walk this afternoon I thought about a language of grace that I could use in talking about my relationship with God. There seem to be two perspectives on this. The first might be an attempt to communicate to others the experience I have had of a personal relationship with the Ineffable One, by focusing on my personal experience. The second might be to use other literary techniques such as indirection or suspense to tell a story that stimulates an imaginative relationship with God. These approaches might help people to get a sense of what it is like to stand in awe before something that is beyond being logical or empirical and is truly overwhelming.

November 16, 1990

We are told that we do not know what or who the deity is in an objective sense. We are told that God is love, light, spirit, consuming fire and from this we fancy that we know what love is, what light is, what a consuming fire is. We think that we know what spirit is. At least we talk as if we knew, but we are really using metaphors about what we assume to be attributes of God.

Yet, we claim with little difficulty (at least many do) to be capable of knowing and doing God's will. How can I know his will or love him when I have no objective knowledge of him, just metaphors. Is subjective, personal knowledge enough? If I don't know what God's will is, the best I can do is to be optimally receptive in my personal relationship, and like the wise virgins be prepared to be ready to be his agent when and if the time comes for me to act. The problem is to know when the time has come.

November 24, 1990

I wrote a letter to Michael today as a substitute for a face-to-face spiritual direction session. When I get back to Ohio over Christmas, I will need to assess his feelings on how this type of spiritual direction is working out.

Right now Olga and I have three weeks before we return home to be with the kids over Christmas. John will call on Monday to tell us about his session with his doctor. It is strange how keeping this journal over the last few years has plotted the rhythm of my emotional state as it relates to his health.

November 25, 1990

In the letter I wrote to Michael yesterday I said that I wanted to have an advent discipline of meditating on the incarnation as it relates to the people around me. This morning I was thinking that if Christ is alive within each of us, then we all become an incarnation of God.

Yet, I find people to be both bothersome and necessary for my existence. I can usually get along with them one at a time, but in a group they constitute a threat to my comfort and my security. Even meeting new people one at a time can be threatening to me. I only feel really comfortable with people who are family or friends that I have known in a long term, personal way. It would be easy for me to chalk this up to being introverted, but if this separates me from the Christ that is in people what then? I need to make this part of my Advent meditations, if I am to focus on the incarnation.

December 2, 1990

I have decided on my Advent discipline. Briefly described it will be *lectio divina*. The discipline will involve daily meditation on the meaning of the incarnation. The prayer structure has four steps: First, I will identify scriptural references in *The Word is Very Near You* that are related to the incarnation. Then read the Scripture slowly several times. For example, "Those who eat my flesh and drink my blood abide in me, and I in them," (John 6:56). Then meditate on the passage in context for about twenty minutes, and finally allow myself to move to wordless waiting and accept what is revealed. This will be followed by using my journal, and trying to capture the essence of the meditative and contemplative experience.

December 4, 1990

"I am the vine, you are the branches. Those who abide in me and I in them bear much fruit. . ." (John 15:5). The creator seems to be the root system from which the Christ, who is the vine, grows. I grow from the vine. I am a branch. And, flowing through the plant is the Spirit that is the vital sap of life. God wants me to produce fruit. To do this I need to be rooted and supported by the vine from which the branches grow and are nurtured by the vital sap that flows through the whole plant. All of the parts are tied together as one.

December 8, 1990

Thoughts racing through my head. God as love. God as love energy. God as the word existing before the world we know. God, as the Word, living among us as the exemplification of love. Jesus set aside for the service of love. Each person who accepts God's grace of love set aside for the service of love. Each person nurtured by love energy and giving off love energy to nurture others. Love growing within individual humans and thus in humanity. In this way is humanity becoming God? Is this what Catherine of Siena meant?

Is this the essence of incarnation? Is this the Word made flesh? Is this perfect union in God? Is this the ultimate equation of God and man? Is this God's reality? Is this what Teillard meant?

December 20, 1990

I meet today with Michael for our second face-to-face spiritual direction session. Shall I bring to him my confusion with regard to Jesus on one hand and the Christ on the other? How do I just stand aside and let the Christ that is in me show forth in love? Is this just a way of avoiding the responsibility of doing my own loving? Is there really a Christ within me who wants to love and live if only I will let him, if only I will unlock the door and stand aside?

And so the Advent season of 1990 came and went, and apparently no Christ was going to be born from within me that year. I became increasingly aware that I still lacked a systematic way of thinking about God. I had taken on one approach after another, used it and left it behind. It was time to bring some sense of closure, if only temporarily, to my divergent and in some sense undisciplined spiritual life. I had been wondering here and there for some time. I had lots of experiences that I thought were useful, and I still think that most of them were, but I could only stand so much divergence. Sooner or later I needed to regroup, take stock and see where I stood.

I thought that more education would be useful in getting some closure so I went back to school. This involved participation in the Group Leaders program at the Shalem Institute for Spiritual Development and The Education for Ministry program offered by the School of Theology at the University of the South. It was my hope that this formal preparation would help me bring some systematic organization to what I had been experiencing for four years.

As I look back on these educational experiences I am more than ever convinced that God was acting as my spiritual director. For me to have forced closure at that time would have pushed me prematurely into a spirituality that would have been grounded in the logic and the theological thinking of others rather than in a direct experience with God. The more I learned the more I realized that it was indeed a very big universe, and that God didn't want me to develop a spirituality that brought closure to my spiritual life. God wanted me to keep the future open, to keep my mind open, to keep my senses alert, to read the trail markers that led the way to him.

## NOTES

1. Brother Lawrence, *The Practice of the Presence of God* (White Plains: NY, Peter Pauper Press, 1963), 19.

2. Thomas Merton, *The Asian Journal of Thomas Merton*, eds. Naomi Burton, Patrick Hart, and James Laughton (New York: New Directions, 1975), 338.

3. Merton, *The Asian Journal*, 338–339.

4. Joseph Campbell, *The Power of Myth*, with Bill Moyers (New York: Anchor Books, 1991), 45–46.

5. Catherine of Siena, *The Dialogue*, trans. Suzanne Noffke (New York: Paulist Press, 1980), 53.

*Chapter Five*

# Contemplative Revelations

Several years earlier Susan had talked with me about the Shalem Institute for Spiritual Formation as the place to go if I wanted to learn more about contemplation. At the time I was a little intimated by the thought of studying with Tilden Edwards, Gerald May and Rosemary Dougherty, but I knew that I still had a lot to learn, and that I had not yet found my own spiritual voice. My conception of a secular contemplative was still strongly influenced by what I thought the life of a monk at Gethsemani or St. Gregory's Abbey would be like if he suddenly found himself living in society as a married man with family obligations. And as one might have expected, it hadn't taken long for my fanciful ideas about a contemplative community based on Little Gidding, nestled in the midst of a busy, materialistic, postmodern world to meet much the same end as most of the other utopias that had preceded me. I soon realized that if I were to adapt the contemplative life to my world, I would have to create my own synthesis.

I was then, and probably always will be, a product of the dominant culture in which I have lived for most of my life, thus when I thought about learning more about the contemplative way and how to use that learning, it was no surprise that I thought that the best way to do that was to go back to school, and so I applied to Shalem for admission to the Group Leaders Program.

At the same time, I was working on several theological issues that I had formed as questions but had not answered: "Who is the Christ?" and "Who was Jesus?" As I attempted to address these questions, the historical Jesus, the historical Christ, the living Christ, and the cosmic Christ became four different people. The Group Leaders Program at Shalem was not designed to address those issues. It was built on the assumption that I would have already dealt with matters like that and have resolved them before I came there. But they were appropriate questions for spiritual direction and I planned to share them with Michael.

December 21, 1990

I never did take my confusion about Jesus and the living Christ to Michael at our session yesterday, but I did bring up the matter of standing aside and letting the Christ within me show forth in love. His reaction to that was that I was talking of a matter of method, and that Brother Lawrence probably had as good a method as any he could suggest. He also recommended a book by a Quaker, Thomas Kelly, *A Testament of Devotion*.

December 23, 1990

For the last two days I have substituted just sitting in God's presence for meditation on scripture. The time has gone by very quickly. It was as if I were in a different time frame, and of particular importance, I didn't bring an agenda to prayer. I just rested in God's presence. Michael is right. I will never experience God fully if I limit myself to my head. Even meditation on God's word will not get me there. Thinking my own thoughts is not a relationship. However, being with God in thought is a relationship.

December 27, 1990

Christmas has come and gone. The kids have arrived in Florida to use our rental place for a short vacation. During this time I received a letter from Shalem saying that I have been admitted to the Group Leaders Program, and I have written Tilden Edwards a letter of acceptance.

Christmas passed without any real emotional high. Just three days of intense family interaction; there were no signs of depression, but no joy either. Why no joy? In reflecting on this it seems as if we just did Christmas. We didn't celebrate Christmas. We just did all of the traditional things. I have some thoughts about this for next year including more focus on the quality of events rather than so much emphasis on quantity. I'm not sure if I can convince the family to try, but who knows.

January 3, 1991

Yesterday I got a letter from Michael dated December 11. It had been sent to Florida and arrived after we had left to come home for Christmas. It was then forwarded to Ohio. It could not have arrived at a more perfect time. If I had gotten it in Florida before my recent meeting with him it probably would have had less impact. In that letter Michael said, "Faith and willingness constitute an attitude, a stance which is not dependent on an external condition or psychological state. It is a stance simply stating, God is, God is present whether I feel it, or am aware of it, or not. Contemplation is simply relaxing, waiting, and watching to see and hear where God is; to quote Brother Lawrence, 'It is the loving gaze that finds God everywhere.' So my counsel for you is to relax, watch, and wait to see how you are opened by God so that you may indeed gaze on God."

Now I understand how Brother Lawrence came into my last session with Michael. I can't force myself to take that stance; I must somehow become that stance. He also enclosed a quote from Thomas Kelly's *Testament of Devotion*:

> If you slip and stumble and forget God for an hour, and assert your old proud self, and rely on your own clever wisdom, don't spend too much time in anguished regrets and self-accusations but begin again, just where you are.... Don't grit your teeth and clench your fists and say, 'I will, I will.' Relax. Take hands off. Submit yourself to God. Learn to live in the passive voice — a hard saying for Americans — and let life be willed through you. For 'I will' spells not obedience.[1]

I am my own worst enemy in that regard. I allow myself to take on the active rather than the passive voice much too often. I have a choice, and I get the feeling that God is doing everything he can to help me to see that choice. I just can't take an active voice stance while living in the passive voice. I must choose who I want to be and live that life.

January 10, 1991

I met again with Michael this afternoon. We used my recent journal entries based on insights I had into what Brother Lawrence and Thomas Kelly had said. The session proceeded in a compatible and caring way. Michael seemed to recognize that in our last session I had felt rushed. The session this afternoon was scheduled for 3:00 to 4:00 and we did not end until after 5:00. We also agreed to continue spiritual direction by letter after I returned to Florida.

January 16, 1991

The war in the Middle East has started. Olga and I were watching the news and Dan Rather said it had been confirmed. We are packed and ready to leave for Florida tomorrow morning. There is no way we can do that now. We went over to have dinner with the family as we had planned. We will see what happens tomorrow and the days that follow. This is not the end; it is just what's happening today. At this moment I know that God's love for his creation (including Saddam Hussein and George Bush) is beyond my capacity to understand as is my capacity to understand the depth of God's sorrow.

January 17, 1991

Today was spent in normal activities. We did not leave for Florida. It is a time for families to be together, a good place to keep the energy of love flowing in the world.

January 24, 1991

Finally, we decided it was time to leave. We left on Saturday morning and arrived early Sunday afternoon. In the short time we have been back, nothing, and yet much, has happened. Within me is a feeling of wholeness yet outside there is no sun, no blue sky, no brilliant sunset. There is a dark rain, heavy rain and an angry and powerful surf filled with energy. I feel no desire to tame it, or harness it for the good of mankind. I am satisfied to see it as a metaphor for the violence of the world.

January 29, 1991
My kingdom is not from this world. (John 18:36)
Since Sunday my thoughts have been overshadowed by thoughts of the worldly kingdom. Certainly, kingdom was an appropriate metaphor to be invoked in the time of Jesus. Today it carries a different meaning for the people of Iraq, Saudi Arabia and the United States. Each nation lives under a different jurisdiction. I feel the conflict that is created by the clash of these jurisdictions.

February 1, 1991
The prayer for me is not as President Bush says, "God bless the United States of America" but rather, God bless the people of the United States of America in spite of all that we do to make you so sad. We do these things as citizens of the secular world not as citizens of your kingdom.

February 3, 1991
The sermon at St. Thomas today hit the mark time and again as the rector preached on Mark 1:21–28, the exorcism of the evil spirit. His contention was that some of what we call evil spirits can be identified as psychosis and neuroses and some can be traced to the ego. What caught my attention was substituting the concept of ego for the concept of an evil spirit.

Is nationalism a metaphor for the collective ego of a nation? Is it a social disease of which psychoses and neuroses are symptoms? How long will we allow this social disease to plague us? How long will we allow greed and power to masquerade as love? I remember these thoughts that ran through my mind at this time. But, in February of 1991, I pushed the conflict between love and evil to the back of my mind and turned my attention to the work ahead of me as a participant in the Group Leaders Program at Shalem.

At the time I took the Group Leaders Program it was composed of six components that were distributed over a year and a half. The first component consisted of guided self-study, and made use of tape recorded exercises and selected readings. The second part was a residency experience in Washington, D.C. in which what had been learned through self-study was applied in a practicum setting. This was followed by more self-study, and then preparation for leading a contemplative spiritual development program at home. This phase was then followed by a second residency, and finally by the summary and evaluation phase.

February 5, 1991
Yesterday a package of materials arrived from Shalem. Today, I talked to our deacon about working with me in developing a contemplative formation group

at St. Thomas next Advent. He said that he would be interested, and would discuss the project with the rector. He will get back to me in a week or ten days.

February 6, 1991

Olga and I went to the Mall today to get some of the required books for the Shalem program. Most of them were not in stock at Walden Books and had to be ordered. If they are in the central warehouse I should get them in about a week.

I did get a copy of *Living in the Presence* and later today I read the first two chapters and listened to and did the first taped exercise, "Presence For God Through Bodily Alertness, Relaxation and Posture." The exercise was a bit rushed for me. I will try it again tomorrow.

February 8, 1991

Again today I did the "Presence for God through Body Alertness, Relaxation and Posture" exercise. This time doing the exercise did help me to relax and become more aware of the skeletal and neural complexities of the body. I had a greater awareness than I previously had of the marvel of the human body as a creation of God. There was no resistance to letting go of self-inflicted tension. It was interesting to realize how much tension I can release when I am asked to do so. Following the use of the Shalem tape, I used the de Mello tape on "Body Sensations." The physical awareness invoked by the tape was much less dramatic than that invoked by the Shalem tape, but the de Mello meditation produced a greater feeling of peace.

February 17, 1991

First, the "Presence for God Through Breath" exercise and then I did the de Mello breathing exercises. In neither case can I say that I had a keen sense of the presence of God.

February 20, 1991

Tonight I did prayer form #3 "Presence for God Through Sound and Silence." This was to be followed by twenty minutes of silence. But it was not silence. It was a busy period of interior noise. Some prayer times are like that.

February 25, 1991

"Presence for God by Invoking The Name of God." Invoking God's name as a mantra was associated with a sense of space. I thought about time being present in space, past time in space experienced as the present, future time in space experienced as the present.

February 27, 1991

Met with the deacon today. The contemplative formation program at St. Thomas is definitely on for next fall. Tentatively we set the time period as November 6th through December 18th. This will provide opportunity for six sessions.

March 19, 1991

Back from Florida since yesterday. The trip home was difficult. A back pain I have had for a number of weeks seemed to drain energy from me, and Olga drove for three long stretches. I slept last night for twelve hours and awakened with the pain this morning.

Later I was reading one of the required books for the Shalem Group Leaders program, *Prayer and Our Bodies* by Flora Slosson Wuellner. The content seemed to me at the time to be on the fringe of magic, and a tent meeting healing service. In spite of my attitude I made a concerted effort to give it a chance. One of the exercises had to do with thinking of some part of the body that is under stress, is uncomfortable, or in pain. And so, I turned my attention to the pain in my lower back. There was an almost immediate sensation of tingling similar to the sensation one gets when muscles relax following a muscle spasm. I felt a throbbing of blood going through the area as if it were carrying away whatever it was that was causing the pain. In less than ten minutes it was almost all gone. The moment was real and now I remember my thoughts about magic and tent meeting healing services. I had participated in a healing experience, one for which I give thanks, and stand in self-conscious wonder.

This afternoon I did an exercise that is an adaptation of *lectio divina* and Ignation meditation. In doing this exercise I was surprised to find myself with Jesus on a path leading to a place far from a crowd we had left behind. Rocks provided seats for us and we rested. I talked with Jesus about John and his seriously elevated white blood count that was a threatening complication in the frequent surgery he had for bladder cancer. Thoughts went back to the clashes of willfulness that John and I have had for over eleven years, and I found myself praying that his doctors would be able to solve the white cell problems, and continue with the program of surgery that had been so successful.

The guided prayer, study and exercises that make up the content of the first three or four months of the Group Leaders Program were in part designed to help each participant teach a session to the training class when we assembled in Washington in May for our first residency experience. I developed a number of Ignation meditation exercises that I could use with my formation group the following fall at St. Thomas. During the residency I used one of these exercises as an example of Ignation meditation. Though all of the lessons were in some way related to contemplative prayer, not all used formal meditation techniques.

One student's project that turned out to be very provocative for me involved the use of artist's clay to create a piece of artwork in collaboration with a partner. I chose to work on a bust of a man. After working for a while I traded my work with my partner who in the spirit of co-creation, was supposed to add her contribution of creation to my work.

May 5, 1991

Yesterday the student presentation illustrated seeing God's presence in co-creation. Using the clay that was provided, I created an abstract bust of a human and titled it Man Weeping. My partner and I then traded our sculptures, and each of us was asked to work with our partner's creation in the spirit of co-creation. When I got my work back I was shocked at what my partner had done to it. My work, and thus I, had been violated. My partner had "heard God" and had done "God's will" by modifying my interpretation of Man Weeping. Thoughts ran through my head and gushed out:

- Who are we in co-creation?
- What are our limits in our work of co-creation with God?
- When do we leave willingness in co-creation and move into willfulness?
- When do we commit idolatry by presuming to become God?

I did not feel as if I had been a partner in co-creation. I felt as if I had been manipulated by an evangelist, and shaped by the evangelist's conception of Man Weeping.

My journal contains no entries during the period from the residency experience in May until the end of August of that year. Over the next several years this pattern of lapses in the journaling persisted. But though there are extended voids in the journal, the pattern also shows that I always returned to journaling as a prayer form. I tried a number of techniques, practices and ways of approaching contemplative prayer, but two have had the greatest long-term staying power, journaling and meditation on the Psalms.

More than any other approach to prayer, I seem to have a natural and uncontrived relationship with God when I am journaling or reading the Psalms. At these moments it is obvious to me that God is present and participating in the experience. I don't consciously think of it, but I am aware of it. The only other type of prayer that has similar characteristics for me are those moments in the social or the natural world when there ceases to be a distinction between God, myself, and another person, or between myself, God and some object of contemplation such as a thunder storm. I think of these moments as natural prayer.

August 21, 1991

One of the requirements for the Group Leaders Program is to do a retreat, and so here I am on retreat at St. Gregory's again. It's been three months since I used my journal, but I'm back again. It's almost like I've been "out of it" since May, but that isn't quite true. Ordinary time can be so ordinary. It seems as if life is often not made up of highs and lows but rather long strings of commas broken by occasional question marks and exclamations. While it is true that much of life is one comma after another, it is also true that each day is fresh and new and pregnant with God's presence so long as it is seen in that way. Is that the deep message of the incarnation?

August 22, 1991

While on retreat I have been asking, "What am I doing here?" "What does all of this mean?" Tonight, as I end my retreat, I tend to think that the answer is obvious. No answer to the big question that leads to the big moment, just lots of commas. Just an ordinary retreat during which I was touched by God in more ways than I can count.

I was beginning to experience contemplation as an accepting gaze at God's world. Sometimes it was with joy and celebration and sometimes, with sadness and compassion. When I did this, prayer became a release from willfulness and an acceptance of willingness for God's transformation of the self.

August 23, 1991

The trip home from the retreat was a delight. God seemed to be everywhere. At a Frish's Big Boy restaurant a number of us were served by a joy filled waitress who turned everybody around her into joy filled people whether they wanted her to or not. She seemed to see each of her customers as an individual. She said things and treated each of us as a special person. What a gift!

Later at a roadside rest I watched an Amish, or perhaps a Mennonite, family as they practiced their unique customs. They, like the waitress at Frish's, were special people, as was a teen age girl who worked for the state emptying trash containers at the rest area as if she had a real sense that her work was important. She seemed to do it with joy.

As I sat at a picnic table drinking coffee I found myself gazing at a trail that led to a grove of trees; the trail was bordered by black-eyed susans. Each object in the scene radiated light in a way I seldom see. Each object shown with a special clarity. Each was transfigured as was the small teenage girl as she emptied trash-cans.

September 12, 1991

I awakened this morning with a clear picture of how I swing from focused clarity, sharpness, and high energy level to a dulled perception and a low energy level where living becomes working around sadness and self-doubt. When this happens, I find that my best coping mechanism is to withdraw and thus cut down on the barrage of unwanted stimuli around me to which I am asked to respond. If I do this, I seem to snap back more quickly than if I try to tough it out. When I am able to withdraw and contemplate the world around me, I often see it differently than I may have seen it just a few minutes earlier, in its (or perhaps my) hectic state.

In the fall of 1991 Olga and I returned to Florida earlier than in past years so I could get ready to offer the contemplative formation program at St. Thomas in November. In retrospect, I see the program that I offered as a success at the organizational level, but a failure at a deeper level. It was an opportunity to demonstrate to myself that I was still able to teach a class as I once had. And at the same time it demonstrated to me that my approach to conducting a contemplative formation group was flawed. I fell into the trap of teaching the way that I had been taught. I now believe that I should not have conducted the formation group like most people conceive of teaching (I've got it-I give it-you get it). Rather, I should have structured a place where people were invited to be free from their previous conceptions of God and prayer and were encouraged to develop a personal contemplative spirituality to guide their personal selections of prayer forms. In introducing contemplative approaches to prayer such as chanting, mantras, breath prayer, *lectio divina*, Ignation meditation or the use of art forms, I should have presented them as a means and not as an end in themselves. For example, I should not have asked people to learn to use the Jesus Prayer unless using the Jesus Prayer could have, in some way, encouraged them to approach God in a way that was consistent with how they felt at the time, or their evolving conception of God. A person does not need to learn to maintain concentration in prayer by blocking out all distractions, unless they believe that a state of solitude that frees them from distractions is necessary to enable them to focus on some topic of prayer or on their relationship with God. Just learning how to do *lectio divina* doesn't go anywhere unless doing *lectio* becomes a way to God. A way to God should be guided by a developing and evolving spirituality of contemplation not just by mastering the use of techniques.

I should have emphasized that contemplative prayer is a way of encouraging a willingness for God to enter one's life rather than a way of hunting for God, capturing him and putting him in a cage of one's own making. But at this time I hadn't developed a contemplative spirituality that included these understandings. Perhaps I just missed it, but none of my preparation, up to the time that I offered the contemplative formation program at St. Thomas, had been grounded in developing these understandings. I saw my preparation as being grounded in the mastery of prayer methods. Thus it should not be surprising that I taught people how to use contemplative prayer without an opportunity for them to ask the fundamental question, "Does learning to pray like this in some way free me to let God approach, and for me to experience God in a way that is consistent with who I am and who I believe God to be?" If the prayer that is used doesn't do these things, then a person needs to recognize this and select ones that do. I did not help participants formulate their own conception of a relationship with God, and then help them to select prayer forms that were consistent with their conception of God and their relationship with him. I did not help participants learn to monitor their relationship with God and then to use prayer forms that would enable them to be more open to the God they knew.

In spite of what I now consider to be a serious flaw in the design of the course, I had ample feedback that people were interested. They did learn some things about contemplative prayer, and they did consider the course to have been a worthwhile experience. But, I never saw evidence that people were choosing ways of prayer on the basis of their conception of God or their relationship with God. I never saw evidence that their prayer facilitated their openness to the God that they knew. I never saw evidence that people's understanding of God or their relationship with God was in some way related to their prayer life. I never saw this evidence because I never asked people to address these issues.

November 11, 1991

Yesterday was the first session of my spiritual formation course, "Praying The Scriptures: A Contemplative Approach." Up until yesterday I had serious doubts that I could do it. I tried to keep an even keel and largely succeeded. But as far back as last summer when I was doing the planning I was filled with doubt. When the time approached for the session the doubt turned to anxiety. Awareness of this didn't allay my anxiety all that much, but yesterday I did what I could. I showed up and taught using an indirect teaching style. I strongly believe that the first session was satisfying not just for me but for the participants as well.

November 21, 1991

The pacing of the class yesterday was less hurried. To achieve that, I cut out the second Ignation meditation and did just one. In retrospect it would probably have been better to have used the second one. This would have led more naturally into the meditations they were doing this week. Other than these mechanical matters and planning to do more than I was able to accomplish, things went well. I was not anxious and I found myself asking, "Where did the time go?"

November 27, 1991

Today was the fourth session of the spiritual formation group. Again I felt very much as if I were an instrument being played by God. If it is possible to talk of progress being made in prayer, we have clearly made progress in learning about contemplative prayer and how to do it. I cannot think of anything that was done that did not feel as if it were a part of a whole. I do believe that many of the people are experiencing satisfaction.

December 6, 1991

The fifth session last Wednesday was again effortless. Some modifications were made on the original plan that I developed last summer, but in general the plan holds up.

In planning for next week's session I have incorporated a way to illustrate the creative and repentant sides of prayer by using a model as a metaphor that seemed to fit two of the chants that we have been using—"I Thank You God For

The Wonder of My Being" and "Lord Jesus Christ, Son of God, Have Mercy on Me a Sinner". The model is in the form of an infinity sign, and shows the flow of the energy of the Spirit oscillating through us from creation and thanksgiving to repentance and reconciliation and back. The purpose for using the model will be to illustrate that creation and reconciliation work in our lives in a repeated pattern, and that we can attend to our creative and redemptive moods equally well by using different contemplative prayers for each. I hope it works.

I used the model in the final session of the group in conjunction with chanting breath prayers. I am not at all sure that they understood the point I was trying to make, at least I got little feedback that they did. Nevertheless I thought that it was one way to help people make use of contemplative prayer in a way that reflected two common experiences in life.

Not daunted by my relative lack of success, I continued working with the idea of the model in preparation for a presentation during the second residency in Washington in February. This time the model showed two typical human conditions as represented by (1) life and light (as portrayed in willingness, wholeness, hope, co-creation and joy) and (2) death and darkness (as portrayed in willfulness, brokenness and despair). Before I could move from the model and chant the two breath prayers, "I Thank You God for the Wonder of My Being" and the second breath prayer "Lord Jesus Christ Son of God Have Mercy on Me a Sinner," the leadership of the group was snatched away from me by several program participants who took exception to my use of the metaphors of light and darkness. They saw my use of these two metaphors as an expression of racism. I was totally flabbergasted. I never considered the use of light and darkness as anything but a naturally occurring dichotomy found in nature. But they saw the use of these words as symbols used as racist code words. There was no way of bringing the group back to the original purpose of the presentation, so I let the discussion go where it may. In the end, I felt as if I had been beaten up by a couple of thugs.

Two attempts to engage people in a consideration of the selection of contemplative prayer types based on their conception of God and their attitude toward life at the time had failed. I still believe that both raising people's awareness of their conception of God, and a consideration of their mood and feelings at the time, can positively influence their approach to prayer, and can be a useful aspect of contemplative formation.

I returned to Florida at the conclusion of the residency to write a final paper and a program evaluation. The final paper was one in which I was to think ahead to using the experiences and learnings that I had gained in the program, by applying them to future spiritual formation events in which I might be involved. I chose future contemplative formation programs that I might use at St. Thomas. In the paper I chose St. Thomas as the site for the programs because as I said,

"The age and maturity of the congregation, many of whom were retirees, would provide a ready pool of people for this type of program. Older people, being closer to the death experience, would be more receptive to contemplative prayer formation than younger people who were still frantically involved in child raising, making a living, and being an active part of the community."

When my final paper was returned it contained a stinging comment that awakened me like a slap on the face, "Got them all figured out, don't you." In fact the comment was right. I had done just that. I had fallen into the willful trap of assuming that I knew what made these people tick, that I could give them what they needed, and that all they had to do was to get what I had to give. I had failed to take into consideration their willingness for God to lead them toward a contemplative spirituality and a contemplative prayer life if that's who they were.

My work with the Shalem Group Leaders Program was over. It left me with a lot to reflect on and in that sense it was a very challenging personal experience. I wrote my spiritual director.

March 1, 1992

Dear Michael,
I have finished the Group Leaders Program and I am still sorting out the meaning of some of the experiences there. They are not likely to be resolved in the near future, nor do I feel a sense of urgency to do so. For right now, suffice it to say that they seem to be issues that point me even more directly toward contemplative prayer that focuses on God in the present. Gerald May's treatment of discernment, as that which happens with God in the space between an event and one's response to it, rang true and seems to integrate well with a prayer life that focuses on the present rather than what was or what the future might bring. I sense even more deeply that our relationship in spiritual direction depends on the presence of the Spirit, and discernment in our active life and our prayer life where the Spirit works within us. When I return to Ohio I look forward to sitting down with you in the spirit of Gerald May's conception of discernment. In the meantime we have moved, and I include my new address and phone number here in Florida.

In response to this letter, I received a letter from Michael in which he told me of health problems that he was having and his need to cut back on his workload. I responded to his letter by expressing some disappointment, and at the same time affirming my acceptance of his need to take this action.

March 20, 1992

Dear Michael,
When I received your letter I read it with some mix of feelings. I found sorrow in learning that your health requires that you cut back on aspects of your

work, and that I was one part that was to be cut. I had fresh hope that we might form a sound basis for communication in our spiritual direction relationship. But, I found joy in your wisdom to recognize the symptoms and do something about them in a positive way. Your priorities are straight. You can best serve God by attending to yourself and your family and your parish.

As you suggest, in your letter, it does make sense to have one more session together when I get back to Ohio.

I was again without a spiritual director. At this time we were spending more and more time in Florida, and I was unable to find a person locally to serve as a spiritual director. The closest places that I could identify where a shaman type of person was available would have been Mobile or Montgomery, Alabama, and both would have involved a full day of travel going to and returning from a meeting with a director. I decided to go it alone for the present. In time, I used the theological reflection sessions of the Education for Ministry course (E.F.M.) as a stand in for group spiritual direction. At least I hoped it would serve that purpose.

My journal shows that I again stopped using journaling as a prayer form in March of 1992 and I resumed journaling in June of 1994. During this two-year period Olga and I started E.F.M., and Olga had a heart valve replaced. These were two very significant events in my life, but I never took them to God in the form of Journaling. And then in June 1994 I bought a notebook and started again.

The first entry suggests a drifting from the contemplative life. This period of drifting was marked by a kindling of the awareness that I still needed to resolve the active-passive conflict within me, as well as the "Who is the Christ?" issue. Both seem to have been re-activated by my participation in E.F.M.

June 8, 1994
The beginning of a fresh resolve to again discover Jesus and the Christ in a deeper way after weeks of "sharpening pencils." This is a direct result of E.F.M. and also an awareness of a deep sense that I still have not resolved the issue of the active and passive life. In order to do that, I need to get back to a full and disciplined life of prayer. For me without contemplative prayer there can be no surrender of self to the passive life and the full influence of transformation under God. Perhaps a good place to start will be to start meditation on the historical, living and cosmic Christ.

On one hand was the magnetic pull of seeing God through the contemplative life, and on the other was the pull of the active spiritual life. This was illustrated by my getting a small group of ecologically concerned people at St. Thomas to sponsor a two-mile strip of Front Beach Road under the Adopt A

Highway Program. We met on Saturday mornings and picked up trash that people had discarded on the side of the highway, trash that we felt defaced God's creation. It was a never-ending job. Even as we picked up the trash that stained God's work it was defiled by the trash of the next wave of excited vacationers.

June 9, 1994
As we picked up the last of the trash along our two-mile strip, tourists were already defacing it with a coke carton, a McDonald's cup, and beer cans. Cleansing God's creation is a never-ending job.

June 10, 1994
I read yesterday's journal entry and was again reminded of the intertwining of the cosmic and the living Christ in our lives. Here was an opportunity to realize that perfection exists nowhere except in God. The two-mile stretch of highway is like our lives. Resolve as I may to walk a straight line, before the day has ended I have blown it again; I have trashed a moment of purity, one more drop of pollution to be absorbed and purified by the cosmic Christ.

June 18, 1994
The Word existed before time and became love in the world. Cosmic love becomes fulfilled in the universe by overcoming hatred and entropy and thus pointing to the realization that the universe is slowly moving toward becoming God's love through the process of evolution.
Certainly I have experienced the historic Christ in scripture, in *Lectio divina* centered in the acts and words of a man called Jesus, and in person after person in the history of the church. I have experienced the living Christ in working with people in the Adopt a Highway Program and in some programs of the church such as, believe it or not, vacation Bible school. I have experienced the living Christ in people around me growing and evolving into love in the world. Yes, we have an eternity to go, but oh the bliss when I realize and accept that giving and receiving love are a part of the same graced act.

June 26, 1994
Wait and watch; be faithful, as God is faithful, and remember that beneath the evil, the dysfunctionality and willfulness of the world is the Word, waiting for those who see through the smoke and flames to the historic, living or cosmic Christ who is love. But we will not evolve into Christ until we give ourselves to God willingly and completely, then Christ becomes us, not the other way around.

A significant influence on my prayer life at this time was a book of meditations by Blanche Gallagher that was composed of excerpts from the writings of Teilhard de Chardin. I used this wonderful little book of over one hundred meditations in the tradition of *lectio divina*. It was a powerful stimulus to meditation and contemplation. For almost three years I read the writings of Teilhard and reflected on the application of his theology to my life. This intense experience with Teilhard had a substantial effect on my developing spirituality.

June 27, 1994

As I was meditating on a passage from *The Heart of Matter*, I was called back in time to three epiphanies of God that remain with me: (1) a light around a bend in a trail I was walking one snowy day in a woods; (2) another trail through a woods that led to a clearing where I sat on a fallen tree, and became aware of God's presence behind me; (3) the realization of our shared compassion for the world one afternoon as I realized how much sadness both God and I felt for it. Today, I saw God as an energy field in the universe that draws together and energizes those who seek him in themselves and in others. I have a sense that this image will become a way of giving direction to my prayer life as I search for the historic, living and cosmic Christ.

In reflecting on Blanch Gallagher's meditation from Teilhard's *The Heart of Matter*,[2] I was caught up in thoughts about my existence in the universe, and the physical and social forces that have pressed on me and shaped me from my beginning. These are the forces that have made me so dependent and predictable, and these are the forces that, at the same time, have helped me to break free and become my own person. These same forces have simultaneously operated on millions of other people, and yet how different they are for me.

June 29, 1994

The summer 1994 issue of the *Abbey Letter* arrived from St. Gregory's Abby today. I had a feeling of disappointment as I read about the loss of another member of the community, and the current climate of disinterest in the monastic life. Yet at the same time they continue their building program started under Fr. Abbot Benedict. Thus they will have a facility for those who, in time, come to the realization that the monastic life is a viable alternative to the active secular life and needs no defense for its existence.

In the long run, however, I know that the contemplative should be well suited to a period of waiting. I am not in despair. I have hope. I am waiting.

June 30, 1994

The cosmic Christ lies beyond my capacity to understand. Yet, I believe that the cosmic Christ has, and always will, live as the Word that was before the beginning, and will be at final fulfillment. I look forward to that time of fulfillment when barbaric man and self centered man will have evolved into loving man. I seek the historic Christ of the Gospels and still believe that Christ is love in the world and in the universe.

July 8, 1994

"Human prudence" and "Divine providence," these two notions are very different, yet often confused. I do believe that I should have more respect for human prudence than I give it. Not as much respect as for the Divine providence that created life, but more respect than I give it. Each moment of God's fulfillment along the way must be considered as mystery. Each step along the way including the life of Jesus, the historical Christ, has been a part of a never-ending process for those who could see it.

July 9, 1994

The last few weeks and again in meditation today, I sensed that often in the past I have not heard Christ call to me out of the torrent of the flash flood that I was caught in. How different things might have been if I had gotten out of the torrent and rested on the bank while I got my bearings. This week the Christ that I met was a deeply committed, faithful, and playful Christ who also enjoyed life as he called to me.

July 10, 1994

The subtle subversion of God by the Prince of Evil is found in three misguided assumptions. These assumptions are that God can be found: (1) by descending into the past and resting there; (2) ascending to a transcendent space beyond the earth and resting there; or (3) being caught up by the belief that one will only experience God in the future. All three avoid the immediacy of God's presence.

What I often missed in the past was that the incarnation was not a once occurring isolated event in cosmic history. It is a continually occurring, evolving event in an ever expanding and organizing cosmos. And we are here to participate in that evolving event, but not give direction to it.

July 30, 1994

Thursday, my prayer time was interrupted constantly by things to be done in relation to the move of Pam, John and Kate to their new home. By afternoon Olga began to feel the stress associated with the move and cried out, "Let's get Buster and get out of here for a while."

After supper I found time to meditate on a passage by Teilhard: " I am afraid, too, like all my fellow humans, of the future too heavy with mystery and too wholly new, toward which time is driving me."[3]

August 1, 1994

Not having enough faith, not having faith through to the end, these are ways in which we inhibit the evolution of God's creation, but what has this to do with Christ? Today, I worked with Pam as we installed a simple landscape around the patio of their townhouse. So much union, so much love that the pain was hardly noticed; joy was dominant. This was truly prayer. This was Christ in the world.

August 2, 1994

A day of being for others: making breakfast, taking Kate to the dentist, then taking her and Olga shopping and finally playing a new card game with them.

A day of being for Kate, and thus helping Pam and John as they move and get settled. I fell asleep doing a mantra. No meditation on Teilhard today, just the feeling of love within the family. Has today been living Christ? Has this day been prayer?

August 3, 1994

The focus of meditation today was on transformation. I was startled at how openly and directly Teilhard put it: " What I want, my God, is that by a reversal of focus which you alone can bring about, my terror in the face of nameless changes destined to renew my being may be turned into an overflowing joy at being transformed into you."[4]

August 4, 1994

I must never believe that meditation is the only way of praying. Nor can I dare to assume that doing things that I think need to be done is the way to interior peace. It will be well if I never lose sight of the reality that I am always on a search. I am always being transformed when I say "yes," and that contemplative prayer has a role to play in saying "yes."

August 5, 1994

Today I did not feel the burden of either my sins or the sins of the world. Yet, if I pray for transformation I must be ready each day to bear the sins of the world.

August 20, 1994

Love is a splendorous gem of many facets. When it is seen as Christ fulfilled, it is the most powerful of all energy. The most brilliant gem is the one with the most facets of reflected light. A one-dimensional love, like self-love, is dull at best.

August 31, 1994

Back to Florida and the first day has passed. Meditation on Teilhard points the direction to the future: " Love alone can unite living beings so as to complete and fulfill them, for it alone joins them by what is deepest in themselves. All we need is to imagine our ability to love developing until it embraces the totality of the people of the Earth"[5]

The future will not be built through man's willfulness, it will be created by the process of transformation and evolution. Will I be there? Who will be there other than God? If only God is there we will have come full circle, and when we come full circle, will there be another trip around? The second year of E.F.M. starts tomorrow. Christ will be there. Will I recognize him?

September 3, 1994

The incarnation was not just something that happened, it is something that is happening in all of our lives so long as we allow the forces of creation and birth to move within us and to do so in ways that support and nurture God's love. The incarnation of Jesus was an expression of God's love in the world. The incarnation of each of us is also an expression of God's love in the world. It is a continual process brought about through transformation, evolution and birth. Teilhard said:

> The more I reflect upon the profound laws of evolution the more I am convinced that the universal Christ would be unable to appear at the end of time at the world's summit unless he had previously inserted himself into the course of the world's movement by way of birth in the form of an element.[6]

There can be no Christ (other than an abstract, platonic ideal) without a continuing incarnation. Jesus was a reflection of the continuing process of God's love revealed. So are we when we are willing and say yes. I think that is what Teilhard meant when he said, "By virtue of the creation and still more of the incarnation, nothing here below is profane for those who know how to see."[7] The human species must think in order to adapt to the world around it. It must also love.

If I had been going through a period of spiritual apathy the previous year, my experience at Shalem, and my interest in the implications of a continuing incarnation got me back on track. I began thinking about a number of aspects of the secular contemplative life that I had not previously considered, and I became less sure that the life of a secular contemplative was really for me. My year and a half with Shalem certainly taught me that I had a lot to learn about myself as a spiritual person, and that there was a lot of transformation still ahead of me. Also ahead of me lay the continuing process of the deconstruction of my old belief system and the reconstruction of one to take its place. The ideas of Teilhard de Chardin were working on me and were slowly contributing to the reconstruction of my beliefs.

I was particularly drawn to de Chardin because his thoughts contained the elements of a theology that tied together the past, present and future with the themes of the continuing incarnation, and the continuing evolution of man as he became God's love in the world. The fact that de Chardin was a process theologian and an internationally accepted paleontologist led me to consider his ideas to be as good a basis for a theology as any that I had previously encountered. I was back on the trail and ready to be challenged. I was ready for another year of E.F.M.

## NOTES

1. Thomas Kelly, *A Testament of Devotion* (San Francisco: Harper and Brothers, 1969), 34.

2. Tielhard de Chardin, "The Heart of Matter," in Blanche Gallagher, *Meditations With Tielhard de Chardin* (Santa Fe, NM: Bear and Company, 1988), 36.

3. de Chardin, "Mass on the World," in Gallagher, 71.

4. de Chardin, "Mass on the World," in Gallagher, 74.

5. de Chardin, "The Grand Option," in Gallagher, 100.

6. Christopher Mooney, "Tielhard de Chardin and the Mystery of Christ," in Blanche Gallagher, *Meditations With Teilhard de Chardin* (Santa Fe, NM: Bear and Company, 1988), 104.

7. de Chardin, "The Divine Milieu," in Gallagher, 109.

*Chapter Six*

# Beliefs in Transition

I was eight years into my journey and I still had not resolved my uncertainties about the true identity of Jesus or the Christ, but there was evidence of progress. That progress was in part attributable to studying the theological writings of Teilhard de Chardin. The more I read by him, the more God, Jesus and Christ came into focus, and as time passed, my beliefs changed dramatically. Experience told me that it was going to be necessary to have a spirituality that I could own, and that I could use to guide my day-to-day life. Intuition told me that this spirituality would have to be grounded in a theology that fit my contemplative leanings, and my experience with God, both in prayer and in my active life. Teilhard de Chardin helped me do that.

In the fall of 1993 something else happened that eventually became very helpful in resolving my uncertainties about who Jesus and the Christ really were. Olga and I enrolled in the Education for Ministry Program (E.F.M.) offered by the School of Theology at the University of the South. One of the strongest parts of this program, called theological reflection, uses a process in which principles of theology are applied to daily life experiences. In this process members of our E.F.M. class re-experienced, through recollection, prior events in their lives, including what they thought and felt at the time of these events. These thoughts and feelings were then generalized for members of the class by creating a metaphor for the experience. Then, the class would reflect on the metaphor and on the original experience from four perspectives: the influences of culture, values and attitudes, tradition, and what we had learned in our E.F.M. lessons. This emphasis on developing a working theology that could be applied to day-to-day experience eventually helped me develop a living spirituality. But that took time. I still had ahead of me the process of finding closure on the Jesus issue.

## Beliefs in Transition

October 1, 1994

I have had to give up reading *Meditations with Teilhard de Chardin,* and for that matter almost all reading, for the time being. Since my recent TIA, my vision has been affected significantly. Apparently it damaged a muscle in my left eye, and I have been unable to read since Saturday. In addition I am experiencing a reduced ability to sustain concentration even in meditation. To my surprise the rosary has carried me through so far. The repetition of the prayers and the mnemonic assistance provided by the beads has been very helpful. Not only has it been an aid to prayer, it has kept before me a resolve to sort out my confusion about the historic, living and cosmic Christ. Jesus has become much more believable than my previous conception of him. In addition, saying the rosary has again brought me face to face with the differences between willfulness in my relationship with God on one hand, and a willingness to say "yes" and let my life follow the "yes."

October 6, 1994

What does it mean to say that faith is a precondition for saying "yes?" Desperation might also be a precondition. But, if it is faith, then first of all this means the existence of a God who I would answer. If I did not have faith in God then I would not respond with "yes." I would not even run and hide. Fortunately, faith is free and as available as the air we breathe. But, as free as faith is, I do not always recognize its abundance. Faith is not conditional, but there are consequences for taking a step in faith, or not taking that step.

October 11, 1994

An early sign of faith may be seen in the first steps toward self-emptying. From that moment on, living becomes a process of going with or swimming against the tide of life. We float like a cork in our self-emptying, or we are drawn down by the weight of the consequences of our separation from God.

October 21, 1994

The E.F.M. project that I started last spring has taken me a long way toward seeing the historic, living and cosmic Christ in my life, and continues to be a part of the unfolding process that I experience as I integrate new cognitive beliefs with a life of experiential faith. But I am far from closure, and Jesus remains a big issue.

By the end of October, I had gotten corrective lenses for my double vision. I started reading again, and I was able to complete Blanche Gallagher's book, *Meditations with Teilhard de Chardin.* Christ began to take on a whole new meaning, a more personal meaning. In an attempt to get an equally useful perspective on Jesus, I turned again to de Mello's meditations in *Sadhana: A Way to God.* De Mello and my E.F.M. project were helping me with this, but I had not yet grasped the breadth and the depth of the thoughts that would, in time, break forth so clearly.

In order to comprehend something of what I was experiencing at the time, it may be useful to understand what I meant when, in my October 1st journal entry, I wrote that my practice of prayer at that time (the rosary) ". . . [had] kept before me a resolve to sort out my confusion about the historic, living and cosmic Christ. Jesus [had] become much more believable than my previous conception of him." At that time I was working with incomplete concepts that would eventually become an integrated whole and would enable the cosmic, living and historic Christ and Jesus to come into focus, however, that moment had not yet come.

In time I would come to understand the *cosmic Christ* to be the energy of God's love in the universe that predates and continues to drive creation in the world. I would also think of the cosmic Christ as being as expansive as the infinitely expanding universe and as timeless as infinity as it moved toward a future of perfect love. The *living Christ* would come to mean the presence of God's love in people, and the expression of that love by people in the world. The *historic Christ* would become the manifestation of God's love at particular moments in history, especially as it had been expressed through the lives of people. Thus Christ would become synonymous with God's love. The word that is used for a manifestation of God in the world is *theophany*. For me, Jesus would become a theophany of God's love. When that happened I would know that I had come a long way on my spiritual journey, and a new belief system and theology would begin to fall rapidly into place.

The next step would be to turn these insights into a living spirituality that could guide me in the days ahead as my spiritual self continued to be transformed by God's love.

October 31, 1994

Teilhard has been a good teacher, and I know that de Mello will be a good teacher once again. Today the meditation on "The Riches of Interior Silence" was filled with distracting thoughts. This was discouraging after all the practice in the past to attain interior silence.

November 2, 1994

As I finished de Mello's third meditation, "Body Sensations. Thought Control," a familiar awareness surfaced: I need to see these exercises in the context of building a belief system and having a faith experience. Until I do this, the exercise runs the risk of just being an exercise in self-control.

November 17, 1994

The de Mello fantasy exercises seem to be holding my attention better than the awareness exercises. But, I must not forget that I am doing these exercises as a part of a process of meeting the historic Christ. How do these fantasies reveal that Christ?

November 18, 1994

How do these fantasy exercises reveal Jesus as the historic Christ? Today, Exercise 17, "Return to Galilee" would have been a perfect place to find Jesus as the historic Christ, but it didn't happen. It was just God's love that was present. Where was Jesus?

"The Return to Galilee" meditation is structured so that I was asked to recollect a moment in the past in which I experienced spiritual joy and consolation. Then I was asked to relive such a moment in my imagination. When I returned to such a time and place, and allowed my imagination free rein, it was God's love that I felt, not Jesus'. My fantasy and recollection took me back to a chapel in the atrium in The Ohio State University Hospital several years earlier where Pam and I sat together in a Eucharist service celebrated by a hospital chaplain. Olga had just been transferred from the operating room to a cardiac intensive care unit following a surgical procedure to implant an artificial heart valve. At that moment I was with Pam and a number of other people in a Chapel in the hospital. I felt bathed in love. Jesus was not there. I think the reason for this is that I seldom had a personal relationship with him, and thus it is hard for me to find such a recollection to return to. For me, Jesus had almost always been a character in a book or a person in a dream or a fantasy exercise. He was a materialized spirit on the road to Emmaus and in the upper room with Thomas. At the wedding in Cana or walking on water, he was the Jesus of Bible Stories, not a person with whom I had a personal loving relationship. The de Mello meditations were serving an unexpected purpose. They were helping me to meet Jesus as the historic Christ. They were helping me to sort out the historic Jesus from the historic, living and cosmic Christ, and from a mystical Jesus who pointed to the ineffable God of love.

December 10, 1994

What is the one distinguishing characteristic of human beings that separates us from all other living beings? Some say our brain, some say contemplation of our own death, some say language, some say the prehensile thumb. It seems to me that only humans are concerned about being separated from God. Are we really built that way or have we invented the story of sin to explain our unhappiness and pain, the dark side of our life? What would the human being do without sin? What would the human being do without willfulness? Perhaps we have invented sin as an explanation for our willfulness.

December 11, 1994

The de Mello Exercise 37 in *Sadhana*, "See Him Looking at You" is a fantasy exercise designed to see Jesus looking at me lovingly and humbly. Could it be that by looking lovingly and humbly that I would see the world as Jesus would have seen the world? If I were to practice the presence of God, would I see the world as God sees the world?

December 13, 1994

Exercise 39 "Name as Presence," another fantasized meeting with Jesus. I want to call him Master but seem to be asked "What's wrong with Jesus?" Suppose I use the names Master and Jesus interchangeably, is this a compromise with my will?

December 16, 1994

Again, Jesus in imagination, de Mello Exercise 43, "Gospel Sentences." At once I wanted to say Master, but Master gave way to Jesus without much of a fight. I like Master. It rings of "times when." But this is me coming out. This is my raw spot, my stumbling block.

December 21, 1994

Who is Jesus? And from deep within me comes what seems like an answer, "You may never know." I accept this as inevitable, but I must continue to search. Seven years ago I told Susan about what I thought was a vision of a snow-covered road in the woods. Around the bend in the road was a bright light, and I wanted to know what it was but I didn't look. I don't know even today. Do I have to know? Like Thomas in the upper room, I want to know. I want to be able to say, "My Lord and My God." Who are you Jesus?

December 22, 1994

I have finished the de Mello exercises again in search of Jesus, Christ and God. Time for a new approach. In meditation today I still wanted an answer to the question I asked yesterday, but a quiet voice within asked if I could wait, and without disappointment I said that I could.

January 5, 1995

E.F.M. was a real community of seekers today, what a gift to be part of such a community. We are all so different and yet so similar in our thirst for God. Tonight an hour with God in prayer – rosary, Jesus prayer, and then quiet.

January 11, 1995

I am unable to be aware of God's presence all the time so I set aside an hour each day to be with God, and I call it prayer. I usually begin prayer by asking for the grace of transformation. Today, I became aware that if, during the process of transformation, I were able to see the world as God sees it, then at that moment I would be practicing the presence of God.

January 18, 1995

Yesterday, I started using *Intimacy With Jesus*, a set of thirty meditations. Again, I return to the search for a personal Jesus. If Fr. H. had only written his meditations as intimacy with God, I would be fine, but no, he had to write the meditations as intimacy with Jesus. The words stick in my throat, but isn't that why I started this particular leg of my journey last June – to find out who Jesus is, who the Christ is? Is Jesus really God?

January 21, 1995

This evening's meditation, including the rosary, seemed like I was just going through the motions (objective prayer just to be faithful). Again I found myself to be more comfortable when I was thinking "Holy Mary Mother of Jesus" rather than "Holy Mary Mother of God." I will be faithful and see where the meditations take me. At this point I think that I am still missing something. Perhaps I am missing it because I am fighting it, fighting you God. Perhaps I am letting my faith be overruled by my tendency toward being a realest.

January 25, 1995

The issue is not prayer vs. works but the balance of prayer and works. It all starts with faith. For me I must start with faith expressed in prayer, time spent individually with God. When works flow from prayer, works become an extension of prayer and when done with an awareness of God's presence, my works become prayer.

January 30, 1995

Busy, Busy, Busy! Just finishing meditation and it is almost time for bed. Rosary and intercessions interrupted twice today. This is a hard place and these are hard times to find space for being alone with you Lord without violating Olga's agenda. Her agenda drives the activity, with her things, kind things, nice things. These are Olga's things and I have only been enrolled, and I am not aware of God being present.

February 1, 1995

Perhaps E. F.M. has come to my rescue – rescued me from Fr. H. and his *Intimacy With Jesus* meditations. We have moved from a study of Hebrew Scriptures to that part of E.F.M. that deals with New Testament scripture and the Gospels. So now I will be working with the story of Jesus of Nazareth. This frees up prayer time for free meditation. "Free meditation," what a wonderful chance for a play on words.

Went to vestry meeting today and only once thought about God. There were six other people there and I noticed them. I presume that God was there; I think I recognized him once in the midst of the activity, but only once and that was just a glimpse. St. Thomas may be a holy place, but not during vestry meetings.

Earlier today the bishop called. He said that he wanted to appoint me to the Diocesan Commission on Spirituality. We talked about what I would be doing. I never thought about God's presence once during the conversation. So much for "God is everywhere." He must have been there, but he might as well be nowhere if I don't notice him.

February 2, 1995

I can't imagine a more ridiculous thing to do than to count fifty-nine beads while saying a mantra based on significant moments in the life of Jesus drawn from Luke's version of the "Jesus as God myth." There Lord, I said it! I can't go on with a prayer discipline that has lost its objective and subjective relevance and in many ways has ceased to be alive. I can't go on doing this when I am not aware of you when I am doing it.

Almost none of my beliefs remain untouched, but I still have faith in you, God. I can't lose that or I really will be lost. I must start again in a new way. The present way is just not doing it. Don't let me become who I was eight years ago, I don't think I could climb out of that hole again.

February 3, 1995

Jesus, not God but a theophany of God. No virgin birth, no physical resurrection, just mystery. No Jesus in a box to theologize, dogmatic, analyze and then know. Just the unknowable, just mystery. And now where to from here? Where to go when God never had a son, only a theophany others made into a God so fanciful that they had to be believed.

As I reflect back on my journal entries at this time it seems to me that I am still experiencing the dark night of the soul. Certainly, I was still going through a radical transformation of my believe-system. When a person who was raised as a Trinitarian Christian says he no longer believes that Jesus is God, that's an important moment in his spiritual life. Today I believe that I am more staunchly Trinitarian than I ever was during the early days of my quest, but my conception of the Trinity has been tried in the crucible of the dark night, and it has changed, and what has come from this is, for me, much more believable.

February 12, 1995

Working on the "Jesus Metaphor" exercise for E.F.M. This has taken me back to my confrontation with Jesus that came out so violently almost two weeks ago. I am much more ready for this exercise now that I have gotten some of my problems with Jesus out in the open. I have questioned my understanding of Jesus in the past, and I never thought that I would come back to that again, but perhaps it is inevitable as I go deeper and deeper into negation. If all of my beliefs must die before I get to the source, then Jesus might be a good place to get on with it.

February 15, 1995

I need to remember that last June, I set out to find the Christ – the cosmic, historic, living Christ. I did not set out to challenge the divinity of Jesus. But that happened, and what have I lost – a belief that most of the people of the world don't hold anyway. And what have I gained but a real, believable, substantive theophany of God's love. I believe that God's love will become the dominant characteristic of humanity at the fulfillment of creation, and I believe that I must be willing to participate in that process to the fullest degree that I am capable. I must be willing to say, "Yes, may it be as you have said." "Yes, may your will be done." I believe that this is the first step. Beyond the first step, I believe lies the continued death of my false self, and the fulfillment of my true self. If that ever reached fulfillment, would I also become a theophany of God's love in the world? Only with ultimate faith!

February 22, 1995
Negation is in process: Gnostic leanings, the passive life, the way of introversion, the life of thought and concept, a "yes man." Born to live that I may say "yes" to you so that you may use me to express more fully who you are, you who are love beyond human comprehension. Willing each day for you to teach me more of what all this means, until one day I will have learned what you think I need to know this trip around.

February 23, 1995
I gave up asking for transformation and you said you had heard that I had given up asking, but that it would be given anyhow in your time. I don't know what that will mean but I understand it to be a gift. I am sure that there will be days when I will say, "Some gift!" Look ahead, it is all before you in the present.

February 25, 1995
Time spent yesterday in meditation was constantly interrupted: the telephone, the front door, etc. The issue remains before me, since when do I get off letting God be the one who gets short changed so that I can respond lovingly to aggressive people who are most often peddling their own wares. Is it not proper for God to have some uninterrupted time in quiet with people who he loves?

February 27, 1995
From the subconscious? Impressions like ghosts, like cobwebs flying on the wind. Not distressing but like dreams, gone now and yet I was awake; I was aware; I was with God.

March 1, 1995
Ash Wednesday service 10 A.M. Vestry meeting 2 P.M. Before the meeting there were prayers that our work be acceptable to God. Then I was startled to realize that it was the end of the meeting and up until then I had not thought about God being present even once.

March 2, 1995
Found myself paying attention to God's presence during E.F.M. today. The awareness was intermittent, but he was there. I also found myself in a situation where I felt a need to explain the difference between mystical contemplation and quietism. It was really irrelevant to the agenda, or was it? The agenda was the

discussion of a quote that Verda brought in, "All things start in mysticism and end in politics." I have the uncomfortable feeling that something is going on and I don't know what it is. I remember once hearing someone jokingly say that a quietest is what one contemplative calls another when they disagree with the other one about prayer.

March 6, 1995

Intercessions, quiet, Carmelite monks chanting from deep inside a tape recorder. Solitude but not silence. Rest with God. Is it transformation going on?

March 7, 1995

Buster and I have faith in puppy love. They say that humanity is created in God's image and only man has a soul, a self, a spirit. Yes, a human has a spirit but so also do Buster and violets and amethysts, how can they say then that only humans have a spirit?

March 11, 1995

Contemplation of the material world: sights, sounds, tactile experiences, tastes, smells all become more in focus. The world becomes not just contemplated entities, but also relationships between entities. It becomes real, whole, not just a place for pawns. The view turns inward. The self undergoes contemplation. Aspects of the self are seen in a light never before seen. The past is visited one event, one day, one year at a time and undergoes a contemplative scrutiny. Values, beliefs, connections and relationships do not escape inspection. But for the self to truly see itself as it is, first its masks must be stripped away. Then comes realization. There is a reality that cannot be contemplated so long as the "I" of the false self and its ego protector stand in the way. All that separates me from that reality must go, and when it does there will be a clear view because there will be nothing to stand in the way of that reality. The I becomes one with God. This is negation. The casting off of values, beliefs, tainted knowledge, blurred vision, addictions, pleasures and acquisitions that block the clear view of God, block all that stands in the way of love.

March 15, 1995

It's been ten hours since Eucharist this morning and I am still seething. I need to get hold of my ego. After fifteen minutes of reviewing all of the reasons for my feelings of hostility and anger I want to get on with it. I don't' like the feeling. When I turn to meditation my mind is still wildly active. It is the mind of the ego self. So much for today. All this because this morning before Wednesday Eucharist I ran into a buzz saw. I should have known better than to take on the establishment, and in particular that part of the establishment known as the altar guild. Fr. C. should have known better than to ask me. I should have known better than to set the altar for Wednesday morning Eucharist, even though he asked me to do so in his absence.

March 20, 1995

After all this time E.F.M. is getting around to dealing with Jesus and the Christ. Right now the emphasis seems to be on Jesus. It was just a little over ten months ago that I started a personal treck to find Jesus, and the historic, living and cosmic Christ. Now in E.F.M. we are studying what the historical Jesus means and how an interest in historical scholarship got started.

March 30, 1995

A rich day at E.F.M., I realized again from a comment that was made, that we humans must be a theophany of God's spirit of love if we are to be Christ in the world. As impressed as Teilhard was by the apparent stability of matter, he also realized that matter was always changing, and that The Great Stabilizer (God) could only be found in God's spirit at the core of matter. Jesus had to be real human matter, but he also had to be a theophany of God's Spirit of love in order to endure as the Christ.

April 6, 1995

I apologized to Olga after E.F.M. today and we had a discussion about what happened. I had sacrificed her feelings in the pursuit of winning an argument about an idea. We talked about being loving, and once again as in the past, I said that being loving was being willing to be what God had created me to be, one who supports the growth of others, and that I had not done that, while she said that being loving was living love as a rule of life. The two are not necessarily incompatible, but I think that they are not always the same thing either.

Why do I engage people in idea scrimmages? I am not sure, but the part I find most bleak is that given the opportunity (and just a little encouragement) I am almost unable to restrain myself. I am not as aggressive as I could be, but the potential is there.

April 15, 1995

Yesterday was Good Friday. There is something about the ultimate act of self-sacrifice, the ultimate act of saying "yes," the ultimate act of being what one was created to be. It's not common, but it is very human.

April 16, 1995

Easter Day. I prayed for you, God. I can't imagine why anyone would want to be God. It must be a really tough life.

April 20, 1995

Being faithful, being present, being transformed. Today at E.F.M. I was feeling good about the realization that I don't need to assert my beliefs, my ideas, when to do so runs the risk of diminishing others. We were discussing the resurrection. For me it comes down to believing the impossible that Christ lives in the world. Without Christ in the world, humanity is going nowhere, because

Christ is God's love. I don't feel the need to argue the point with anyone. I just listened to them talk about what they believed.

April 22, 1995

I left today for the Easter retreat held at the Visitation Monastery in Mobile. I was to have left yesterday but weather was bad, heavy rain and thunderstorms in the area and Olga felt apprehensive. This may be a difficult time for her, but there's a part of her that says she wants me to go. I will only be away one night.

Visitation Monastery is old and charming from the outside, old and barren and depressing from the inside. The wing that the retreatants use was once used for novices. It must have been privy to a lot of tears. I feel no particular joy in being in the building. The Sacred Heart of Jesus is everywhere.

I was sitting on a bench on the lawn until the rain began. Now I sit on the ornate, wrought iron second floor balcony. Rain falls on the trees and an expansive lawn that looks like it was just cut and never needs cutting, on which stand huge live oaks, and southern magnolias. They stretch their branches as far as they are tall and the lower branches are twenty feet from the ground. Spanish moss is ever present. The lawn is as large as a football field and there are only fifteen or so trees on it. The point of focus is the obligatory statue of Mary with arms crossed over the heart. As I went back to the retreatants' wing, the building smelled old, stale and sour. I wondered what Olga was doing and how she and Buster were making out. I'll call them this evening after supper. For now it is time for prayers before the afternoon session.

This afternoon meditation continued with the theme of love. To love, one must experience love. We don't experience a lot of love in our world today. We experience the use of willfulness and power as a substitute for love. We experience the destruction of others, seldom the nurturing of their fulfillment.

The way to the spiritual life is to acknowledge who we really are—including all that we are afraid of, proud of, ashamed of. Offer all this to God and then set it aside. Be honest with God who accepts us, wants us, needs us as we are. And when we can relate to others as God relates to us then we relate to others by accepting their fear, their pride, their shame. This is the living Christ grounded in faith. This is love. O.K. it's true, I have had and still have a lot of trouble feeling and expressing love. Maybe I didn't have very effective role models when I was growing up. O.K. but I'm not through growing, and I can learn. To be transformed by God into one who loves as God loves is the work of contemplation. My part in that is to be willing to be transformed.

April 24, 2995

Back home from the Easter Retreat to daily meditation, the experience of God's faithfulness, and the experience of my faithfulness in my every day life. This is where the stuff of retreats gets worked out day after day.

May 7, 1995

Humans did not invent negation in the abstract. Humans discovered what God has always known, namely that his gift of will to human beings can be expressed as either willfulness or willingness. It was then that humanity discovered that the negation of the ego self, and the false self occurs with the negation of willfulness.

May 8, 1995

Willingness to let God transform. Willingness to give my willfulness to God. Spirituality, religion, the Church, God, these are not the same thing. When we allow their distinctions to blur, we take a terrible risk of being deluded. Yesterday, I saw the Church practicing its religion, and I wondered where God was. It's O.K. for the Church to practice its religion and to protect its religion from corruption. It's O.K. for the Church to do things that protect and perpetuate its conception of religion. It's O.K. because we give the church the responsibility for doing those things. But, what would the Church be like if its primary reason for being was to support people in their search for God as God reveals himself to them? I wonder if the Church would be all that busy? I would hope so. I think that there are a lot of people who want to discard a God that they cannot relate to. Why can't the Church spend at least as much time on those who want to find God in their own way, as it spends on delivering it's conception of God to those who want to learn about the Church's God?

May 20, 1995

There is no drive, nothing to strive for, yet I do not experience the anger of depression. Am I experiencing the natural consequence of negation? With luck I am near the end of the walk, but I am afraid that's only a mirage. I have a long way to go. If this is the dark night, I recommend it only if there is the promise of a bright morning ahead.

May 23, 1995

There is a great deal of difference between trusting God and having a system to explain God in the world and in my life. One is called faith. The other is called theology.

Negation got me to unknowing and to the discovery of a faithful and loving God. The process of rebuilding my belief system led me to a need to explain God for myself because God wasn't going to do it for me. In the process, Jesus died and the Christ of the logos rose from the depths of the cosmic darkness, and the living Christ came out of that darkness to explain something more than human failure or success. He came out to explain love.

In the spring of 1995 we came back to Ohio to liquidate the nursery and sell the land. I was truly surprised at how painless it was. One day it was there and a few weeks later it was gone: plants, tractors, greenhouses everything. It had served its purpose and now it was gone. Along the way it became obvious to me that the nursery was an albatross around my neck and that it was becoming a chronically losing enterprise. The economics of the times created a climate in which the small, independent production nursery in central Ohio was becoming increasingly less viable. John and I talked about this, but no decisions were made. And then, something happened that was totally unexpected. A close friend of John's during law school proposed an opportunity for John to practice law with him in Columbus, Georgia. The nursery was liquidated. Olga and I sold the property and moved to Florida.

For nine years my Journal had been filled with entries that revealed that the nursery was often not a very loving place to be. Over time I found myself caught up in a real love/hate relationship with all that it represented. I often commented on what I saw as being the spiritual implications of practical matters in the nursery such as production, personnel and financial issues. Then, one day it was gone; there was nothing left; I no longer owned the land let alone tens of thousands of plants and all of the structures and equipment to propagate, grow and market them. All that was left was a memory, an electro-chemical residue that appears in my dreams to this day. One day, a challenging and often painful reality just disappeared. It no longer existed, and much to my surprise there was only the most offhand reference to all of this in my journal. As with my exit from teaching there was no grieving. I just walked away. If I had experienced a more conscious grieving period things might have been different, but I didn't. Whatever went on occurred below consciousness. As the nursery went from an ever-present worry to nothing but a memory, I slowly realized the depth of commitment that I had made to it. I had become its slave as surely as one becomes a slave to any addiction.

June 6, 1995
Two days driving and then re-entry shock; we are home in Ohio. Home is where the kids are. Soon home will be Georgia. That's where the kids are going.

June 18, 1995
There was a time for buying and now it's time for selling, not a time for journaling. I have thought "another day and no entry in the journal." But what would I have said? I have nothing to say.

June 27, 1995
It seems as if faith burns brighter these days than at almost any other time in my life, and my new beliefs are becoming part of a personal spirituality. Most of what I believe is pragmatic – useful so that I can have a belief system if I need one. More and more I take an agnostic position toward beliefs, they become less and less central in my life.

Bep once said that the path of *via negitiva* ultimately led to agnosticism and a faith crisis. It didn't for me. My faith is even stronger; it's my old beliefs that I am leaving behind. I have fewer new beliefs, but they make more sense, and I hold them more closely.

August 2, 1995

The age of enlightenment did not teach us to leap the moat of the ineffable God. But, it did give us the potential to see man in the universe in perspective. It has given us the potential to experience, and appreciate what our cosmos has been like since the beginning of time. It has given us the opportunity to appreciate God as timeless, faithful, ever present. It has given us the opportunity to sense the interconnectedness of creation, its wholeness and oneness, and man's niche in that universe.

Whenever I experience the absence of wholeness and oneness I almost always experience it as a violation of human relationships or of creative human productivity. Humanity has a lot to learn about the big picture, and a myth that would help us understand humanity's niche in the cosmos rather than the centrality of humans on the earth would give our created institutions a lot more reality, and limited, but more realistic credibility.

August 31, 1995

For several months now I have had a dream so real that I have awakened not only in an anxious state, but I have had to forcefully tell myself that I had no need to be concerned—it was only a dream. In the dream I am a student who is taking three courses, English, math and science. I am always faced with an examination, final or midterm that I am not prepared for. I have been cutting classes, not studying and I am going to fail the exam for sure. There is no way that I can prepare for the exam; it's too late. Each time I have had this dream I have awakened in a state of anxiety about the test, and then I have had to convince myself that it was only a dream. I would say, "I am not a student, and there is no exam not today or any day."

Last night I had the dream again, and I got all the way to the point of knowing that I was going to fail the test. Then instead of awakening in anxiety I continued to dream. I continued to dream that I was dreaming. It was all a dream. There was no class, no test, nothing. It was all a false reality. And then a strange thing happened. All of the other people in the dream, other students in the class, denied that it was a dream. They insisted that they and the class and the test were real. I was the one who was dreaming. I was seeing reality in a dangerous and distorted way. They were suspicious of me; they distrusted me; they were angry because I was saying that their reality was only a dream. What should I do? Should I just ignore them and let them continue in their dream, or should I try to convince them that their reality was nothing more than a dream? That was when I awakened.

Wow! How closely this seems to fit my struggle with the St. Thomas adult Sunday school class. What was my reality is still theirs, but I no longer see God, or religion or the Church as I once did and presumably they still do. Should I tell them that they are dreaming, or should I keep my council and let them live in their own reality? The answer is clear. I must remember that my view is just that, my view, and to suggest that God can be understood as a subjective reality who is experienced differently by each person is my reality not their reality.

September 29, 1995
  Faith, this is a personal word. For all practical purposes I can believe what others believe. But, I cannot have the same faith experience as anyone else. As I have unloaded one article of belief after another over the past year or so, my faith has become even stronger. My faith in God's love and fidelity increases.

September 30, 1995
  I have faith in God. I do not have faith in my beliefs about God, or faith in the beliefs that others have about God, or faith in what the Church believes about God. If I have faith in God because of my relationship with God, that's one thing, but, if I have faith in what I and others believe about God that's something else. One is faith. The other is religion. As I begin to build a new system of beliefs about God to replace the beliefs that I have challenged and discarded I must be careful that they only represent my religious beliefs. I must be careful not to put my faith in those beliefs.

I have often thought, what would have happened in the process of negation if my faith had been shattered? Transformation had unsettled my beliefs, but fortunately about this time I became increasingly aware that beliefs and faith were not the same thing even though many people use the two words synonymously. It was then that I realized that if in fact they were not the same thing, my beliefs could change without necessarily affecting my faith. The more I thought about it the more I realized that beliefs and faiths were different in ways I had not considered before. First of all, the same belief can be held by many people. In fact, religion, nationalism and the practice of science depend on commonly held beliefs. My faith on the other hand is a private matter. My faith may be similar to another person's faith but the two are not the same. Secondly, my beliefs come from sources that are outside of me. My beliefs come from other people, from books, or TV. They come largely from my parents or from school, or church, or from my friends. In each case someone or something outside of me is the source of my beliefs. My faith on the other hand comes from within me as a result of a trusting relationship that I have with God, with people or with things. A third difference is that beliefs depend on a common language. Without a common language with which to communicate, institutional sources of beliefs such as schools, or churches, government or the economy could not exist as we know them today. But faith can exist without a common language because it is built on a personal and private relationship that does not need to be communicated to others. If a person tries to communicate their faith to another person it is often done by using metaphors or symbols that point to something beyond the finite world or beyond definitions or even commonly experienced evidence. When Julian of Norwhich said, "Sin is inevitable, but all shall be well, and all shall be well and all manner of things shall be well,"[1] she did not make a prediction about something specific that would happen in the future and could later be verified, she expressed a trusting, faith relationship with God that in the end all would work out all right. The fourth difference between beliefs and faith has to do with authority. I consider my beliefs to be true when they are supported by a reasonable source of authority, are commonly held to be true by a lot of people who I considered to be reasonable, or pass an empirical test of reality.

My faith, however, is not subject to a test of empirical evidence, commonly held agreement, the tried and true processes of logic or science or institutional authority. It depends on a personal test of trust that grows out of a relationship, often one that has existed for some time. I do not use scientific evidence, common agreement or even logical argument to support my faith. My faith grows out of my personal relationship with the Ultimate.

When I finally realized that my beliefs and faith were not the same thing it felt very freeing, and my concern that transformation would challenge my faith diminished. But I also realized that there are two kinds of faith: *limited faith* and *ultimate faith*. My faith in social institutions, well-known authorities, established leaders or the scientific process necessarily involves people, and no matter how spiritual these people are, how hard they work, how lofty their ideals or how smart they are, they are temporal, imperfect and corruptible. They are limited by their humanness. It is OK for me to have faith in people and social institutions so long as I remembered that my faith in people or their institutions will always be limited by my and their humanness. People and social institutions can be and frequently are wrong. In order to transcend the limitations of people, my faith needs to be something that is incorruptible and infinite. It needs to be in something that is ultimate. I soon realized that this position on faith was similar to a position taken by Paul Tillich[2] when he defined idolatrous faith as an ultimate concern that is put in material and temporal things including the self. When Tillich talked about idolatrous faith he was talking about limited faith. Beliefs and limited faith would be helpful to me at many points in my life, but they would always be fallible. Just realizing this was exciting in its potential.

I can always change my beliefs if I get new information. I can have limited faith in my pastor, the president or my best friend even though I know that they might be wrong. But it makes no sense to me that something that is ultimate can be considered wrong. It may make me feel uncomfortable or it might even threaten me, but it will not be wrong. My relationship with the Ultimate might change. I might even fall out of relationship with the Ultimate. I might even lose my faith, but this was not what was happening to me at the time. My beliefs were undergoing change and I was leaving a number of old beliefs behind because they no longer squared with reality as I knew it, but my ultimate concern for God was holding steady, even increasing. I had faith that all would be well.

October 21, 1995

I have no faith relationship with Jesus as God other than as a theophany of God's love, and I do not believe that the authority of the Church, historical research or logical argument support the belief that he is or was anything else. For me, the strongest support for the divinity of Jesus comes from belief in a myth. Jesus as the son of God seems to have grown naturally out of humanity's deep longing for an all knowing and all powerful messiah figure to identify with and relate to. Jesus fills this role well as a mythical person who is fully God and at the same time fully man. Even the Pharaohs of Egypt, the emperors of Rome and the kings of the Near East pale in comparison to the mythical Jesus as God's son and King of the Universe, or at least heir to God's kingdom.

October 22, 1995

If God is ineffable, all powerful, all knowing and infinite then why is it that we are surprised when people express different conceptions of God? It is reasonable to assume that the cultural institution that people entrust with their religion would want to put limits on the diversity of beliefs that people hold about God. In many respects the job of the Church would be a lot easier if everybody believed the same thing.

But, in spite of the pressure to shape man's religious beliefs, a diversity of beliefs, not to mention an infinite diversity of faith experiences, has persisted. There must be a lot of people who have rejected the doctrinal claims of the Church but who resonate to one of the most deeply instinctive needs of man dating back to the earliest times – the need for an ultimate hero figure to whom they can relate. Why can't the Church participate openly in this myth as one source on which to build beliefs? Would this not be a loving and humane thing to do?

November 16, 1995

I am fighting what I perceive as despair. I feel as if I am fighting for self-preservation. Could this be the dark night of the soul? I don't believe that God would create a dysfunctional self – an anxious self, a self that feels inadequate. Of course it could be a change in my chemistry, or it could be my false self fighting for survival. God wants me whole not broken. That much I can count on.

I believe that God would say, "I want you to fulfill the image that I have in mind for you. I want you whole. Have faith in our relationship. Be creative, be redeemed, love others and you will sense that you are walking with a faithful friend, you are even now being created, you are even now loved. Soak up the love that is around you, take part in your own redemption, participate actively in your creation, continue in faith with me. Don't allow yourself to be suckerpunched by your false self."

December 17, 1995

In Church today I realized that I can have an experiential, mythical and institutional knowledge of God at the same time. These are three ways of looking at the same thing. One is my personal story, the story of my experiential relationship with God. The second is the story of humanity's relationship with God – the collective hopes, fears, dreams and needs of humanity of which I am a part. The third is the institutional experience of God that is taught by the Church. Religion must somehow champion all three of these sources of knowledge about God if it is to be a truly human social institution. Direct personal experience of God and the mythical and institutional experiences of God are not the same thing, but they all can be valid when they touch the depth of the self.

Constructed knowledge of God is knowledge created by us to explain who God is. But constructed knowledge comes alive when it squares with personal knowledge and the collective knowledge of myth and the Church. What part of my constructed knowledge of God corresponds with my personal experience of God? What part of my constructed knowledge about God corresponds with the mythical knowledge of God that is held by humanity? What part is the teaching of the Church?

My theology must include my personal experience with God and the knowledge of God experienced by humanity over eternity. And as a useful theory of God, my theology, must be modifiable by both my personal experience and my understanding of humanity's experience. When these experiences change, my theology must change if it is to remain relevant in my world.

January 14, 1996

God is who I believe God to be. God is who I experience God to be in faith, and beyond these, God is who God is. These are three faces of God.

April 20, 1996

I note that my last entry was on January 14th. I am also aware that the last few months have been spiritually active. I seem to be building back up from my challenged beliefs to beliefs gained partially from myth. To this extent I am a part of humanity's relationship with God, and, smiling over all of this is the Ineffable One.

I am on retreat again, and I am back at the Visitation Monastery. Earlier today I read the journal entry from my retreat here last year. So much has happened since then. The nursery and our home in Ohio were sold and we now live full time to Florida. Pam and John were divorced, and Pam and Kate still live in Columbus, Georgia. Hurricane Opal happened. E.F.M. continues to have an impact on me as

I let go of much of my old belief system and start the rebuilding process. I am calmer, more positive in my outlook than I ever have been. Thank you God.

April 29, 1996

Back home after an evangelical silent retreat. During the singing of hymns during the service of Eucharist yesterday I sensed the magic of the pull of the evangelists toward the personal walk with Jesus. I didn't go on that walk with them, but I sensed the power of the presence of Jesus in others around me. I am fully comfortable with Jesus as the mythical Son of God, but I did not sense the joy of his presence in the way the evangelicals who were present did.

July 4, 1996

The God that I worship must be God, not be a super man. Theology should not be used to define an ineffable God, but rather to recognize and interpret signs of God's presence in the world. The purpose of religious ethics should not be to develop and interpret laws of human behavior, but to help us recognize and emulate God's love in the world, in our lives. Law is one thing; love is something else.

July 7, 1996

God is, for each of us, what we believe God to be. God is for each of us what we experience God to be in faith, but God is ineffable, beyond knowledge and comprehension. God is sticks cracking in the deep woods; God is the grass matted down in the meadow; God is the hair raised on the back of my neck when I sense that he is there, right behind me. God is the tone of a voice, the yip of a puppy, the calm half smile of a dying woman whose jaw is set firmly in hope, the eyes of a friend who just yesterday was an adversary or a stranger. All of these are signs of God. In contemplation we can attend to them.

How could Andersonville, the holocaust, or Hiroshima have happened in the world of a loving God? They seem to mock God. It is not satisfactory to say that they are a mystery. Better to be honest. Say that people – depraved people, D.N.A. run amuck – did those things. God would have preferred that they didn't happen, but they did. We took a step backwards, and God knows it. How many of us do?

September 12, 1996

If people could only understand that their God of yesterday and today must die before their God of tomorrow can live, then they would not fear evolution or even a revolution that causes their God of yesterday and today to be challenged. But each person must do that challenging individually or invite others to participate. We must not impose ourselves on others. When religion takes the stance of imposition or coercion or majority vote or judicial decision then it ceases to be religion and becomes politics. Politics is about power. Religion should be about hope and love.

## September 19, 1996

God's love was crucified by the law and power politics, but God's love was raised from the dead. God's love could not be contained by death. The potential for this love lives in all people. Without this love humanity would have little hope for anything but eventual self- destruction.

## November 6, 1996

Daily contemplative prayer continues. It has become that part of the day that I look forward to most of all.

## November 7, 1996

Pure awareness of God for no utilitarian purpose. This is what it is like to be in his presence. Is this a natural consequence of being human? Do the animals and trees have a pure awareness of God's presence?

## December 28, 1996

Back from spending Christmas with Pam and Kate. All sorts of reasons for it not to have been a calm and peaceful time, but it was.

## January 2, 1997

A calendar for the new year, a clever invention of human beings. Music playing on a C.D. player, very clever. Musical notation, the generation of electricity, musical instruments and a concert orchestra, the C.D. player, amplifiers, speakers and so much more are all very clever. The song that is playing, "Oh Little Town of Bethlehem", is a song about a child who is God. Another clever invention? An invention to explain that which we would want to explain but cannot? It goes on seemingly forever, our artistic, social, scientific, linguistic, mathematical, social inventions, very clever. But, we cannot explain God. If we ever touched an understanding of God it would be found in the awareness of how totally dependent we are on the God who created us.

## January 15, 1997

The cloud of unknowing is the cloud that separates us from knowing God. But we will always be separated from God if knowing is our desire. To pierce the cloud of unknowing is to put knowing aside and to experience God in relationship. My beliefs tell me about what I, and others, think we know about God. My faith points to my relationship with God.

## March 3, 1997

No more feelings of annoyance and indignation aroused when others talk about God in a way that says that I should know God as they do. For me to think about the ineffable as an objective reality is unthinkable. Of course there is a God, an ineffable God, not a knowable God in the sense of an objective reality, but a subjective reality.

April 26, 1997

Yesterday I started another retreat sponsored by the Commission on Spirituality. It seems as if Ruth's work was completed when she delivered Fr. C., our retreat leader. In other words, the job of retreat coordinator went begging for a while yesterday until it became clear that I was the only person on the Commission who will be at the retreat all three days, and who has been to an Easter retreat at the monastery in the past. So far all is well. People do what they are capable of when it is necessary.

This morning there was a leak in the ceiling in the entry hall right over the registration table. Water was dripping all over the table. The retreatant at the table went to find a bucket, tell the sisters about the leak and find out what to do. Soon a sister (enclosed, I would guess, for forty or more years) came out, looked around and said to the person at the registration table, "The first thing I would do is to move the table." A good idea! People do what they are capable of doing. A plastic ice chest in the hospitality room overhead cracked and water was running out all over the floor. I poured the remaining water and ice into another ice chest, got towels and mopped up the floor. Then replenished the food in the hospitality room, selected tapes to be played at meals, tried to get an old woman with a walker to the bookstore, checked with the night person about turning off lights in the women's area at night, checked on readings for worship services, got people to be lectors, moved people around who had been paired with snorers, got compline organized (it had been left off of the duty roster) arranged for an announcement to be made on Sunday morning at Eucharist about a free-will offering to defray costs for unexpected expenses, got a check to pay the retreat leader, got someone to take him to the airport, and on and on until everyone had left and gone home on Sunday afternoon.

All of this is ministry, but only indirectly does it have anything to do with God. It has to do with greasing the skids so others can presumably have a retreat with God.

July 17, 1997

Finished *The Cloud of Unknowing*. Something has been happening. It always seems to when I get serious about contemplation. Why don't I stay with it then in spite of all else. But no, it seems as if I turn to everything else. Then in time I return as if there were nothing else.

There were a number of times during the deconstruction and then reconstruction of my beliefs that I got off the trail, got turned around and lost my way for a while, but I always seemed to find my way back. And then one day I realized that I had done more than just wander off the trail. Previously I have described the experience as being more like losing my navigational system and my ship to shore radio. Unless someone knew I was out there I would be in big trouble. I said that I had faith that someone knew who I was and where I was, but just in case, I set out to fix my navigation system. Shalem and

E.F.M. helped me to do that. In time I was able to rebuild my belief system to the point where it could provide me some bearings and some security about direction. Then one day I saw land again. It was a different port than the one from which I had left, and it was not my intended destination. But the people there were real. If I stayed for a while it would give me a chance to work with them and also to re-supply, and charge my batteries. I never realized that I would stay so long, or that this place would be so different from the destination that I originally had in mind, but I walked ashore and entered an active ministry of service. Martha was there waiting and I noticed her immediately. She made me feel welcome, and it wasn't long before I was once again more involved and busier than I had ever planned to be. I stayed for almost five years, and during that time I tried to honor my contemplative commitments, but it didn't always work out that well. I became more of a secular active than a secular contemplative.

## NOTES

1. Julian of Norwich, *A Lesson of Love: The Revelations of Julian of Norwich*, ed. and trans. John-Julian (New York: Walter and Company, 1988), 61.
2. Paul Tillich, *Dynamics of Faith* (New York: Harper and Row, 1975), 1–34.

## Chapter Seven

# Community Ministry

There were days when I was able to live as a contemplative in the busyness that buzzed around me. These were some of the most satisfying days of my life. I felt whole, balanced and alive. And then there were days when I doubted that I could ever live that way for more than a few days at a time. I wondered if I was not just kidding myself.

At this stage in my journey I did not have a spiritual director to turn to, and role models were available to me only through books, some written by contemplatives, some by people who wrote about people who were contemplatives. I had no one to ask questions such as, "Is my experience typical?" or "What is my experience telling me?"

As I reflect back on the years when I was involved in community ministry, I can see now that in spite of my service commitments, I continued to undergo a slow process of transformation. My true self was growing, my faith remained strong and, my beliefs continued to undergo change. Yet, again and again I realized that in spite of all my talk about God as love, I still wasn't sure that I really understood what spiritual love meant in either the active or the contemplative sense. But I did sense that there was a lot of difference between knowing about spiritual love and practicing it. There is no such thing as spiritual perfection, but I was in process.

Now that the Jesus matter had been settled, ahead of me still lay at least two more issues. I needed to resolve the Mary/Martha issue, not just listen to people around me talk about it, and I needed to experience real solitude for extended periods of time, not just read about it. I needed to find out if the solitary life was really consistent with who I was. At this time, however, contemplative life interfered with my active life, and my active life interfered with my contemplative life. In both cases I experienced continual distraction caused by a constant dialogue between Mary and Martha, and I remained aware that without the experience of real solitude I would forever be one who worked at, or even played at, being a contemplative. In time I would realize that I had to make up my mind. I couldn't wear two hats comfortably at the same time. That wasn't who I was.

For now, though, I had an agenda to keep. I had spent several years in E.F.M. preparing for a ministry to others, and now it was time to use that preparation. Or, perhaps it would be better to say, begin the process of testing which of two vocations I was really better suited for: the vocation of a socially active person, or the vocation of a contemplative, living in solitude on the margin of society with a clear understanding of responsibility for my neighbors, particularly those in need. I never seriously considered becoming a hermit, and withdrawing from the world. I always believed that I had an obligation to my fellow humans that went beyond just being civil. I realized that my degree of social involvement would be influenced by how close I lived to the margin of society, and that this was a choice that I could make.

Slowly it began to dawn on me that there was a lot more to being an active or a contemplative person in the world than how I prayed and whether or not I actively served the needy. The real difference was grounded in how I looked at the world, how I saw God acting in the world, and how I reacted to what I saw. Of course it was easier to see this in retrospect than it was at the time. In fact it has always been that way from the beginning. Much of what I have described thus far might look like a plan unfolding, but it was not. At various points along the way I could have said yes or no, and I did, but that was about as much control as I exercised. Things just seemed to happen.

Thus, when the opportunity to serve the needy by working at the Beach Food Pantry came along, all I had to do was to say yes or no. Olga and I started by distributing food to needy residents and transients who showed up at the pantry in numbers. The Beach is a common stopover for homeless people who are on their way from Texas to South Florida and points in between. They come through the Beach twelve months a year. The regular Beach population has high summer employment, but it also has high unemployment in the fall and winter when the vacationers go home. Hunger is a year-round problem for both the transients and the residents.

In addition to food, many people also have need for shelter, electricity, medical attention, transportation, and counseling. For years Ken C., the minister at the Presbyterian church on the Beach, had helped individuals when they came to him for food, but he knew that the needs of a large number of people on the Beach were far greater than just food. He had tried to enlist help from pastors of other churches on the Beach in an effort that became known as Beach Care Services, but help remained mostly at the talk level. When a young priest at Grace Episcopal Church became president of the Beach Care Board, he was able to help the board think more expansively, and action was taken to raise funds to help the needy. Until then, Beach Care Services remained just an idea.

As a member of the Beach Food Pantry volunteer staff, I learned a lot about how and when to contact Family Services, the Salvation Army, the Rescue Mission, Public Health, United Way, and other services available in Bay County. I didn't know it at the time, but this would serve as a preparation for me when Beach Care Services would spring into action. In the meantime it remained an organizational nightmare on the table of the Board of Directors. There was anything but full agreement on whether or not there was a need, and there were a lot of people in the community who thought that making provisions for the needy would attract undesirable people to the Beach, and be bad for business. A previous effort by the board of Beach Care Services to do a needs assessment study to document a case for need had been talked to death and died quietly. But the new president of the B.C.S. Board resurrected the idea as a way to give focus to their work. When asked if I would take on the job of doing the survey I said yes. But, I said that I would not draw implications from demographics taken from census data as had been previously tried. I would contact individual members of the community and transients, and I would talk with homeless people. That was acceptable to the board, and a needs assessment survey that took six months to plan and conduct was under way.

The needs assessment study clearly documented that there were real needs on the Beach, and the nature of those needs pointed the direction that an organizational plan should take. That organizational plan included setting up an office in an unused Sunday school room in the Presbyterian Church, training volunteers to be intake counselors to assist clients, mounting a publicity effort, and developing an ongoing fund raising campaign. In March of 2001 the doors of Beach Care Services opened. Everything was done by volunteers. The first year B.C.S. had eleven thousand dollars to use to assist needy clients. Two years later it had a yearly budget of fifty thousand dollars, two paid part-time employees, and its own office paid for by donations from the community. It had developed recognition on the beach, and the respect of the social service community across the bay in Panama City. We were serving between seventy- five and one hundred clients a month. This rapid growth was made possible largely by volunteers from the community. It was a classic job for Martha's with all kinds of talents. I found myself directly involved for six to ten hours a day with B.C.S. activities, and twenty-four hours a day dreaming, thinking, worrying, planning, scheming. How many thousands hours of volunteer time were spent in this effort no one knows. We never counted.

My prayer life shifted dramatically from the life of a secular contemplative to the life of a secular active. Some meditative prayer continued, but the prayer of the active, the prayer of doing, became dominant.

In addition to B.C.S., I became involved in church politics. I agreed to serve a second term on the vestry of my church and in addition was appointed senior warden at a time when the vicar was due to retire soon, a new bishop had just been installed, and our church was fractured by the clash of two factions, one that wanted progress now, including a substantial building fund effort, and the other that wanted to wait and see what happened when our vicar retired.

When I agreed to test my vocation as a socially involved volunteer, I was unaware that I had so little prior experience to fall back on that was directly related to the task. I just jumped in and got started doing what needed to be done. I had ahead of me a very busy time.

October 28, 1997
One of the few truths of my life must certainly be that the harder I push my way toward God the further I get from touching him.

November 6, 1997
Can't pray. Haven't been able to pray recently. Where is God? The Commission conference on spiritual direction is tomorrow; I am looking forward to the conference and a chance to get away even if for just a few days.

November 8, 1997
Camp Beckwith: spiritual direction conference. God, you and I have not been talking for a while. It's not that I am angry with you or disappointed in you; I'm not. It's just that as a transcendent God we're not connecting, and as an immanent God perhaps we have become too familiar. But this is too beautiful a day to fuss about us, and our relationship. I just want you to know that I really appreciate the peace and the quiet here. You practice the ministry of silence with great skill. You really are good at it.

Over the next eight months my journal shows only one entry. I am not sure why. Perhaps my active life of service with the Beach Food Pantry served as prayer for me at that time. There is no record of a fight with God or with the Church. There is no evidence of another extended bout with depression. I looked forward to the annual Easter retreat to get me back on track.

April 26, 1998
I should be getting home about now from the annual Easter retreat at the Visitation Monastery in Mobile. Pam and I were going to go together, while Olga was going to stay with Kate. Instead Olga and I came home from Columbus, Ga.

on Friday. What the retreat might have brought I will never know. Faced with Pam and me going on retreat for a few days Olga had another anxiety attack. She has agreed to talk with Dr. P. next Friday. Whether or not she will level with him I don't know. I had pictured myself as using the retreat to get psyched up and pay more attention to prayer. We'll see how I feel about it tomorrow.

July 7, 1998

Tomorrow is today—almost three months later. It has been a good three months. Olga and I have never been so at peace with each other. We live in each other's presence and enjoy just doing that. Since April I have read *Why Christianity Must Change or Die* by John Spong. I wonder if I would have appreciated him even more if I had read him during my long years of frustration with the church, or did I need to come to terms with the church and God before I could really appreciate Spong? I think that Spong is closer to the truth than many of us would like to admit. But, I have no desire to be caught up in more church controversy. Actually I am more at peace when I realize that I am celebrating a myth.

July 24, 1998

During meditation today I read "The Body of Reality" in *Living Buddha, Living Christ*. This should be a comfort to all who wonder what would happen to the Eucharist if we ever really got serious about being ecumenical. The only thing that I can see that would change is that we would invite to the communion rail all baptized Christians, Buddhists and anyone else who believes in the sacrifice of the self on the altar of God's love.

July 27, 1998

I sense the expansive freedom of being one with God—perhaps this is what Merton sensed in his last years. He had become a living Buddha, a living Christ, an enlightened one and he knew it. I begin to sense what this might have meant to him.

July 28, 1998

To live aware of the moment of eating, working, reading, loving, singing, walking, and being thankful for the moment, thankful for the awareness of the moment, this is to live in the presence of God.

September 4, 1998

If I want to find you, I must look in at least three places. I must continue to look inward to the unconscious ground of my being. Here I will find you welling up from the deepness that is the spiritual self—the grounded self that I and all other members of the species share. And, I must look outward to see you in the others living in this world around me. And if I can look beyond, I will see this world evolving to become love as it has been since the beginning. There I will find you. But, I will be no more informed about who or what you are or are like. I will only be more firmly and deeply convinced of your presence.

October 29, 1998

God does not always speak to us individually and personally in an exclusive way. Often God acts in the world, and those who have eyes to see notice his presence. God speaks, and those who are listening hear him. God loves, and those whose hearts are disposed feel him. Wanting an exclusive relationship with God is a natural feeling. Many have the experience of wanting and waiting when all they need do is to be mindful of the world around them.

October 31, 1998

I waited for a long time for a personal invitation and then I realized one day that it was not going to happen. I had already been invited. I believe that there are many others who share with me a similar experience. We wait and we want a personal invitation and we fail to recognize a world that craves to be noticed, a world that wants only that we are willing to take a long, loving look at it, to see it as it is and accept it. How do I notice that God is there all the time? How do I sort out God from all the rest? Perhaps the first thing to do is to stop looking for what I want, and to remember what Tennyson said at Arthur's passing, "God fulfills himself in many ways lest one good custom may corrupt the world."

November 17, 1998

In Walker Percy's novel *The Second Coming* Allie expresses a certain apprehension about the 4:00 P.M. hour. She didn't want to be alone from 4:00 to 6:00. It just occurred to me today that my most comfortable prayer time is in the late afternoon. I look forward to meditation around 4:00; it's time to be quiet with God.

At this point in my quest something happened that I have no explanation for. I mislaid my journal. Actually, I had put it into a large, unmarked three-ring binder that I then put in my bookshelf and forgot about. There it lay unnoticed, unused as a way of prayer while I served my internship in social services work at the Beach Food Pantry and waited for Beach Care Services to take form. Then one day, just as accidentally, I was arranging some books and there it was. My journal had been found.

September 25, 2000

One year and eleven months ago I wrote my last entry in this journal. Since then it had been lost. Today it was found. (I am struck with how much the lead in the pencil I am using matches the pencil I was using almost two years ago. But then again, I almost always write with a #2 pencil.) I looked everywhere I could think of for it and finally concluded that I had mislaid it or inadvertently thrown it out. At first I thought that it would turn up, but it didn't, and I thought that perhaps it was best that I give up journaling. Maybe the spiritual journey was over. Well, this is not so; I still have a lot to talk over with God and a lot of listening to do.

September 30, 2000

The Beach Care Services needs assessment study, or more correctly my compulsion in dealing with it, seems to constantly conflict with my attention to the present. I am spending more time thinking about it and fantasizing about what it could mean in the future than I am spending time in the present. It is as if the study has possessed me. I don't think that this is desirable.

Olga's sister is visiting and this past week has been a marathon of talk and activity that is not normal. It has constantly intruded into the daily routine and created a reality of its own. It is always knocking at my door and invading my silence. Right now I can't find the silence to pray. But of course in doing this journaling I am composing a lament. I am praying.

October 5, 2000

I think that what I am experiencing, in working with the needs assessment study, is the rush of the excitement of doing action research again, and the ego that is so tied up in doing it. My thoughts are so often about what might go wrong and about my desire to do a good study. No wonder that something about it has been bothering me. I have been experiencing the activity of the ego self defending the false self rather than experiencing the Christ in the people involved with me in the study.

October 29, 2000

It's beginning to get through to me. I seem to be separating myself from people by both my spiritual life and my secular life. They seem to be there doing their thing and I am standing off on the side observing them. It's hard to observe in a purely descriptive way so I become judgmental. I find that I say to myself that I do not suffer fools lightly. And, apparently it is seeping out of me. Olga called me on this again today. Do I really have that obvious an attitude? Is this what I really project to others? Is this spiritual pride once again or a more general lack of tolerance?

After a year of laying the groundwork, conducting a needs assessment study to point the direction that B. C. S. should take, and months to develop a training program for volunteers, we were ready. It was time to turn well-intentioned volunteers into effective, compassionate intake counselors. And, after a month of training we had a team people who were ready to meet the needy, listen to their story, and respond with professional sensitivity. The Presbyterian Church opened its doors to the community and provided us with an office. Needy people by the hundreds came from up and down the Beach from the sleazy trailer parks and run down houses a block off the main road. They came from the tents and cardboard shacks of the homeless in the woods off of Rt. 98.

March 5, 2001
   Today the B.C.S. Resources Office at the beach Presbyterian Church opened with real volunteers and real needy people. It was a full morning, a morning filled with focused, caring people. It was Bud working as an intake counselor. It was Paul and Colette at the Food Pantry, it was Ken and Daphne in the church office writing checks for needy people that Bud sent up to them, checks for rent and electricity, and vouchers for gasoline so they could get to work. We were in relationship with people and fully present.
   But, what about the contemplative life of prayer? Working with B.C.S. over the last year has not been a quiet and peaceful time. It has been very active. There has been the adrenalin rush of action, but there has also been the pull to enter the circle once again with God – a time of quiet. A pull to be one with God, free from the needs of the false self. I am aware that there is, once again, a desire in me to be a secular contemplative. There is a need to get off this carousel, get off the dizzy ride, get away from the music of the calliope, the bright lights and clutching for the gold ring. I feel the need for a quiet place where I can get off to the side and be with God as he works in the world, where I can be undistracted. I need a place to be a monk again before I lose my perspective. I need some solitude or I will lose my sense of touching God and being touched by him in ordinary ways that I might, in the rush, attribute to something else. I need to find a place in my life for contemplative prayer again.

March 19, 2001
   I am still at it, but with less intensity today. The volunteers are picking up a feel for the job to be done. And so, freed from the daily feeling that I must "get it to work," I have turned to the piles of details that were left unattended to until there would be time.

Always in the back of my mind was the realization that we were doing the job of professional social workers and none of us were professionally trained to do the job. We were energetic, well intentioned people who had no real sense of the politics involved in a community effort that involved the local government, local churches, business interests and the social work community. For example, we had a client who came to us for financial help in filling a prescription written by a local doctor. The volunteer on duty that morning was unfamiliar with the drug Oxycodone, and he accepted the prescription as legitimate and wrote a voucher for the prescription that the client could take to a local pharmacy to be filled. Later that day a plain clothes security person outside the Wal-Mart store where the pharmacy was located, observed the client peddling the Oxycodone to college kids on the beach for spring break. That incident might have broken open in any number of ways and we could have been crucified. It didn't. We rethought our prescription voucher policy, revised our procedures, and got through a year and a half without further incidents like that, until another client brought a similar prescription to a new volunteer on her first day at work. The red flag procedure we had established worked and the matter was handled in a professional way. But, the possibility of similar or other gaffes always lurked in the wings and we were keenly aware that our inexperience and lack of professional training continually made us vulnerable. In April, our second month of operation, I mused one day on our lack of experience.

> April 4, 2001
> I have not lived enough to know the saint or sinner's life
> of true delight.
> I have not lived enough to know the grip of true enduring
> fright.
> I have skimmed the surface as swallows do in ever active
> flight.
> I have missed the conflict, sorrow, and despair
> of a never-ending night.
> In simple fact I have not lived enough to know true joy
> or deepest plight.
> Is it too late? Have I lost forever the chance to do it right?

In time I realized that at least for the present, if there was to be emergency assistance for the needy on the Beach, we were going to do it or it wasn't going to get done. There was no turning back. In reflecting on the question "What on earth am I doing here anyhow?" I tried to answer the question for myself.

> April 30, 2001
> 
> The moment.
> Moments are what they are
> An eternal sea of them.
> 
> Right here.
> Here is where we are
> In countless space adrift.
> 
> The past.
> A place to float to
> Where there is no now.
> 
> When.
> A time to bathe in
> if tomorrow is all there is.

Here and now is where we are
A drift
In a sea of life.

Seeking not to do the good
There is no good to do
Just here and now to live in.

Seeking not to make it right.
There is no right or left
Just distance from the middle.

Seeking not to set it straight.
There is no line to draw
Just circles in the sand.

Seeking rather space eternal.
A place to live and love
Amid the cries for help.

May 10, 2001

Things have started to get busy at the B.C.S. office. This could be because we are getting better known or it could be the employment dip between spring break and summer vacation. In any event I have felt the pressure of more persistent demands than I am comfortable with. The other day I said to myself "I can't take care of all of this." and a voice said, "Who ever told you that you were suppose to." To that voice I responded, "I thought you did." Then the response, "Not I, you've been talking to yourself again."

In early May a man came to the office and said that he needed some money to go home. He wanted to get to Louisiana by Mother's day. We told him that we never gave money to people, but that we could buy him a one-way bus ticket. He thanked us but said that he had a bicycle and he wanted to ride. He could get home in less than a week but he needed money for food. We gave him food from the Food Pantry, which he tied onto a beat up old bike and headed west. I kept thinking about him, and several weeks later I wrote this in my journal.

May 20, 2001

"Be home for me on Mother's Day." was all she said to me.
   So mad I couldn't see.
It's quite a way from where I am, to where she is I fear.
   It's anger got me here.
If I stay on Route 90 West I could be there next week.
   Forgiveness there I'll seek.
I'll leave today with lunch and luck. You know I travel light.
   Cars pass me through the night.

And when the sun comes up and climbs above the mist and dew.
> I'm damp and cold all through.

A shave, a shower, and wash things out. A meal doled out as pay.
> I'll see her yet today.

The first I seen was cousin John when I came into town.
> I never seen a man so down.

"She couldn't wait" was all he said. "Died Thursday afternoon.
> Didn't think she'd go so soon."

"Buried her today out by the pines. Weren't hardly no one there.
> Just me and Tom and Clair."

"She knowed I'd come, I said I would, I told her so last year."
> I said,"Now don't you fear."

"We ain't seen you for all these years. She hoped and hoped you'd come.
> Then quit. Waiten you was done."

"You done what you have always done showed up past short and late.
> She said she couldn't wait."

"I said I'd come, I wanted to. I often come so near.
> Just couldn't beat the fear."

"I left in anger when I left, didn't seem so big a deal.
> Never thought just how I'd feel."

"Ne'er let it go, I thought I would. It's stayed with me these years.
> My anger and my fears."

"And, I'm too late to tell her now. I kept it all this time
> Like bitter, bitter wine."

"Afraid she wouldn't pardon me for what I did that day.
> Were things I couldn't say."

June 7, 2001

Who are the people that we serve at B.C.S.? Are they the evolving Christ? Are they the one to come? I guess they are in that they are a part of the pool of life that evolves toward a fulfillment of the one who is to be. Giant steps will have to be taken to move from where we are to where we could be. But, who says that we have any conception of what the One who is to be will be? Merton says that the Christian loves his brother because he is Christ. I still seek to find the personal meaning of that, B.C.S. is one place where I might get a real understanding of what that means. But, I fear that I will never find the meaning in words.

June 14, 2001

Things just happened at B.C.S. this week. There was no scheming, or manipulating or the exercise of will. A $2000 gift and an offer to sponsor a fundraiser this summer that could mean $15,000 just happened. This was followed by an effortless process to raise $300 for the first month's rent of a man at Gibb Village. As far as I know B.C.S. is not on any prayer chain. When people consider others with compassion, and then do something about it, that seems to be prayer. At least it seems to work like I always thought prayer was supposed to work.

July 8, 2001

I had a good size cancer taken off of my face this week and that provided a legitimate reason to disengage from what has become the frenzy of B.C.S. The space was welcome, but at first I didn't know how to handle the idle time. Time is a man made concept that best serves us when it matches the natural rhythms of the universe. If not, it's like a noose, the more you struggle against it the tighter it grips you.

> For years on end I've seen the fiery sun
> Arise to meet the challenge of the day
> To point, to gesture and at last to say
> The prize belongs to those who swiftly run.
> Oh yes, for years on end I have believed
> That work is noble, prince and king of all,
> The way in which a man prevents the fall
> Into the pit of lethargy deceived.
> An old man has at least the chance to know
> That race and kingdom are not all there is
> To live for. And at last to find and show
> A light on those who grab for what is theirs
> In darkness that conceals the hidden foe.
> Victory goes to those who ride the flow.

July 26, 2001

The past few days I have been fantasizing about building a cabin in the woods, near where Pam and Graham live. A simple twelve month a year cabin, spartan by today's standards, but not austere. A fantasy.

August 15, 2001

Two great passages from Merton's journal. Both passages seem to say the same thing. One from the perspective of death and the other from the perspective of life. As humans we live between our first moment of life and our death. What is between the two is living in the world, not our world but God's world. When we understand that, we don't try to make it into our world, and by so doing we move toward freedom. Neither idolatry nor license are formulas for living a joyful life or facing death as a free person.

August 29, 2001

Today Merton was talking about a priest, Fr. R., who had lost his faith and was now an apostate. In order to lose faith one must first have faith. One must have a relationship with God. I would like to say that I find God in relationship with people. Thus my affection for working with B.C.S. But, let's be honest! Do I really like working with people, or do I like the idea of working with people? Do I like to be in relationship with God, or do I like to be in relationship with a God that is my conception of God? Some days I perceive people and God to be a nagging bother. I don't want to be in relationship with them. Does that mean that I have lost my faith in them? Do I want to be in relationship with them only when they fit my conception of what I think they should be?

September 23, 2001

It has been almost two weeks since the terrorist attacks on the World Trade Center and the Pentagon. The news broadcasts, the newspaper, and speeches have generated a lot of interest and anxiety. But I have hardly talked about it at all, even with Olga.

I have a very different reaction than I had to other national disasters and crises. It isn't that I don't care, it's that I keep thinking about what Julian of Norwich said, "Sin is inevitable, but all shall be well, and all shall be well, and all manner of things shall be well."[1] That's either faith or apathy. Which?

October 10, 2001

When we all live for self (self perpetuation and self gratification) we will have come to the place where our species faces extinction. The perpetuation of the species is dependent on at least some people who are willing to give their "body and blood" for the species. Is that what the terrorists and the people in the world trade center thought on the morning of September 11th? That's a sobering thought.

The demands of Beach Care Services were taking their toll. More and more I yearned for solitude. In reflection, I wondered if my turn of attention toward solitude reflected a desire to escape from the demands and pressure of the job, or if it was a growing awareness that the modest gains that I had made toward willingness were being sacrificed to the willfulness that I applied to the job. Was it my false self being protected in its position of comfort by my ego self, or was it running cross grain to who I had been created to be?

October 18, 2001

At the Beach Care Office this morning there were the phones, the intercom, clients, things to be done. I left them in good hands and came home for an hour of peace. The phone rang several times. They needed this or that. I picked up Olga at the Food Pantry at noon. She was exhausted. I came home and the phone rang six times. Too busy for my liking, too much going on.

I was having second thoughts about the active life. I began to sense that solitude was calling me. I began to fantasize about what the life of a contemplative living in solitude would really be like. I began to debate with myself and build a rationale for the solitary life. But I continued with the active life because I thought that was what I was supposed to do. I was up to my neck in it and the water was rising. My thoughts about solitude became more and more elaborate, but they were still just thoughts, my thoughts.

November 3, 2001

Finding solitude will not be easy because solitude is not just one thing. Solitude can be refreshment in the middle of frantic activity. Solitude can be an escape. Solitude can be an environment where possibilities can grow and mature. Solitude can be a place where the mind plays cruel tricks on itself. Solitude can be a place where one grows, or a place where one languishes and goes crazy. I had better know how I will relate to solitude before I close the door. Solitude is what happens when we build the right kind of a semi-permeable membrane around our self to protect against distractions, interruptions, and demands of the world. If it is the right kind of a membrane it allows awareness of the world to come in, and compassion to flow out to the world. If it is the right kind of a membrane it does not nurture smudginess, insensitivity, and isolationism. It becomes the boundary of a nurturing place for insight and prayer.

This is what I think, but I will only know if I experience solitude on solitude's terms, not on my terms. To experience solitude I must leave the frantic world behind and let solitude work on me as it will.

November 7, 2001

Solitude must not be a narcotic that puts a false glow of pleasure on the world by covering up that which is painful. Solitude must be a place where the distractions of the world are put aside thus allowing me to see the world as it is, to see creation and the incarnation in the world, to see the true and the false self with clarity. Solitude should be a place that enables me to view the world with compassion and see the pain that is created when one person causes another to fall short of what he or she was created to be. The world is not all pain. There is much joy and pleasure in the world. Perhaps solitude is a place where I can see love, joy and hope with clarity. I think it is, but I need to find out.

November 16, 2001

Blood pressure is back up again — not good. I am not really sure why, but my involvement with B.C.S. has got to have something to do with it. Tonight is the B.C.S. fall fundraiser. The phone has been constantly ringing in or calling out for the past two weeks. I have been to the office every day. Day after day. I realized last week that I am stressed. I almost lost it at this month's B.C.S. board meeting. Lord, I am not sure that this is what either of us had in mind when I started. I really need to get in touch with my true self to hear what is going on. For too long now I have been listening to messages inside and out that tell me how important I am to the success of B.C.S.

November 27, 2001

Olga and I went to Alabama to spend Thanksgiving with the kids. A wonderful four days of relaxation. Now that I am back in Florida my mind is buzzing again with a fantasy about solitude. It could be done, but what would Graham and Pam and Olga think? What do I really think when I get past the fantasy? Where is God in all of this?

December 2, 2001

Today, I realized that I am not the person that I am capable of being. People are definitely a bother. I am constantly on guard for fear of antagonizing anyone. When others, Olga included, put the slightest pressure on me to do something I have a definite avoidance reaction. I have feelings of indifference, or anger or irritation. I just want to be left alone. Olga is in a holiday mood and I am down, flat, unanimated. I don't care.

December 10, 2001

Previously, I have said that sacrifice involves doing what the situation calls for even though it is not what I would have preferred to do, and then doing it without self interest—that is, doing it without interest in the consequences to the self. I think that this is what Beach Care Services calls for at the present. I have good days and not so good days at B.C.S. Taken as individual instances each day is just a day, but in the long run I wonder what effect the work is having on me. I wonder if this work is really my vocation. Right now I do what I do because it is called for, but what about another year or so? I need to come back to this.

December 11, 2001

Merton says I will find solitude when God gives me solitude and when I recognize it and accept it. If this is so, then the only thing I can do is to pray and wait.

December 25, 2001

So far, this is the most enjoyable Christmas that I can remember in a long time. Olga and I are alone, but Olga is still reaching out to others—Helga, Maggie, Bertha, Rose, Carol, Bobbie, Virginia, Ernie and who knows how many others. The phone must be hot. She's reaching out because she can't help herself. It's her nature. Me, I'm finding Christmas joy in no phone calls, no intrusions, no demands except the minimal demands of living. Strange, finding comfort and wholeness in solitude on Christmas day.

December 29, 2001

Beach Care Services is on my mind too much. Where are we going to get the volunteers to sustain it? And now being on the vestry and being senior warden at church, I never wanted this. What kind of a test of faith and will is this?

At first my rather nebulous fantasy took the form of a guesthouse, a cabin in the woods where I could go for a few days or a week at a time and get away from the pressure that I was under. Though I didn't see it that way at the time, the guesthouse idea was an "I can eat my cake and have my penny at the same time" solution. But ahead of me was a "one or the other" decision. In spite of my awareness that ultimately I was going to have to make a decision, I kept thinking that perhaps I could have it both ways.

January 1, 2002

I felt better today, not so jangled inside and I realized that my tendency to "not suffer fools lightly" really means that I am a rational, left brain, logical, empirically oriented, driven person in a world populated by less cognitive, more affective, more people-oriented, less driven people. I question my ability to work effectively with such people. Or at least I wonder how long I will be able to keep this up.

I talked with Pam earlier tonight. She and Graham are still positively inclined toward the idea of a guesthouse on their property in Alabama.

In time I was able to face something that kept coming up over the years but for the most part I had skillfully avoided. Some days I liked the idea of working with people but I couldn't honestly say that I really liked working intensely with people for an extended time. I had the skills, but I didn't have the disposition.

January 3, 2002

Let's be honest. I don't really love the people that I work with at B.C.S. or at church. I respect some; I tolerate some. I try to be non-judgmental, but I don't think I love them. Either that or I still don't know what love means in a spiritual sense. In reality, I sometimes feel annoyed with them. Most often trying to love them comes down to relating to them in a decent, non-judgmental, unselfish way because that's what is called for. I get the feeling that love is not a many splendored thing but a loosely over-used word. But if I don't love these people then what is love? What does it really mean to love one's neighbor?

January 10, 2002

Another wave has passed and I didn't drown. Today the B.C.S. board meeting was followed by my first vestry meeting as Senior Warden and the vicker is out of town on vacation. I didn't crumble. Last night I did have a wild anxiety dream about losing control of the vestry meeting and having people walk out in anger and I awakened in a sweat. But in general the meeting turned out better than I expected, given the opposition and frustration that seems to be boiling between factions in the church. I have started reading *The Art of Loving*, an old classic by Erich Fromm.

January 12, 2002

I wonder what I would have thought if I had read *The Art of Loving* in a thoughtful and deliberate way when I first got it. I tend to think that it might have been perplexing. In any event I am now blessed with a gift from Fromm. It is giving me a structure to make some sense out of the questions about love that I have tried to deal with for the past fifteen years.

January 18, 2002

Not a good day. Is the "beast" still with me: low energy level, loss of appetite, depreciating thoughts about self and others? Blood pressure still up. Just got up from an after supper nap and I am now looking forward to going to bed in an hour. Drinks before dinner have crept up to four. This is too many.

January 24, 2002

Finished Eric Fromm's little book, *The Art of Loving*. I am not sure that anything has happened in the almost fifty years since he wrote it. It certainly could be discouraging for many. It almost left me feeling that there is no hope, but not quite. It should crack the complacency of some. It exposes many false loves that I'll bet a lot of people never question. It is very forthright in saying that unless humanity takes the search for real love seriously we can expect serious consequences. He is realistic in pointing out that real love is not impossible, it does exist in the world, but it takes openness, effort and self-sacrifice. It takes work. I would say that it takes a willingness to be transformed.

January 31, 2002

I was struck today by the monthly B.C.S. staff meeting, a quiet celebration of the efforts of the past year. One year ago there was no B.C.S. Resource Office to serve the needy. There were no volunteers. Through wrangling, positioning and dedicated effort it was born, and it lives, and it's there to serve the needy of this community without consideration for the ethnic, ideological or religious perspective that the clients hold. Some would say that this is one of those examples of God's love in the world, God working with people in community.

Then later I was struck by Merton's journal entries of May 20th through 31st 1961. They are a testimony to God's work in solitude in a world almost void of human interaction. Merton is finding God's love in solitude.

February 2, 2002

Got back today from a vestry retreat. I processed the Friday evening and Saturday morning sessions. The vestry performed magnificently. They made decisions because they were committed to what they were doing and they did this fully aware that God was watching. I never thought that I would spend the better part of two days enjoying the doing. There is hope.

February 9, 2002

Today clear. Nothing in the blue but a blinding sun. Temperature in the lower seventies, almost warm. So different from yesterday with low fleeting clouds and flashing moments of sunlight, but the comfort of the sun was always broken by a cloud, another moment of coolness. Each cloud a shiver.

More examples of the prostitution of the word love by fast food advertisements on billboards: "Love food?" and the other one "The food you love at the price you like."

February 11, 2002

> Born on a breeze,
> Lifted by another,
> Letting go of the burden,
> Being nothing.

What if letting go is nothing? Then all shall be well. Nothing meets nothing where it all started. Merton's journal entry of September 8, 1961, reveals his real struggle with not being able to love those who he knows that he should love — some members of his community and particularly his abbot. Reading this was too close for my own comfort.

February 17, 2002
    Back from Alabama. Long trip up (we had a flat tire) and the drive back was at the edge of my driving comfort. But the time up there was excellent. Looked at sites for the cabin and discussed related issues. Solitude seems within grasp, perhaps within twelve months. It will not be pure solitude any more than Merton's solitude was pure, but it will be real and substantial. If Olga and I stay well, it will be a step toward wholeness.

It would be over a year before I would be able to say it to anyone, even to myself. But, over the next year and a half I would slowly realize that I wasn't going to be able to integrate my conception of a contemplative life with society's conception of a life of service. As long as I maintained substantial ties to society I would have to play by its rules. I would have to do it their way. I came to realize that I was not a person who enjoyed making waves nor was I a person who walked in step with the person beside me. I was a person who wanted to be reasonable, and responsible to the person I walked with, when I walked with a him or her, but most of the time I wanted to walk alone. I really didn't want to be a highly involved social person. I wanted to be a responsible person when I related to society, but I needed a lot more solitude than the society that I knew would let me have. It was no longer the Mary/Martha issue that was at stake. It was no longer the contemplative/active issue that I needed to resolve. It was finding the niche that had been prepared for me. It was being the person I had been created to be that I needed to give birth to and nurture to maturity. Coming to understand this, and accomplishing it in a responsible way was what lay ahead of me.

Why didn't I just accept society's expectation of how to live the good life, and finish out my days living that life with my friends and neighbors as I had done all of my life? As I look back on that question from today's perspective, I am startled to realize that the thought never seriously occurred to me.

## NOTE

1. Julian of Norwich, *A Lesson of Love: The Revelations of Julian of Norwich*, ed. and trans. John-Julian (New York, NY: Walker and Company, 1988), 61.

*Part III*

# LIFE COMMITMENT

## Chapter Eight

# Thirsting for Solitude

It would not be publicly announced for almost a year, but in my mind a decision was all but made – I would leave my active life on the Beach for a life of contemplative solitude. Before I could do that, however, I wanted to play my part in finishing what we had started, the building of a stable and lasting social service presence for the needy on the Beach. For at least another year I would continue doing some things such as fund raising and publicity that sometimes gave me feelings of satisfaction, but I really did not enjoy doing. What I enjoyed most was coordinating and facilitating the work of our office volunteers as they worked with clients who came to us for assistance. And because I did not delegate responsibility well, the workload and thus the pressure of the job, increased each day.

I no longer thought about solitude as a fantasy or as a weekend retreat, and began considering practical matters that might arise when it became a full time reality. By February of 2002, I began to see what I thought would be realistic issues that we would need to consider before that time came. Most of these dealt with potential problems of adjustment to the solitary way of life that Olga and I would be entering. Some of these concerns about the future actually did materialize, but none turned out to be an occasion for a major change in course. For the time being, however, I had a commitment to keep to Beach Care Services, and a full life to live each day.

February 18, 2002
    The more I think about it the more it seems that my desire for solitude is leading to something more complicated than I first imagined. Olga is a person who finds her reason for existence in others. If she lost that she would lose her meaning in life. But before she did, she would smother anyone she could get a hold on with her conception of love. This will put a lot of pressure on the people

around her, particularly the family, unless it can be recognized up front and dealt with productively from the start. I may need to adjust my concept of solitude to meet the situation, and accept that to have solitude at the expense of her need to reach out to others would not be fair to her. The question might become how to recognize our individual needs and reconcile these in a positive and productive way in which we can both grow.

A realistic approach might be for Olga to work out her own life and find fulfillment in pursuits that will be enriching and personally growthful for her. In this way we could each follow our own bliss while being present to support each other. Clearly, it will not work if we change our environment and the people who put demands on us, and then proceed as if nothing had happened. Something radical is going to happen and it needs to be seen as an opportunity for both of us to grow and not as a cross to bear. If Olga sees this as something "she will do for Jack," a sacrifice she needs to make because "it is Jack's turn to have his way about how we live," this will be a disaster for both of us.

February 20, 2002

Every so often the voices that say "know thy self," "unto thy self be true," and "allow for growth from within" get through to Olga. She senses that she should listen to these voices, but it is not easy for her to do. On the other hand, I still hear voices that admonish me to consider the advantages of society and to be a self-sacrificing and productive member. Certainly there must be some wisdom in what these voices are saying to us. If we both leave the door open to what we hear, we both will experience the tug and pull of some conflict, but we might grow as a result of it.

February 22, 2002

Solitude is a state of being free from internal and external demands, real or imagined, that disturb the wholeness that comes from knowing that though I am alone, I am an integrated part of the universe, and that I am alive and participating in a process of growth that comes from within.

March 6, 2002

I know, but I need to remember, that there is little chance of successfully living a life of solitude by simply announcing it to myself and to the world. I expect to spend a while finding out how much solitude I can take and how much I can negotiate with family and friends. I must be ready to accept the possibility that I may not be able to take too much without having serious emotional problems. I must be able to accept that my family and friends may not allow me to have solitude. If this happens I must not use them as an excuse to back off, but I want very much to find out. I want very much to have the experience and tell it for what it is—a wild dream or a whole new world to venture into and experience in depth.

March 9, 2002

An active day, starting with a two hour meeting involving the vicar and the junior warden on financial matters and the conflict between factions within the church over building expansion. The B.C.S. office followed this. One of our clients, a woman from Tennessee, was being stalked by her estranged husband, and was found by him. She refused to go to the local police, said they wouldn't help. We helped her get out of town. The afternoon was spent assembling and stuffing envelopes with the five-year plan survey for the church. Dencie called just as we were finishing the stuffing, Milt was lost; he must have gotten confused again. We called the police then went to be with Dencie. By the time we got there Milt was home.

On January 25, 1962 Merton wrote of being utterly regular and devoted to the ordinary common life. He said, " . . . I haven't taken time to myself in the woods all week." He was being a good, conforming member of his community. Yet, he speaks of being starved, and strained even though it has been good in many ways. But, he asks ". . . have I any other satisfaction from this other than the satisfaction of having done what I did not want to do?"[1] There are days when I could have written that myself.

March 15, 2002

Further insight into Merton's lack of solitude as a member of the monastic community of Gethsemane:

> . . . I only meditate for the 1/2 hour in the morning and 1/4 hour in the evening. We do not normally have sufficient time or silence for meditation here. But I have a special opportunity at the hermitage and I must take it seriously, for my own soul's sake, for the novices, for the entire world. Today, I have become aware of the importance of this work and this vocation.[2]

I too have plenty of time to do God's will, if there is such a thing, but I use little of that time for solitude, and when I am tired, contemplation leads to sleep. I am not at all sure that this is that bad; I must need the sleep.

March 16, 2002

Spent most of the morning working on labels for the *B.C.S. Newsletter* mailings. Then spent the afternoon composing a second draft of the vestry letter to the congregation about the building fund drive. My temper is short, my nerves tight and I fear I have lost perspective again. There has not been one moment of solitude today, just external pressure and internal anger. A good night's sleep will help, but this can't go on much longer.

March 20, 2002

First day of spring. Good prayer time; some meditation before supper. Signs of creation are all around me. Earlier today I did think about the future—the Alabama woods—perhaps this will be a reality yet. Things at B.C.S. have slowed down, a consequence of full employment during spring break.

March 27, 2002

I read a short article today that was written by Gerald May for *The Shalem News*. In this article he reflected on "God's will" and concluded that we really can't know God's will in any complete sense because we don't know who God is in any complete sense. The best we can do is to have faith and the humility to let God work through us.

April 8, 2002

Things do change, but seldom for the reasons we expect, and seldom because of what we do to effect change, further evidence that we do not really carry the burden of the future on our shoulders. I need to remember this in regard to my feelings of responsibility for B.C.S. and St. Thomas. I can use them as an excuse to never enter solitude, or I can let uncertainty about solitude become the reason for not choosing it, or I can say, " The time has come." I really do have a choice. I can walk the trail of relative security with knowledge of what will come because I have been there before. Or I can step out on a stretch that I have never walked before. I hope that I don't miss the rest of my life because of fear of the unknown or an over developed sense of importance.

April 17, 2002

Right now I can only believe that I want to take the step into solitude. In some respects it seems like the first time I jumped off a high diving board. I remember that moment in vivid detail. It was not an act of will; it was an act of abandonment. I think that my false self knows that if I step into solitude it will have been dealt a serious blow. If I open its cage and just let it out it will want to stay with me. But I must leave it behind. There will be no place for it where I am going.

May 3, 2002

Pam called last night to say that they have found someone who is interested in building our cabin in Alabama. It will be about 1200 square feet, and she and Graham now need to go to the planning commission and get a building permit, etc. We are under way. Thank you.

May 5, 2002

I continue to feel a strong call to solitude. At first I was bothered by the thought that this was just an attempt to avoid facing social reality. I now feel that the self-transcendent and socially transcendent urges that I have felt and tried to suppress for much of my life are real, not just a fantasy about who I might become. I am thankful to recognize that I have been a part of a transforming process that has been working on me. I want it to change me.

May 8, 2002

I found an interesting passage in Merton's Journal entry of January 15, 1963. It seems as if healing is taking place. He expresses almost none of the frustration and anger that he has previously expressed toward his abbot, his community and himself. He seems to have been healed rather than setting out to heal himself. I am aware that I am feeling healthy, less angry. I wonder if it will last.

May 12, 2002

This is from Merton's Journal of January 20, 1963:

I have been absurdly burdened since the beginning of the year with the illusion of "great responsibility" and of a task to be done. Actually whatever work is to be done is God's work and not mine and I will not help matters, only hinder them, by too much care.[3]

What really good advice and wise counsel is summed up in that statement. It seems that the universal law of gravity applies not only to material things, but spiritual matters as well. What goes up surely must come down. Just a few days after my delight at feeling the transforming power of love, my false self counter attacked and my true self took another shellacking. The self inflicted pressure of my work for the vestry at St. Thomas and my work at Beach Care Services got to me again.

May 14, 2002

There are several phone messages on the answering machine. They all imply, or openly request, that I do something for the caller. It would be very easy to believe that these people in some way think that I am important. The next step would be easy—to think that in some way I really am important. I don't want to think that is true. I want to think that I am only convenient. For tonight I have no intention of returning any of the calls.

May 18, 2002

The phone calls continue. The demands of St. Thomas and Beach Care Services continue and I begin to feel resentment and repressed anger. I don't know if this is a return to depression or just the beginning of burnout. In any event I don't like it. I don't like the feeling.

Now, after forty minutes of undisturbed meditation I am feeling better. I am still capable of the prayer of silence. This at least is good to know.

One of the most effective ways that I have found to deal with tension and constant demands from others is contemplative prayer. I do not know whether contemplative prayer provides a medium in which to recognize that I have choices, or whether it provides a medium for me to realize how really small and insignificant I am and how big the universe is. But it helps me to regain my balance and perspective. Certainly it is a good medium to help me see God's love in the world, and that I have a choice of being a part of that love. There were lots of times during my period of active service when I failed to take the time for contemplative prayer, and I have no question, in retrospect, that I paid the price for it. I lost my balance. Certainly, contemplative prayer is a part of a process, not a quick fix. Transformation takes time.

May 20, 2002
In his journal entry of May 20, 1963 (thirty nine years ago to this day) Merton records that once again he is feeling frustrated by his abbot. His response is anger and loss of sleep. He recognizes this to be neurotic:

> So it is that the Christian and monastic mind is admirably fitted to be a seed ground of neurosis. This is at once a weakness and strength. Unfortunately I can't imagine, for the moment, where to find any kind of strength in this futility.[4]

I was periodically reminded, by reading Merton's journals that his life as an enclosed monk, who professed to be a contemplative, was anything but a life of interior calm and placid meditation and prayer. It seems to me that in 1963 Merton was questioning whether or not his vocation was being compromised by his laxity to commitment, and by his reaction to his abbot's decisions which Merton saw as constantly frustrating his freedom and the appropriate autonomy of his spiritual life. He saw his condition at the time to be a potential seedbed for neurosis.

And now, almost forty years later, I was experiencing a period of frustration that, in my case, frequently led me to question my choice to follow an active life of service. I was questioning if my fantasies about solitude were not just an escape mechanism to get out of a situation in which I felt over my head. I was questioning whether or not this was what I should be doing. I was wondering if my behavior was also symptomatic of neurosis.

As I reflect on Merton's reaction to his life in 1963 and my reaction to my life in 2002, it seems to me that both of us were grounded in largely unrecognized reactions of willfulness to follow a way that we each saw as being more personally fulfilling than what we were currently doing. At the same time I believe we were both aware that we were doing what we were doing because ultimately we had made that choice. We were the ones who said "yes." Yet, we were being forced to face up to whether or not some modification in our reaction to our life was called for.

As I look back on my life at that time through the perspective of my journal, I now think I understand what Susan meant when she said to me some years earlier: "Jack, God doesn't want you to be perfect, God wants you to be obedient." I think what she meant by this was that when I said "yes", my "yes" should proceed from ultimate faith. It did not mean that I would succeed, let alone do the task perfectly. It only meant that I was willing to try. No one ever said that I or anyone else would ever be transformed into a full expression of God's love in a lifetime. I think that Teilhard believed that it could take millennia for this to happen to humanity. But it seems that people continue to perpetuate their willfulness by putting faith in themselves and their fallible creations rather than recognizing the choice that they have to say "yes," in a love that follows from ultimate faith in God. If this willfulness continues, then humanity may very well become an increasingly self-serving species that could destroy itself and a number of other species in the process of self-destruction. What a blown opportunity and waste that would be.

When I get so involved in doing what I chose to do and I think is best, and don't stop to remember that I am the one who made the choice and that I can unmake it, then I do not use the potential that I was given by virtue of being human. It is easy to fall in the pit of believing that if I work hard enough I will change humanity for the better. This willfulness can be destructive to myself and to others. I believe that this is what had begun to happen to me. This was a good time for me to consider a period of solitude and then regroup, and this was what I did.

May 23, 2002
From Merton's Journal of June 4, 1963:

Solitude—when you get saturated with silence and landscape, then you need an interior work, psalms and scripture, meditation. But first the saturation. How much of this is simply a restoration of one's normal human balance?[5]

Long hours, days on end having no agenda, no objective, just being saturated by the natural world uninterrupted by the demands of the social intrusion of man. Believing that it is right because it feels right. Will this be what solitude is like at first?

May 26, 2002
When I get to a place of solitude and start practicing it much of the day, I must be myself, and not a reflection of the image of someone else's discipline. Mine must be what is right for me in that situation.

May 28, 2002
I cannot assume that demands made on me by others make sense for me. In many cases they only make sense to the person who makes the demands. But, if the demand does not occur, then there will be no obligation to respond. When I get to solitude, ground rules will need to be made. But the consequences of making an issue out of violations is likely to be as disruptive as the original demand. To live even marginally in solitude on the edge of society means to subject oneself to the possibility of demands of society, at least to some degree. That's a reasonable

expectation. If I wish to benefit from at least some of the advantages of society, I must open myself to some demands from society. But, when I pursue solitude, then it seems reasonable to create buffers to societal demands that offend others as little as possible. Doing this will require some social skill and sensitivity.

June 8, 2002

Without some solitude I never will have the opportunity to get in touch with my true self. Without solitude I always will be subject to the voice of the world telling me what to value, what to dream, what to hope. I need some solitude to maintain a healthy balance just as I need some experience with the social world for balance. It is always a matter of degree. Solitude is like any other growth component. Some people need more of it to remain sane, some less.

June 14, 2002

Whether it is on the Beach of Captiva Island hundreds of miles from New York City, in the woods near Concord, Massachusetts, in a hermitage in Kentucky, or in a monastery kitchen in France is not the central issue. Any place that provides an opportunity for solitude will do.

June 17, 2002

I must realize that all that I have said about solitude is at arm's length. My knowledge comes from secondary sources. I have not experienced long periods of solitude, and until I do I am only dealing with hopes or speculations. I need to find out from experience, but in the meantime I need to hope.

June 18, 2002

At present I am not willing to make a radical rearrangement of my life so as to be able to devote long periods of time to living in solitude. I just talk about it to myself and to God and carve out a bit of time now and then. I wonder if this is not the behavior of a dilettante.

Olga has gone out shopping and I have an hour for meditation if I want it. I do. Got off to a good start, then ten minutes into centering prayer the phone rang. Better get it. Kate is driving down for a visit and she's on the road. It might be her. No, it's Jan on B.C.S. business. Back to centering prayer. Phone again; it's Margaret. She says that Bill B. wants to meet with me at 11:00 about 600 square feet of office space that B.C.S. can get in a good location. I agree to meet him. It's now 10:30 and Olga isn't back yet. What if she doesn't get back with the car in time? Back to meditation, but now I can't concentrate. Phone again, Kate this time. She's on the road and all is well. Olga just got home; I have the car and off I go to meet with Bill B. about office space.

June 23, 2002

Spent a half hour in contemplation on the back porch ingesting a mosaic of forms, light, shadows, color, movement, bird sounds. Quiet, peaceful. No demands on me, no one wants me to do anything. Spoke with Pam earlier today, house plans seem to be back on track again.

June 26, 2002
By October 12, 1964 Merton was still not living full time at his hermitage. It was not until mid-October of that year that he was able to sleep there for the first time thus giving him his first opportunity for 24 hours of solitude. I need to remember that.

July 11, 2002
Talked with Pam on the phone last night, the land survey was too late for the July meeting of the Planning Board. Decision put off until end of August.

July 23, 2002
Today I go in for cataract surgery. Reading is a central part of my life so I have some apprehension but not really anxiety. In just a few hours it will be over.

July 27, 2002
By last Friday I began to get signals that all was not well with my eye and by Saturday morning I had a serious post-operative infection. I could not see. Our neighbor, Tony, drove Olga and me to Tallahassee to meet with a specialist. Connected with him at his office and had a procedure done that involved having an antibiotic injected into the eye. Right now it's up in the air whether I will see again out of my right eye.

July 28, 2002
Went to another specialist today and his judgment is that the bacteria are dead and all that remains are their bodies and the toxins they produced. If I am lucky these foreign materials will dissipate, if not I will need to have the eyeball flushed out. There is nothing to do now but to wait and see what happens. How about prayer?

August 4, 2002
As a result of my eye surgery and the complications that have followed I have been quite inactive. I am beginning to feel the consequences of this inactivity. I am lethargic. I have no energy.

Hindsight is always so clear. As I look back over my journal entries for this period I realized that my lack of provision for adequate solitude and periods of contemplative prayer was having serious consequences. Rather than get off the carousel and regain my balance and my bearings, I pushed and acted as if my push and my drive were needed to keep St. Thomas and Beach Care Services afloat—what a presumption on my part. I am convinced that if I had spent more time listening and less time almost compulsively pushing and driving to accomplish what I thought was right, I would have been a more loving, sane and healthier person. But, I didn't see that at the time. (Incidentally the last I heard, both St. Thomas and Beach Care Services were alive and doing well without me.) I do believe, however, that the brief periods of solitude and contemplation that I did snatch from the daily activity may have kept me afloat for a year.

August 6, 2002

Things are starting to heat up again now that I have learned to function with one eye. Phone ringing again constantly, appointments, things to do to keep up the Beach Care image, vestry work to keep us from going broke or falling apart as a parish. It's easy to become seduced into believing that I am of far greater importance than I am. How much I would like to be in the Alabama woods in solitude. But that's not going to happen in the near future. Until then I will need to work out as much solitude as I can in my daily routine. Even a bit each day seems to help me to keep some semblance of balance.

August 9, 2002

It seems that to live in solitude, devoid of any solidarity with anyone else, would deny the reality that we are all interconnected and that we are all a part of an infinite system that defines our reality. If I ever lived a life that denied that reality it would be like breaking my tether to an orbiting spacecraft and drifting off into an infinite void. I cannot long exist unconnected to anything else or anyone else. Even if I were at the extreme margin of our social system, I would in some senses be a part of that system. The question is how far out on the edge can I live without losing my orientation? The companion question becomes how far toward the center of the system can I live without self-destructing.

August 15, 2002

Two more weeks before any radical decision can be made about my eye. At present there seems to be some improvement but I am still not able to see out of it.

Yesterday was filled from morning till evening—too busy. Hunger and Homeless Coalition, arrangements for the service award for Bill B., Office Depot for B.C.S. office supplies, eye doctor, pharmacy, vestry meeting, home by 9:30. No time during the day for solitude. One might say "much accomplished" but I was drained by the end of the day. Is that an accomplishment?

August 16, 2002

Another full day. Spent the morning at the B.C.S. office, then over to Panama City to see about Bill B.'s service award and was reminded again that without Bill's generosity and efforts I doubt if B.C.S. would ever have made it. Got the car serviced, had a late lunch, and then a call from Marian G. about a B.C.S. family, two parents, four children who needed food, and the food pantry was closed. Marion is so dedicated and effective in working with our clients. We need to find more people like her, but where are they? We got the Food Pantry open and got food for them and then I had a little time before dinner for prayer. Typical day? No such thing as a typical day but there is a representative day—busy.

The needs of people are far beyond what we can meet and there are far more people than we can serve, and it will go on forever. Every person I met today was a reasonable person. It was easy to find Christ in each one. Some days it is not so easy, but I suspect that this is because I don't know where to look and how to look or even, if I am honest, what to look for. I suspect, however, that it's a lot easier for me to find my conception of Christ in people than it is to find Christ.

August 20, 2002

Why do I journal? There are things I want to complain to God about. There are things that I want to say to myself in God's presence. Not that I expect God to do anything about them. I just want to say them. It's like having a friend I can talk with about anything. I feel better when I share with him.

August 23, 2002

No news about the property in Alabama yet. All of this business about surveys, subdivision of property, easements, building codes, things that have to be decided by the planning board, etc. baffle me.

August 24, 2002

Today Olga and I have been married for fifty-one years. There is still life in me and I want to live it; I do not look back on my life with regret. I look forward to my life to come as an opportunity. I have no idea what tomorrow will bring, but I know that all will be well.

August 27, 2002

Thank you! The Planning Board approved our request to build a guesthouse on Pam and Graham's property. We are on the way.

September 12, 2002

Went to Tallahassee on Tuesday for a vitroectomy; it was a very difficult day. The doctor said that he got lots of stuff out of my eyeball but that in closing, a drop of blood got in and lodged on the retina, this should be absorbed by the body. When the blood is absorbed my vision should start to improve. Pam came down from Alabama to help us get through the operation. I did not expect that it would be as big a deal as it turned out to be. Further evidence that our move to Alabama, where we will be closer to the family, has advantages beyond just solitude. I am getting older, faster than I had previously admitted to myself.

Just woke up from another nap—second one today. That vitroectomy on Tuesday was more of an insult to my body than I had expected. Everything still seems to be in slow motion especially my thought process. It's as if the building blocks of my thoughts are being put together by a robot whose batteries have run down.

September 13, 2002

Was able to read a little bit in Merton's journal with my left eye. He notes striking differences between the monastic life and the hermetic life, particularly the need to develop a new pace in life, a new rhythm, and not to let old habits, useful in community life, rule the hermetic life. He talks about his need to slow down, be more deliberate, less frantic.

September 18, 2002
  Saw the doctor today. No good news, but hope remains. He thinks that in time my eye will regain some sight but not soon. We are talking weeks or months not days. He may have to operate to remove the blood that got into the eye when he was closing the incision. Right now I have hope, but I dread the day when I will no longer have hope.

From the middle of September through the end of the year my life became a fugue defined by four themes: Beach Care Services, the vestry of St. Thomas, my eyesight, and the details of winding down a life on the Beach and starting a new life in Alabama. The four themes were played over and over again with minor variations while the same bass rhythm thumped day after day. I was grinding it out, and it was taking a toll on me that I didn't recognize at the time. It was the Sisyphus syndrome. It was rolling a rock up hill day after day because I didn't dare let go of it. What kept me going was the belief that it had to be done because it was the right thing to do. The spontaneity of each new morning was replaced by, "Pull up your socks and put on your boots." It's what happens to so many people before the bottom falls out.

September 24, 2002
  There is nothing really to be concerned about. Certainly, I don't want to get myself to the point I got myself into with the nursery. That was unhealthy. My most vivid memories of the nursery in its last few years, and perhaps always, were memories of talking about and conceptualizing organizational solutions. For example: getting the right people, and organizing things logically and clearly. Sounds good, but it never really worked for me. People never quite fit the molds that I created for them. I invented the nursery and as I went so went the nursery, or so I believed. I shaped the present form of Beach Care Services, and I need to get out before I start believing that as I go so goes B.C.S. Either it goes because people want it to go and believe in it, or it won't go.

September 25, 2002
  "Playing movies" of how the day went and how I did is most often the work of the ego self, done to justify the false self. The problem with this is that it puts the "I" in the center when it's really the "Thou."

Since June my journal has no mention of meditative prayer let alone wordless contemplation. There must have been some. I don't recall. But there was frequent lament about my eye, talks with God about solitude in Alabama, and the prayer of service. As I sustained the prayer of service, without taking the time to check in with my true self or with God through contemplative prayer, I ran the risk of losing my way again. I was becoming too concerned with myself, my physical condition and my priorities, and confusing service to others with well intentioned activity. Perhaps more than anything else I had lost sight of the willfulness that was inherent in striving for perfection.

September 26, 2002
  A day of attending to the structure and operations of B.C.S. I can see how a person can keep busy doing things and convince themselves that they are doing something important. It's the life of an administrator. It's not me.

October 1, 2002
  Yesterday and today were filled with getting the B.C.S. satellite office in operation. Getting phones installed, ordering food, getting a schedule of volunteers, duplicating forms, finding a person who can qualify for the Senior Workforce Program to act as day to day coordinator on the spot. All of it is busy, too busy and far too much of a temptation to confuse the thrill of being a mover and shaker with what I should be doing.
  Tomorrow I go to see the doctor again about my eye. The vision is beginning to improve a bit, but it is nowhere close to being acceptable. This is clearly one thing that I can't do anything about.

October 3, 2002
  Started this morning at 8:00 by preparing a talk about B.C.S. that I gave to the Women's Civic Club at noon, then had an hour and a half meeting with key community people to get the satellite office for B.C.S. going. Found out at 3:30 today that my candidate for the day-to-day coordinator at the satellite office fell through. It's back to square one, and we open the office in two weeks.

October 6, 2002
  Today I spoke on stewardship and the work of Beach Care Services during the 10 o'clock service at Grace Church. This afternoon I wrote letters of resignation from the position of Resource Office Director at B.C.S. and as Senior Warden at St. Thomas. Both will be effective as of January 1st. After that it's move to Alabama and solitude.

October 8, 2002
  I tried to read tonight rather than looking at the baseball playoffs. This gave me a chance to test my night vision for reading. I still have lots of difficulty but it was possible for a short time. Thanksgiving sings within me. I may regain my sight after all or at least a fair portion of it.

October 14, 2002
  Worked for B.C.S. all day today covering for the staff who had Columbus Day off. Tomorrow is the opening of the satellite office. Blood pressure up today. No

room for denial—I am my own worst enemy. It's time to become my own best friend. Lord show me how.

In mid October B.C.S. opened a satellite office at the Laguna Beach Christian Retreat. We had worked out an arrangement with them that resulted in our using some of their facilities (kitchens, sleeping quarters etc.) that are not used during the winter months. By opening the satellite office we were able to provide beds and hot meals for transients who were passing through on their way to South Florida.

October 16, 2002
The satellite office was open for the second day. We have two transients staying at the retreat. One is a Native American Sioux and the other is a depressed, Anglo-European drunk. The young Native American man is of interest to me. I would like to ask him lots of questions but I can't. It would not be appropriate. All of our clients at B.C.S. are entitled to their privacy. The drunk doesn't interest me as much. I have seen so many of them in the last few years—damaged goods in a world created by God and broken by man.

October 26, 2002
Saturday afternoon, and the week is all but ended. This week I submitted my letter of resignation to Fr. C. at St. Thomas and Ken at B.C.S. and of course told Ben and Margaret at the office. The word is out. Jack and Olga are moving.

October 28, 2002
I'm going to solitude in Alabama not to seek and find God (I think I know where he is), and not to put God in a cage and say, "Come see, here is God." I am not out to satisfy years of doubt once and for all, or to justify following the question wherever it will lead me. Nor do I start out questioning the presence of God in the world. That is a given. I just want to spend my time noticing God and savoring our time together. Olga just came in to say that we needed to find cooks for this afternoon at the satellite office by 4:00. The people who had volunteered for this afternoon couldn't make it. Where are you in this God? I sense that you have been in Beach Care Services from the beginning. There have been times when I have sensed this more than other times, but recently I have not taken the opportunity to just step back and see how much you are present. I would like to do that.

October 31, 2002
Spent an hour and a half this morning just doing nothing, well not quite nothing. I read six pages of Buber's *Eclipse of God*. But, most of the time I just closed my eyes and did nothing. Then I went to this month's B.C.S. staff meeting and told the most dedicated group of volunteers I have ever known that Olga and I will be moving. Beach Care Services will go on as usual. I want very much to believe that.

November 6, 2002

I will not write about the flock of sandpipers that I saw on the beach this morning. Rather, I will write about being one with the ebb and flow, and the perpetual motion of a hundred or more little legs of a flock of sandpipers at the water's edge. From this experience came knowledge of sorts, but beyond that I stood in awe of the work of the Creator. That's as close to solitude as I have been in a long time.

November 9, 2002

It occurred to me today that work on behalf of the church and work on behalf of the needy have not taught me to love. They have taught me about love, and they have taught me about the need for love. They have taught me about the commandment to love, but they have not taught me to love. Work in the church and work on behalf of the needy has taught me to respect and have good feelings about others who share my views of service, but not those who don't. I must frankly admit that engaging in this work has brought me in face to face contact with lots of people who don't give a damn about the needy because the needy are undeserving, or because acknowledging them in public is bad for business or politics in the community, or because the church should be directing it's energy and money to those who deserve it, not to the poor who make them feel uncomfortable. These people have not taught me to love, they have taught me that I am capable of having negative feelings about many of my neighbors. I need to get away from this temptation to be negative and judgmental about others. I need to experience solitude for at least long enough to heal so that I can again enter the world with real charity for others, a charity that I don't have right now.

November 11, 2002

As I think about leaving the Beach, two things keep coming to mind. One is that I want to get away clean while the almost idyllic aura of the success of Beach Care Services surges through me. The second is the increasing realization that I am caught up in what Albert Camus called the trial symbol in a life in which we are both judge and defendant. It seems that there is no realistic escape from this condition of malignancy. It's a game that people play, the game of judgment in order to shore up our false self.

December 2, 2002

Back from another Thanksgiving trip to visit with the family in Alabama. A year after first dreaming of a retreat in the Alabama woods, that dream is close to fulfillment. Our cabin is under roof and our hope is that it will be ready by the first of January.

December 3, 2002

Go there and experience as much of a life of solitude as possible. Describe the world of solitude around me as well as I can. Describe my awareness of things happening within me as richly as I can. Be aware of the distinctions between being influenced by the world around me and the world within me that I bring to the experience. Be aware of judgments and values and where they come from. Be as descriptive as I can, not judgmental.

December 12, 2002

Throughout the ages, people have seen reality through the flavor and characteristics of the era in which they have lived. During the age of enlightenment and baroque period people tended to see the world through intellectual structures mixed with passion. The romanticists saw the world through heroic emotions of a great transcendent spirit moving through the universe. The modernists saw the world through theory and the predictability of man's behavior. The post-modernists see the world through a created perspective of the way they want the world to be at the moment. When I go into solitude I want to try to put aside previous thoughts and presuppositions of what my world will or should look like. I just want to try to describe it as it is. I don't know if this is possible or even how to do it. If I can't do it then that's O.K., but at least I want to try.

December 27, 2002

We are here in Alabama for Christmas. Progress on the house is slow. In one sense this is good. It gives me some opportunity to assess what I am doing rather than getting completely caught up in frantic packing, moving and such. One thing seems clear now. I will be going to Alabama to just be and be surprised by the awe. This is more like what I expected prayer to be. But first I will need to recognize that I will probably become anxious because I am not "accomplishing" something. I need to learn not to be anxious or feel guilty at just being.

January 6, 2003

Strange thoughts breaking out of meditation today: one of them had to do with God and the Devil as metaphors that describe different aspects of a single reality. I need to retain this for future meditation. The concept of God and the Devil, presumably as polar opposites, in a relationship of oneness and wholeness disturbs my western sensibility. Are peace and conflict, love and hate, dynamic growth and entropy not polar opposites at all, but aspects of the same thing? Earlier today when I thought about polar opposites being one, I wondered if I had not experienced a crack in the wall that might become a window or a door revealing a different view of the world.

January 14, 2003

We made settlement on our house in Florida last Friday but we won't leave here until the end of February. Ahead of us is packing and moving. I am wiped out. I didn't know how much I had really invested in this.

January 27, 2003

I pulled my back packing boxes and have been in bad pain for two weeks. This was aggravated by a fall I had a couple of days ago. It was after dark and

I took Buster out for a walk. He was on the leash. All of a sudden a Boxer from down the street appeared and started chasing Buster around me in a circle. Dogs barking and snarling, me yelling and before I knew it, I was hog-tied by Buster's leash and went down like a tree in the woods felled by a logger, hit my head, bent my glasses and took care of my back once and for all. In between going to the doctor for pain pills and muscle relaxants, having x-rays on my head and getting my glasses fixed, came a shaft of light. My C.D. player, a fifteen year old single disc model, died and I got a replacement that loads five discs and cost less than the one disc model. Now I can put all the psalms for the day on the C.D. player and have them sung by English cathedral choirs while I read along in King James language with an old 1928 Prayer Book. What a wonderful way to do the psalms from the Office morning and night. I get a real sense of God's presence in human history dating back for over three thousand years. It gives me a real sense of perspective.

January 30, 2003

My back is still giving me lots of grief. I am convinced that I did hurt it packing, but it was the fall I took with Buster that did it in.

I was reading Merton's Journal entry of July 8, 1967. It gives me motivation to live each moment to the fullest including the moment of death. It gives good reason to root my faith in unknowing. There is no scientific reason to do otherwise. I carry this with me as I prepare to enter solitude.

We left the key with Tony and Judy next door to give to the new owners, got in the car and drove to Alabama. The Beach became a part of the present that we called our past. Alabama and solitude lay ahead of us as an unknown present. When I said my goodbyes to friends, neighbors and people I had worked with, I did not say "goodbye, see you soon." I said, "Goodbye. You and I need to realize that we may never see each other again." To some, in addition, I said, "I will miss you."

## NOTES

1. Thomas Merton, *Turning Toward the World: The Pivotal Years*, ed. Victor Kramer (San Francisco: Harper Collins, 1996), 197.
2. Merton, *Turning Toward the World*, 218.
3. Merton, *Turning Toward the World*, 291.
4. Merton, *Turning Toward the World*, 321.
5. Merton, *Turning Toward the World*, 327.

## Chapter Nine

# Solitude at Last

The year began like almost every other of recent memory. When I got up it was New Year's morning. Once again the time had come to start a new calendar and remember to write the new-year on my checks. It seemed that nothing much had happened, but it had. Our house on the Beach had been sold, and we had started packing in preparation for a move to a cedar cabin in the woods off a dirt road in Eastern Alabama. Martha had her day in the sun; it was now time to give Mary a chance to try her hand in shaping a spirituality that was more consistent with who I was. Until the late 1980's my spirituality had been grounded in the beliefs of the Church, but it was wanting in personal relevance. It lacked a faith that grew from a personal relationship with God, an understanding of creation as a dynamic and ongoing process that I was involved in, a way of thinking about God as an expression of love working in the universe, and the idea of a spiritual self. Years before when I began my spiritual journey, I first became aware of the feelings of transformation that are associated with the practice of contemplative prayer. More recently I felt the stimulating rush that comes with helping the needy and working on social problems, but I had not experienced the long term effects of solitude on the transformation of self, or the awareness of each day unfolding, largely free of a willfully oriented agenda often imposed by others.

Perhaps the first hint of what my new life was really going to be like came with the early realization that the life of solitude that I had chosen was a lot less austere and a lot more enjoyable than I had imagined. From my view I had not been very successful in being a secular contemplative while living in the midst of a driving, over busy, materialistic society. Perhaps I could do better living on the margin of that society.

In solitude, each day became a revelation. Without the constant conflict caused by challenges to my true self by society, my true self found new energy with which to develop in its own direction, and my spiritual self grew. Each day became an opportunity to live in a setting in which it was less and less difficult for me to distinguish between the false gods of the world, and the Master of the Universe. I thrived on an awareness of God's presence, and I knew what it was like to feel whole and at peace days on end.

One of the most revealing discoveries to come out of extended solitude was how much it had in common with *via negitiva*. Both the negative way and solitude required the divestment of old beliefs and habits. During my ongoing experience of *via negitiva* I had challenged and discarded many of the beliefs and values that had served me for so long in my religious and spiritual life. Then one day, I realized that I had little left of my original religious beliefs, and that I needed to develop a new belief system that I could use to guide me up and out of the void, and point me in a new direction. I found that the old ones no longer helped me chart the new path that I was on.

Solitude quickly made it clear that many old ways of living, old habits and understandings, and old values that once had a place in the intense encounters of society, were of limited use in solitude. My first thought was that I needed to build new understandings, habits, and values that applied to my new existence, an existence that was largely internally directed rather than an existence directed by the people, institutions, and cultural values that surrounded me.

There were some new habits related to self-directed behavior that I needed to develop, but of equal importance, there were many social habits that I needed to give up. Many of these were ways of living that I had spent a lifetime practicing. Perhaps the most obvious was a dependence on clock time and the calendar. I now had little use for these social conventions. They had been necessary to keep the social world around me from flying apart, but they had little use in solitude. I stopped constantly looking at my watch; finally I took it off, and have not worn it since. I needed to develop my own patterns of life that would get me through the day with an unhurried sense of satisfaction. There were a handful of cases in which I felt some urgency to dovetail my schedule with other people's schedule, but most of the time I was on my own.

At first I found myself with time on my hands and asking, "What shall I do now?" but within a few weeks, a rhythm of moving through the day without stress had replaced meeting deadlines, meeting appointments on time, and getting all the work done for the day. This was replaced with sunup, sundown, the cool of the morning, the heat of the day, and things to attend to as they came up.

One thing that living in solitude required was learning to give up a dependence on motivation that came from the people around me, and to replace it with a motivation for living that came from within me. Fortunately I found this much easier to do than I had expected. Indeed I found that I really enjoyed it. I found new meaning to Merton's words when he spoke of the challenges facing those who would follow a monastic life in the second half of the Twentieth Century, "From now on, Brother, everybody stands on his own feet."[1] Unlike what I had imagined the demands of solitude to be, the greatest demand became assuming responsibility for my own decisions. There was no one to blame for failure other than myself, and no one to fallback on to cover up my inadequacies. Society no longer became a thicket in which to hide. I was on my own in the presence of God. I became responsible for scheduling what I did each day. I developed and enforced my own discipline, and set my own standards. I developed my own goals and monitored my own progress. I identified and met my own needs. I became responsible for my own actions, and for living a life that was personally productive and personally fulfilling. Other than Olga and Buster there was no one else for me to be responsible to.

During the first year we were in Alabama, contact with other people was seriously curtailed. I entered solitude, and for days on end the only people with whom I had any significant contact were Olga and Buster. Olga was amazingly good in giving me free rein. She saved up matters to talk about until late in the afternoon at which time subjects such as doctor's appointments, trips to town for food and other such errands were discussed and planned. But, during much of the day she left me alone in solitude to adapt and grow, guided by my natural inclinations. She gave me the free space I needed even though her choice would have been to subtly remind me of what she thought I should be doing. Giving up social involvement for solitude required a whole new approach to life for her. It required a sacrifice of a big piece of who she had been for most of her life. Her dominant way of expressing love was doing things for others that ultimately placed demands on others by making them dependent on her. Her new approach required a very different conception of love. She opened the circle when her previous inclination would have been to close the circle. It wasn't that she experienced a miraculous, overnight, transformation, but it was much more rapid and consistent than I would have expected. It was almost as if she had been building up to this moment. She became more and more independent of me, and more ready to trust herself than she had ever been. She became, more than at any time in her life, a personification of "All shall be well, and all shall be well, and all manner of things shall be well even if I'm not the one who organizes things."

Buster, on the other hand, would have none of this approach. His philosophy of need gratification was based on a model in which he was the stimulus and I represented the response repertoire that he desired at any time of the day or night, for any need that he chose: attention, a soft place to sleep, a person to take him out, food, and finally at the end of each day someone to turn down his bed where he could make his nest for the night. The next morning it started all over again. I loved Buster, and my feelings of love for him were, in part, tied to fulfilling his needs. After all, I said, "Love is partially grounded in fulfilling obligations to others, and servanthood is an extension of that love." Together they lead to a feeling of wholeness and a feeling of purposiveness that is the hallmark of the true self lived out in the presence of another. It was Buster and Olga who, in different ways, taught me about love in the solitary life.

Then, one day it became startlingly clear to me that solitude was what I had been searching for all along, not just the contemplative life. I had started seventeen years earlier by asking myself the questions, "Is it really possible to be a contemplative in today's world? Is it possible for me?" When I asked those questions I had little real appreciation for what I was asking. I really should have been asking, "Is it possible for me to be a solitary in today's world?" It was solitude that would nurture contemplation, not the other way around.

It was solitude that enabled me to discover that union with God was not only possible, but that it was always available. But, unlike what I previously thought union with God to be, I found that it had nothing directly to do with searching for God. After all, I lived in God's presence all the time. Union with God had little to do with a prayer induced state of mind. Union with God was dependent on my being willing to set aside my agenda and my willfulness and just let myself become engaged in gazing passively at the world around me where God already was present in a bird's foot violet growing by the side of the road, or in Olga or Buster, or people I met in town on my occasional rounds. Union was always a function of a relationship that involved just being in the presence of God, not changing in any way the object of perception in which God was present, but in just accepting it and being totally present for it: the person, the wild flower, the tree frog or whatever it was, then being aware of God's presence, and then losing all distinction between the perceived and the perceiver. When this happened, a relationship occurred that I now recognize as union.

That is what I had been looking for, and solitude made it possible for me to see it. Solitude made it possible for me to experience God in ways that I had hoped to develop previously but seldom experienced. Solitude enabled God to grow into a reality that for me was a lot more expansive than I had previously experienced. God burst the walls of the house of religion and entered fully into the universe. And this happened even as the commandment to love others remained as demanding as ever. Solitude is not a place to hide any more than the thickets of society are a place to hide.

Solitude is not a place to escape from love. It is a setting for bonding with the spiritual energy of the universe. Love, more than any other aspect of the experience of union with God, seems to be the one that is either most distorted, most corrupted, most deformed or just ignored in our society today. In one segment of society after another the sacramental meaning of love is twisted into material, physical, emotional or intellectual self-satisfaction, or simply pushed aside by indifference, anxiety, power or pride. Solitude by its very nature limits the opportunities for society to corrupt the sacramental meaning of love that is an essential component of union with God. The love of the true self is grounded in an awareness of God's unconditional and extravagant love that is showered on each of his creations, a shower of love that makes it possible to give away the true self without losing anything. Only when I accepted the depth of the well of God's love did I realize that the love of the spiritual self, like the well of God's love, is eternally full and it is that love that continually joins with God in the rhythmic dance of the universe.

Solitude enabled me to see the futility of my frenzied interaction with my false self as it fed on the passion fruits so readily available when I was in society. Solitude enabled me to see how the addictive qualities of many of those fruits deluded me into believing that the fruit is there to be exploited when in fact it was I who was being exploited by those who grew and marketed the fruit. Solitude made it possible for me to get a grasp on the differences between being addicted to products of the culture and choosing to creatively use products of the culture as sources of energy for growth. Solitude had a way of enabling me to see both the false self and the true self working in my life. And, with that clarity of vision, I could see choices that I had never seen before. These choices led to growth in my ability to love. These choices had always been there, but for me, solitude finally made it possible to perceive a new world of freedom and choice.

Some people, particularly true extroverts, can live a balanced life in the midst of society today and preserve their integrity. I was unable to do so. It was necessary for me to move to the margin of society to get my bearings, and find my true home.

All of this was ahead of me as I packed box after box in preparation for our move to Alabama.

February 15, 2003

We have been packing on and off for a month. Moving day is six days away. I have been able to keep up with evening Psalms, but all else has fallen away to preparations for moving. I hope we don't try to unpack in less than a month. If this can be done, solitude should start in April.

I can't remember having a day of joy in the past six months. It has just been one day after another, like one step after another on a long march. Pick 'em up and put 'em down one after another. April will come. Spring will come. Things will be different.

What an irony it would be if after all these years I had a chance for the warmth of real solitude and no light or heat was left, only cold ashes.

February 20, 2003

Tomorrow we leave for Alabama. Pam is here to help with the last details of packing. Soon we will be going out to get some supper. Tomorrow we move and a new life begins. I am starting to feel better already.

March 3, 2003

We are here! Since Tuesday we have been unpacking boxes, setting up a washing machine, and moving furniture around. I think that Olga is pleased with the potential of our cabin in the woods, and I am delighted to see her so excited. As far as my office is concerned, only my journal has been unpacked; all of my books and other things remain in boxes. It will be well into next week before they are gotten to. Right now its dishes and lamps, and towels and sheets and blankets and clean clothes to wear that take priority. But even now I can see that this is an environment for solitude. No T.V. yet, and we do not get any cable out here, antenna T.V. doesn't work, and Direct T.V. may be a problem because of the tall trees that surround us.

March 5, 2003

Boxes still to be unpacked, mostly in my office and in the cellar. Life has gone into slow motion. Went shopping today for bathroom fixtures (towel rods, toilet paper holders, etc.). Spent most of the rest of the day installing them without tearing the walls up. The telephone was out all day. Got the C.D. player up and going, but now there are wires all over the place. Need to figure out what to do with them and how to do it, otherwise I'll be tripping all over them. No time yet taken for extended meditation; that was the deal with Olga, first we get the living area up and functioning. I look forward to a disciplined life of prayer. Too little discipline makes a man loose and easy which can be enjoyable for a while but then becomes questionable. So far I don't miss people, and the question of, "Where is God?" has not loomed large as of yet. I am comfortable, not hungry, not cold, not bored. I just am, and I have been so for eight days now.

March 6, 2003

Another cloudy day. Rain at daybreak, and light rain continues through the morning. Still doing things to make a nest for Olga and Buster. Tired, but this is a good day. Progress is being made. Graham is still trying to get Direct T.V. arranged for Olga. No picture yet. Phone has been out for over 24 hours. It will be fixed today they say.

March 9, 2003

Focus still on getting the cabin organized. Worked with Graham today putting in a mailbox up at the road, then unpacked more boxes. I did get a half hour this afternoon for Psalms, and tomorrow I will start Psalms morning and evening. I am really tired, but the internal anger is gone. I have not felt anger, anxiety or any other symptoms of depression for almost two weeks. Buster just came in; he said it was time for a walk and then to bed.

March 10, 2003

Things continue to fall into place. One thing that became obvious today is that some barriers will have to be erected to protect solitude. The family is caring, but can be a bit over solicitous. Olga has her affiliation needs. Buster is Buster. There is still a world around me that creates demands, but it need not do so. I must remember that though some interruptions are self-serving, most of the time people are just trying to be social, they don't violate my solitude intentionally. I have not gotten into a routine of solitude yet. So far only a little time in the morning and evening for Psalms and journaling. Buster usually respects my solitude when we walk before breakfast. He becomes absorbed by the sounds and smells and sights of the Alabama woods, and we both get in a little contemplative time.

March 13, 2003

Settling in is still underway. We are now in the furniture readjustment and picture-hanging mode. For Olga this is important. I still hope to be in a more stable and substantial life of solitude by the time we have been here a month. I am now into a pattern of morning and evening prayer. I am encouraged. As usual the Psalms are very penetrating. They contain so much reason for hope, and yet at the same time they are realistic and down to earth. By using a set of compact disks produced by Priory Records, I am able to hear the Psalms appointed for the day sung by English cathedral choirs. It's a moving experience. Several commentaries and modern translations help me get through the language of the King James Bible as I follow the Psalms in the 1928 Episcopal Prayer Book. All in all it is working out well. I think that it's useful to be reminded frequently that the passions, problems and joys of human beings three thousand years ago are those that we still live with today.

March 15, 2003

Rain last night and it is still raining this morning. The woods are dripping. The Psalms remind me each day that I am among the fortunate. Life was so fearful and brutal for so many of the people that I worked with on the Beach. So many were lost and cut adrift. They truly are needy and really do need help. But they are lost in their own closed circle of despair and don't know how to get out.

Perhaps some day I will return to working with them, but for now I have set a year aside for solitude in which to find new discoveries in life. For now this is my life, and for now I am enjoying every minute of it. I seem to have left my anger and anxiety behind, but it's a little soon to tell.

As I think back on it, there have been many periods in my life when I subscribed to the "no pain no gain" philosophy of self- discipline. But I was never very successful in following that way. The natural sequence almost always followed a predictable course. Pain led to avoidance; avoidance led to guilt, guilt led to anger, and anger led to many emotional states that I would call anything but growthful. The big thing that I learned from this approach is that the world is filled with pain that is mostly self-inflicted.

March 16, 2003

Got the spring issue of *The Beach Care News Letter* today in the mail. It was exciting to share in their work again, if only in words.

It has been another cloudy, cool day filled with deep satisfaction. Solitude was broken only by a brief visit from Pam who stopped in for a cup of coffee, and Thomas who stopped by late this afternoon to see what was going on. We played a game of chess.

March 17, 2003

Another rainy day. It has got to stop raining some day, but not today. Through the gloomy daybreak I hear the stirring strains of the 57th Psalm sung by the choir of The Lichfield Cathedral.

> My heart is fixed, Oh God, my
> heart is fixed;
> I will sing and give praise.

This is a world filled with rain. It is a world filled with pain, despair, selfishness, and ego satisfaction. It's in every corner I look into, if I look for it. But beneath all of this is God's goodness, if I look for it. I will sing and give praise. There is hope, and there is an abundance of it. I have not felt better. Solitude is strong medicine.

I hung a plaque over the front door today that reads *Vocatus atguenon vocatus deusaderit* (bidden or not bidden the gods are present). It is late afternoon and still raining. When we get a few days of sun and warmth the woods will burst into flower and leaf.

March 18, 2003

The fourth week of our life of solitude here in Alabama begins today, and it begins with another cloudy morning. Apparently there is a deep southern dip in the jet stream pumping moisture up from the Gulf. It will be with us for a while longer.

Let my true self be transformed in solitude. Let it work on me and shape me. This is the power of solitude. I did not come here with a plan for restoration. I came willing to be transformed.

Hog plum, yellow jasmine, sparkle berry, and red bud are in bloom. What will follow?

March 19, 2003

Another gray and somber day yet pregnant with possibilities. Our government prepares for war in Iraq again and the cost it will inflict on human lives and the Earth. One editorial in the local newspaper gave subdued support, and there were peace vigils in town. But, cloudy skies and threats of war not withstanding, spring in Eastern Alabama is about to break out. I weep for the sadness that will be heaped on the world by this war.

March 20, 2003

I understand that the Second Persian Gulf War started last night. The government has fulfilled its promise. The collective ego has been released from its cage. There are none who can stop the death and destruction. It will eat a path through Iraq until it gets in its own way. Then it will eat itself.

This afternoon I took a walk with Pam, the first since we arrived here almost a month ago. All previous contacts with her, or Graham or even Olga have focused on the details of moving in, doing house and yard things, getting bank accounts, legal matters like an Alabama will, change of address notices to people, finding out where to go in town for what, etc. In short, living in the woods has not been solitude so far. But it was great to talk with Pam about the plans for solitude that lie ahead. We parted by agreeing to fix some time to get together and talk. It's a bit ironic that we need to plan to get together for spiritual reasons in a place like this.

March 21, 2003

The day has not really begun yet for the sun. It has not risen over the ridge to the East, but when it does it will be one of the few sunny days we have had since moving here.

Another day of getting things done in town and around the house. Olga will make this little house of ours a candidate for the Home and Garden Show even if it eats us up; that's her bliss. But, I must not let myself get caught up in her activity, and yet I must accept her idea of what is real and important for her. But for the sake of this venture into solitude and my own quest for bliss, I must put a fence around her demands for my time and for material perfection before it beats me down and consumes me.

March 22, 2003

The sun has not yet risen, but I can tell that it will be clear and cool with a hint of spring in the air. I have identified the first casualty of solitude. Its name is smugness. From such an idyllic spot it is easy to inflate one's fortune in the world and look with smugness at those who live another life. Solitude is *a* way to God not *the* way. There is no place for smugness on this path that I have chosen.

March 24, 2003

My first day of planned solitude. Awoke at 5:30 and was well into morning meditation by 6:00. I think that Merton had a profound insight into the true nature of solitude as actually being active, not passive. He realized that solitude demands that their be a purposeful drive from within to motivate one's life. In order for that need to thrive I must first break down habits that I have brought with me from the active life, habits that no longer serve a purpose. I need to break free from the restrictions of society that are no longer useful, and develop a reason for being that is self directed and self-sustaining. This seems to be the challenge of the solitary life. This is quite different from the protected, fenced-in life of resignation and quietude with which solitude is sometimes associated. I am not surprised to find that a solitary life requires considerable self-direction. This is a habit that if I do not have I will need to develop. And, self-direction requires self-discipline to prevent life from becoming a candy land of irresponsibility.

The active life, on the other hand, seeks direction from the stimuli that surround us. One approach that the active life takes is to manipulate the world that surrounds us by turning it to profit, or by destroying it, or rendering it impotent if it constitutes a threat. A second approach is to see the world around us as filled with messengers who bring us knowledge and beauty that we can use to enhance the quality of life. In either case the world is still there. The active person turns out for direction. The solitary person turns in to the source.

For a society to exist for any length of time, there need to be common understandings that people will agree on. This is necessary for society because even though living under these agreements may impinge on immediate wishes or desires, in the long run, living by the agreements enhances social freedom. These understandings are called social norms and expectations. They allow a complex society to hold together and work. Regrettably, people being what they are seem unable to live by these understandings on their own. We seem to need the threat of sanctions to keep us on the path. In society we are limited in what we can do in the name of individual freedom without sanctions being invoked if we violate societal expectations. Some social institutions use restriction of privileges, or punishment. Other institutions emphasize the use of guilt. From the beginning, families and churches and schools have been big on making violators feel guilty as a form of sanction.

It is very easy to confuse social norms and expectations with personal values. When I began a life of solitude it was seldom necessary for me to behave consistently with the expectations of society. It was seldom necessary because I lived in solitude on the edge of society. What proved to be more useful were a set of personal values to guide my life as long as I remained in solitude. When Olga and I talked or had meals together or when I reentered society to go to the store, I became a social person. I then needed to attend to what that society expected.

At first I did not understand and apply a distinction between society's expectations and my personal expectations, and their consequences for my life of solitude. When I passed through the door to solitude it would have been helpful to remember that the rules changed. But, for a while I continued to be concerned about such things as what time it was, and I was still oversensitive to the niceties of social expectations. In fact, I had little need to be concerned about how things were done by others, how I dressed or what people thought of me. It wasn't that I rejected these social ways of behaving, it was that much that previously was a regular part of my life in society, and had served a purpose there, no longer applied because I wasn't living in society. I didn't stop bathing or shaving, or eating or sleeping on a regular basis. I valued these things, and they were a regular part of my routine because I wanted them to be. But I did these things in a time frame that suited my daily pattern of life. On the other hand I found that I had a lot more difficulty in leaving the world of "shoulds" behind me. These were the "shoulds" that previously had been invoked by the family, church and workplace to establish and maintain control over my behavior, thoughts and feelings. They no longer applied. And yet, it wasn't long before I found that I was applying sanctions to myself for what I thought was a violation of a principal of social responsibility. I found myself questioning whether I should be living my life in an idyllic setting of solitude when so many people living in society were needy in so many ways. But even worse, I began to feel guilty. If I had continued to follow this line of thought I might have come to the conclusion that the way to deal with my guilt was to return to society and once again participate in a life that I had just left and had said was inconsistent with who I was. Obviously, "misery loves company" was not a useful approach to take. I soon realized that I was not responsible for the dysfunctional lives lived by people, but I was responsible for my own life in solitude. I could have compassion for those people, but I could not solve their problems by feeling guilty or returning to the mainstream of society. What I needed to do was to reach out and help them from the edge, not jump back into their turmoil in order to save them.

I ran into this situation early in my solitude. At first it came out in the form of "shouldn't I be doing something to help the needy like I was doing on the Beach? Isn't that my responsibility?" Clearly, I needed to attend to the nagging feelings of social responsibility and guilt that I brought with me into solitude from society. In time I would work out what I considered to be a satisfactory approach to individual responsibility, but when I first entered solitude I carried attitudes with me that interfered with my life of solitude. Those attitudes were filled with social "shoulds" and consequences that may have worked in society but had no place in the solitary life. It was very freeing to shed that baggage.

March 25, 2003

Sun, blue skies, crisp nights, even a chill in the air till noon. The jet stream has moved. Again this morning I thought, "should I be here in this idyllic world of solitude when so many people need help just to get through the day with some degree of dignity?" And then I caught myself. I am focusing on the world I left behind me. I came here to experience solitude for at least a year. That year has just started. I have much to live for and to learn. My inner directed self says, "You are acting like a spoiled child, you're reaching for something else before you even eat what you have before you, one thing at a time. Solitude will be your life for a year. Then we will see."

March 26, 2003

I have all the time I want to do nothing, or to do something else that I choose to do. The healthy solitary life is found in making life-sustaining choices. I live on the margin of a very complex society. How I react to making those choices will, in large measure, determine the success of my life as a solitary.

I went into town yesterday afternoon to get an Alabama drivers license and automobile tags. At the license bureau and county court house life seemed right out of another time, but the tags and a driver's license were dated 2003. If they had been dated 1903 or even 2103 it wouldn't have made a whole lot of difference because my life would be much the same.

If I reentered the active life that I came from, my behavior and thoughts would be substantially determined by the community: the government, the church, the economic system, the work place, the members of the club and the pace of life lived by people in a fast moving industrial world. But in solitude my choices don't conflict with the standards of modern society. I am free to choose. In society people and institutions don't always agree on standards, and when there is a difference of opinion there may be conflict, but in general, people know what they are expected to do and the society works fairly smoothly. When they violate those expectations they usually know what the consequences will be.

As long as I can stay away from society, there will be little conflict. But this does not mean that I have no standards. I do, but I have to create my own standards and use those standards in making my own choices. If things don't go well I can't invoke, "I was only doing what I thought was expected of me."

March 27, 2003

In some way charity must be an integral part of the healing process I have entered into. This life has too much potential for, "I'll do my thing and mind my business, and you do your thing and mind your business and it'll be O.K. Just let me alone." Society will not let me get away with that for long, even on its margin, and I think that I realize that this attitude would not be healthy for me. To be healthy, solitude must be lived in a state of love. I need to remember that. It may be my greatest challenge.

Today was the day for wisteria. I had noticed some yesterday driving into town. But today I couldn't miss it. My nose, notoriously retarded since my smoking days, was overwhelmed by the scent. Then I looked up, and there were clusters of purple mingled with emerging leaves. Buster and I stopped and just took it all in for a few minutes then we moved on up the hill on our walk.

March 28, 2003

I awoke this morning to see six deer down by the stream. The presence of my white undershirt at the window spooked them. They jumped the stream and made their way up the hill and over the ridge.

Later when walking Buster we discovered pink wild azaleas. I have seen yellow ones before and seen pictures of white ones but these were my first pink, native azaleas. Their flowers are a work of art.

This morning I worked on my journals and realized that I have twenty-seven volumes, including nine volumes that cover the period before my retirement. I had almost forgotten that. The process of reading them and making notes on them goes smoothly. In a month or so I may have a sense of what is really in those twenty-seven volumes.

March 29, 2003

One thing that I have learned so far is that days of the week make no particular contribution to living in solitude. Such meaning as they may have is limited to my minimal contact with society such as setting and keeping a doctor's appointment on Wednesday at 2:00 in the afternoon. I fit into the doctor's schedule, or I don't see him. If church is at 10:00 on Sunday morning, I show up on Sunday at 10:00, or I don't go to church. My choice is defined by society's schedule insofar as I wish to relate to it. It is almost never the other way around.

In a world of solitude, the rhythms and routines of each day are defined by me, and they had better provide a structure, a gyroscope to keep me in balance, or my life could go to hell in a hand-basket very quickly. That structure comes from within. It is not imposed by others. Without the fabric of a discipline, solitary life would be a torturous trip. This is a significant difference between the social and the solitary life. The social world gives structure and direction that is largely defined by others. In solitude the balanced life is given by the gyroscope within me. If I don't have one I better get one.

The more I reflect on this, the more I become aware of the difference between "what time is it" and "it's time for." Right now my stomach says it's time for breakfast.

March 30, 2003

It rained hard last night, but the front has gone through. Also last night I had a very vivid dream that involved people from various past moments in my life. It was a potpourri of experiences in different settings, but throughout the dream I was aware that I was always late in making connections with others in my life. Clearly an anxiety dream, I did not awaken in a panicked sweat, but it was a very vivid dream.

I am now settled into solitude, and I can think of no reason why I should not continue with my life as planned. Things have gone well in so far as working with the journals is concerned. Less time spent in formal contemplation than I expected. Olga seems to be adapting well, actually better than I had even hoped. Today is Sunday and we may go to church—we'll see.

After lunch Olga, Buster and I took a walk and saw coral honeysuckle in first bloom, blood red like the red buckeye I saw yesterday. It's all here, but if I blink I'll miss it, except for the dogwood; they're so thick I couldn't miss them.

March 31, 2003

A clear cold morning, Olga brought plants in last night, it was a good thing. It went down to below thirty degrees. Coffee tastes particularly good.

April 1, 2003

I was working today with a journal that I wrote fifteen years ago. This evening at Vespers I sat quietly just letting my mind go where it wanted, and my discursive, meditative mind focused on my life during the late 1980's. So long as I am able to keep things in perspective, this is probably a good experience. Past moments that I had forgotten about, gushed out from my subconscious. It's not all pretty, and about as close to a reconstruction of that period of spiritual development as I want to get.

April 3, 2003

Pam brought us some information about a food bank that serves the county. The materials included applications for volunteers. I know that the pull of this will be great and that it might end up being the first intentional violation of my solitude. I thought that it would take longer before I had that kind of temptation.

April 5, 2003

After a string of clear cool days with highs in the seventies, it looks like we are in for a few cloudy days with thundershowers.

Birds have finally found the feeder so I need to get the bird book and binoculars out. I can already see that there are some that I have not met before. Ruby throated hummingbirds showed up today so I need to get their feeder up. In spite of the damage done to the woodland close to the house during construction, I saw several trillium that were spared. What a pleasant surprise.

This afternoon I had a stimulating conversation with Pam that centered around Henry James and the fertile environment for though in the United States at the end of the 19th century. She does provide a kindred spirit to rub shoulders with once in a while, and I do appreciate the opportunity.

April 7, 2003

Strong thunderstorms this morning before breakfast they lasted a couple of hours and it is still raining. The creek will be rising again and mud is still up to our ankles.

Today I started the third week of solitude. The time has been mostly filled with work on my journals, and morning and evening prayer focuses on the Psalms and some meditation. So far I have had no sustained, serious time in contemplation. I am aware of a need to fix this. My prayer is too busy for my comfort.

April 12, 2003

Solitude was broken by a phone call answered by Olga. The family back East is in trouble again. The membrane that separates us from the world is semi-permeable.

April 17, 2003

Sweet bush, dewberry and swamp buttercup, how the days and now weeks go by. It is easy to lose track. The dating of my journal entries reminds me of the artificial structure of the life I have left, but the rhythm of the daily routine creates its own pace. The rhythm comes from inside not from Greenwich and the clocks that regulate business. No clocks to punch, no bells to ring and tell me what to do, or tell me that I am late. An interior rhythm has replaced that.

April 19, 2003

Psalm 88 is about as close to an expression of lack of faith as I can imagine. At first it seemed like an expression of ultimate despair, and then I realized that starting with verse one the psalmist really had a relationship with God. For the person who wrote this psalm and the millions of others since then who have read it, there is a relationship. They are all talking to God. You don't do that unless you have some faith, or at least belief

April 20, 2003

Prayer is like resting with a friend. My friend and I sit together just to catch our breath and to relax a bit. Neither says anything. We just rest, aware of each other's presence. There is no pretense, no need to impress. At first I am aware of feeling rushed. My mind keeps running. I want to calm myself before I talk, if I talk at all. But if I do talk there will be no topic of conversation that is taboo. I will share what is on my mind. We both seem to know what the other is thinking anyway.

Today I experienced a bit of disappointment, nothing more, and really no big deal. One of the people that I had worked with closely at Beach Care Services was going to Atlanta to have a consultation on a medical issue, and Olga though that it would be nice to invite her and her husband to visit with us on their way to Atlanta, and spend the night. When Olga and I had a conversation about this I reminded her that we had agreed that we would not have visitors during our first year of solitude. Olga said that she didn't think that something like inviting the couple to stay over night would count, and it became obvious that she was at a loss as to what to do because she thought that they would think it strange that we didn't invite them to stay. She didn't know what to tell them. It turns out that she had only confided in one person on the Beach about my year of solitude because she thought that others would not understand. Other people would think that I was a bit odd to want to live in solitude for a year. She would be embarrassed to tell them that her husband wanted to become a marginal person. I saw this clearly for the first time. Olga hasn't left society yet. It is still very much with her.

April 22, 2003

There are voices that still call to me to join them in the world. There are the voices of the needy in the community; there are voices of friends, previous neighbors and colleagues who we left behind when we came to Alabama. Here in Alabama there will be voices of people from church, the nearby university, groups that Pam wants us to join. If I let them in they will swamp me. But Olga's social needs are great. She needs to reach out into the world to get and receive love. Her need to love and be loved is very real.

I must realize that one consequence of solitude is being alone in a circle drawn by me. Olga is not quite in that circle. She stands the closest to me on the edge, but she is still outside the line. She is my most frequent touch point with the world, but she is not here to seek solitude. She is here as a part of a contract that involves my solitude not hers.

I suspect that for the remainder of the year this reality will linger on both sides of the line that separates us. But somehow we each need to walk on our side without violating the line for the other. This may or may not be possible, but it is a hope.

April 23, 2003

How will standing on the edge of the culture and viewing it from there help me to better respond to the Christ in people around me? Or, does solitude have nothing to do with people? Does solitude have to do with my healing and wholeness so that I can better relate to other people as Christ in the world at a later time? This almost sounds like what Anthony and some of the desert fathers were up to.

April 25, 2003

It has been raining again since late yesterday afternoon, hard rain. Severe thunderstorms and tornadoes are predicted in the area starting about 4:30 P.M. Read through more of my journals and made theme cards. Tomorrow I will sort through the cards again and see if anything is taking form, see if any themes are emerging.

April 27, 2003

The front has passed through and today breaks forth cloudless as the sun enters first on the very tops of the trees that surround our little house. Down here in the hollow it takes the first part of the morning before the sun climbs down the towering pines and oaks that for years have made their way to the top of their world. Beneath them now are the second growth of trees that will grow up to take their place, but for now these young ones are overshadowed by the more mature creatures of the forest. In time though the old will fall and nourish those who follow, but for now they stand tall and catch the first rays of the morning sun. This is the rhythm of the universe. It is the ultimate rhythm.

I feel so right about taking this step to solitude. It was not too late. This has been as close to extended joy as I have ever had and it is clear to me that God looms large in this whole process.

Later: Olga just told me that she has been talking with the family back East again. Things are not good, and she is afraid of what will happen. The membrane is pierced again by society. Now where is God in all of this?

April 28, 2003

I sometimes think that God is nowhere and certainly not in the people of the world, but I know better. In a state of absolute pessimism I can stand around and wring my hands and say, "What can be done, we're all losers." Or in a world of absolute fantasy and unrealistic optimism I can stand around and raise my hands, and say, "Fret not, God will beam us up to a seat of honor guaranteed by the many stars in our crown of suffering." Or I can be realistic and say, "Things can get worse and things can get better, and they will." But history illustrates lavishly that when faith and hope and love are applied to difficult situations along with a little creativity, that in the long run things are more likely to get better than to get worse. I opt for this perspective. But, it may take time. We tend to forget that both we and God have got all the time in the world, and maybe even more.

May 1, 2003

Spending too much time talking during prayer. My active mind leads me to talk too much, and then I spend too little time listening. How can I have a healthy relationship with God if I don't spend lots of time listening? Isn't this what a contemplative is, a listener? Isn't contemplative prayer the prayer of the listener?

May 2, 2003

Symbols, whether they be found in music or the graphic arts or in words, are only ways for a person to approach an indescribable God. They are not representations of God.

The mother and the boy were sitting on the back steps. He had a mason jar and a fish net that came with an aquarium. The back yard was filled with katydids, tree frogs and fireflies. They could hear them and see them all over.

Boy: "Why are there so many fireflies?"
Mother: "I don't know, but there certainly are tonight."
Boy: "Where do they come from?"
Mother: "God made them. God's in everything."

Suddenly the boy jumped up and ran into the yard swinging his net. "I got him," he said as he clamped the lid down on the Mason jar. "I've got God in this bottle. I'm going to take him to bed tonight and talk to him."

Twenty years from now will the child still talk with God? Will he still expect God to talk to him? If he remembers his experience with the firefly will he, in twenty years, think of it as a metaphor for his relationship with God?

May 7, 2003

Thunderstorms again last night, cloudy this morning, and it looks like a warm, overcast day ahead. It has started to heat up, but no 90° days yet. Actually it has been a pleasant spring. The amur privet and wild honeysuckle are in bloom everywhere I look. I saw a new plant today, a little low yellow one that I couldn't identify. But up to now the wild azaleas and sweet bush have taken the spring prize.

Reread Merton's *Contemplative Prayer* again today. I had forgotten that it was not written for the average person. Yet it remains relevant so long as I can get through the quotes from medieval saints and the formal theological language of Catholic doctrine. They were the right words for his audience, but they don't always get through to me until I translate them into my own language. I have been spoiled by his journals that are so much freer and subjective.

Each day so far has been a joy. I am excited beyond expectation. In general Olga is becoming far more supportive and accepting of this life than I ever hoped, and this, of course, makes things a lot more enjoyable.

May 22, 2003

One of the things that I see as I read over my journals and spend contemplative time on the fruits that come from reading them is that I am one of those people who has trouble walking and chewing gum at the same time. I can do one or the other fairly well, but not both at the same time. Yesterday I spent the afternoon doing just one thing.

I took a walk and took the camera with me. It was a time of sheer bliss. I don't know what the pictures will look like, but I haven't enjoyed myself so much in a long time. For several hours I was drawn to the wild flowers along the road. The rest of the world did not exist.

June 1, 2003

I wonder what it would be like if I stopped dating my journal entries, made no days special in any way, Sunday for example, and did not create any other culturally oriented bench marks, and lived this way for weeks on end? So far I don't use the phone; I greet people warmly in town and they seem to respond in kind, but so far I have avoided social encumbrances with people, and my contact with tradesmen and doctors is only that which I have need for. But I still wonder what it would be like if even those contacts with society were eliminated.

June 6, 2003

I took a step toward awareness today. During morning prayer time I realized that any desire, or willfulness or even conscious willingness to be one with God is evidence that I am not one with God. Sometimes I realize that I am tensing myself as if to force something to happen. Then, I remember that I must just relax, let desire, willfulness, or even concern about willingness go, and let God possess me. Any attempt to possess God won't work. For me, union with God comes in those moments when I am possessed by God, forget everything else and become completely absorbed in God's incarnate presence in the living organism or inanimate object to which I am attending.

June 7, 2003

Rain again today and more expected tonight and tomorrow. I continue to be plagued by lower back pain particularly when walking down hill. If I had a membership in the exercise and fitness facility run by the local hospital I would be there today. I am feeling the need for exercise. I am doing too much sitting, writing and reading. But rain and mud are everywhere. I need to get a membership at the fitness center, but that would take me into society, so I better avoid that.

I continue to work with my journals each morning, but I am beginning to lose confidence in my ability to tie all the themes together. I promised myself a year's trial with this, and I want to honor that promise.

June 8, 2003

Pouring rain again for most of the night, and it is still raining. Flooding in low areas all over the state. As usual I am up at 6:00 while Olga and Buster sleep. I wouldn't want to take Buster out for a walk now anyhow. So far I have been able to keep my spirits up, but it is touch and go. Everything is damp and soggy. My spirits are damp but not yet soggy.

I have learned a lot so far in this move to solitude, and most of what I have learned is about me. I have no idea how much of my learning applies to any one else. One of the things I have learned is that entry into solitude should take place slowly, and that the time spent in meditation should not exceed an hour or at the most two hours each day, at least at first. Solitude provides a setting for ego confrontation, but it also provides a place for transformation to take place, a place for time spent deliberately with God, a place for becoming aware of God's presence, a place to build an integrated spirituality, a place to be startled by the realization that for the past few moments there has been no distinction between my world and me. Solitude needs to be filled with lots of down time. Time to just be, and not to be filled with all those things that need to be done.

June 9, 2003

I have no sense of where I am on the path I started on eighteen years ago. Certainly I have not arrived, too much of the false and ego self remain. Yet, I have less and less desire to return to the world I left four months ago, although the memory of my work on the Beach remains strong and positive. That was something that I needed to do, but my ego self was beginning to get in the way. I needed solitude to regain balance and take stock.

Last night I had a foretaste of the experience of union with God. I stood alone and a half moon shone through the towering trees. Whip-poor-wills called to each other in the distance, and the tree frogs sang a robust cantata down by the stream. All else was overwhelmingly quiet. I felt God's presence, but I also was aware of mine in the role of observer. Last night we were not one, just two who were very close.

June 13, 2003

Rain again yesterday and it is cloudy and dark this afternoon. Did heavy food shopping yesterday, enough to last a month except for milk and bread and things like that. This should cut down on trips to town.

Work on the journals continues to go well. There is no question that I am enjoying what I am doing. It is creative, satisfying work which is done each day without pressure. It is a delight to set my own pace and be satisfied to get as far as I get each day.

Among the many pleasures of this life are the daily moments of a continuing revelation of God's work seen in the form of butterfly peas, sensitive briar and trumpet vine—blue, violet, red-orange delights of God's fanciful moments of continuing creation. This place is the Valley of the Gods surrounded by Cain and Able multiplied a million fold, each carrying the stamp of their prehensile thumb and their problem-solving mind.

One of the rainiest springs in recent years became one of the most magnificent displays of plant life I ever remember seeing. Winter's drab woodland exploded in color. But for me, the most moving part of the whole display was the uncountable shades of green that composed our scene from the windows by the table at which Olga and I ate our breakfast, lunch and dinner each day while squirrels raided the bird feeder, blue-tailed skinks and geckoes sunned themselves on the porch railing and birds of every hew and color flashed by. It was both exciting and magnificent. Everyday was the day of creation once again. Then one day I realized something. The more I developed the disposition and the desire to look for God in the world, the more I became aware of being in relationship with him. The more often I paused to gaze at the people around me in town, the more often I became aware of the love that was in the world. There was more evidence of it than I had ever imagined. Of course, it had been there all along, but I had not taken the opportunity to see it. Solitude gave me that opportunity. It gave me the opportunity to climb out of the rushing torrent of daily life that I allowed, and even encouraged myself to swim in while I was in the social world, and to realize the peace and the pleasure that was available in the still waters of life. For me this was perhaps its most significant revelation.

## NOTE

1. Thomas Merton, *The Asian Journal of Thomas Merton*, eds. Naomi Burton, Patrick Hart, and James Laughtin (New York: New Directions,1975), 338.

*Chapter Ten*

# Commitment

One day, quietly and without fanfare I realized that I was seeing things differently. In the woods that surrounded me I found myself not just casually noticing, but participating in what I saw. I stopped and looked at things more deliberately and more carefully; I smelled them; I felt them; in some cases I even tasted them. In town at the post office, or the bank, or the grocery store I found myself deliberately attending to other people; I talked with them, not at them or to them. We became subjects relating with each other, not just objects reacting to each other.

Solitude created an environment in which contemplation of the world around me became involving. I was not constantly distracted by the strident sounds and bright lights of a society that illuminated people and goods that they pressed on me as they said over and over, "Look at me. See what I have. Look at me." In solitude it was easier to pause and look at what I wanted to look at, easier to attend to what I wanted to attend to, easier to become involved in what I wanted to be involved in, rather than to be drawn into a world that others wanted me to participate in, or buy into.

My life on the Beach had been much faster and more hectic than life in my solitary niche in the woods. But that wasn't what struck me as being most satisfying. What struck me the most was how consistently I saw the world in new and fresh ways that I had seldom noticed before. In the past I had experienced a number of momentary epiphanies, particularly over the last few years, but suddenly life became one epiphany after another that revealed God's daily participation in the simple, yet profound drama of life.

I realized that not all of the natural world had been sacrificed to commerce. There were still vast regions of it that were almost as pristine as the day they were created. I realized that not all people were angry, self serving and insensitive. Far from it, lots of people from all walks of life were able to shine flashes of love into the world. I saw person after person who it seemed to me might have radiated even more love if they could only have realized that they were capable of being a theophany for others, if they would only have risked a willingness to be transformed, if they had only believed that they could be God's love in the world.

June 14, 2003

When I see the world through the eyes of a detached observer rather than those of a participant, I see it filled with great globs of matter separated by space—a tree here, a car there, a person coming out of their house and in between the tree and the car and the person and the house is distance, nothing but space as if it were a vacuum, though of course there is air. But this way of thinking limits me to a pluralistic conception of reality. There is me, there is you, and there is my car and your house, etc. But instead of the world being made up of individual chunks of matter that are owned by lots of different people and that have space between them, it can be seen as an infinitely related, flowing field of energy. When I see the world this way, I see all things tied together by God in a great cosmic dance that has been pulsing and throbbing throughout all of eternity. Whether or not such a description of reality is a crude description of things as they are, or just a metaphor, I do not pretend to know, but it does seem to have something to do with seeing myself as being in union with God.

June 16, 2003

It's an escaped, cultivated plant living as a solitary soul in a sunny spot on the edge of the woods on the side of a dirt road in Alabama; it's a garden coreopsis. This morning I stood on the side of that road looking at that one escaped specimen; there was nothing but that one coreopsis. There was no one naming it. There was no one to own it. There were just complex energy fields and we were all related, we were one, we were all one with God.

June 17, 2003

It is still easy for my false self to grab hold of me, and claim me for itself, and tell me that all is well. But you God, are the one in whom I have faith. God as an energy field remains a metaphor. For me to believe that you are literally an energy field is like believing that you are a firefly in a bottle. It is so easy to want to capture you and make you mine. It is so easy to want to grasp you with my mind because then I don't have to give up my addiction to wanting to explain the unexplainable. You are the one in whom I have faith. Energy field is intriguing but I prefer to think of you as catching us when we fall.

June 27, 2003

I had an angiogram done at the local hospital today. It seems that I have significant blockage in a couple of places. They are going to try angioplasty and stents on Monday and if that doesn't work the fall back is bypass surgery. I feel O.K. about this and perhaps this will relieve some of the tiredness in my legs.

July 4, 2003

I was clearing the dishes from the table on Friday night following the angiogram, and I had a heart attack. Stents were put in Monday after a weekend of hospitalization. One of the blockages could not be taken care of, but I took the others in stride I guess. In any event I am still here. I still feel a bit fuzzy headed what with all the anesthesia, but in general I think I feel better. While I was in the hospital Olga brought in the last volume of Merton's journals and I was able to read some in spite of lots of sleep and the constant interruptions for various procedures. One quote from the *Astavakra Gita* caught my attention, but I was not able to maintain concentration for long enough to hold it for purposes of meditation. I look forward to going back to it when my head clears. I also look forward to getting back to a discipline of prayer and writing.

July 5, 2003

I tried to return to writing today but I think that I started too soon. I found it really difficult to hold ideas in my head long enough to use them in a sentence.

July 6, 2003

As I look back on the six days I spent in the hospital I wonder where God was. I don't remember spending a lot of time in meditation. I don't remember pausing before meals to offer thanks. I don't remember intentionally seeing the nurses and doctors and others as being Christ in the world. In short, I don't remember much, not even a lot of time with God. Was that because of the anesthesia and my inability to hold focus as I contemplated the world around me? Or, was that because my surroundings were so different, that they didn't call for the usual reactions? Does that mean that if I am reasonably comfortable, and if the habit and rituals of worship are broken, that God isn't there? That's a sobering thought.

July 11, 2003

Two weeks since my heart attack and I have not gotten back into the routine of things. There is no question that I thrive on routine. I feel most comfortable when I sense that I am a part of something bigger, even if that something is nothing more than a pattern of life I can fit into. I think that my need to be a part of the whole draws me to God. For me, God is the One I feel a part of without having to justify myself. I just am, but I would not be if I were not a part of the One. It's a sense of fit, a sense that there is a place for me. It's an awareness that it all makes sense even if the moment that I am experiencing seems meaningless at the time. I feel better when I remember that my individual efforts are a part of a pattern, a whole, a part of community.

July 12, 2003

I wonder if finding a relationship with God is nothing more than finding my place in the world. Maybe it's finding a place to rest, or a place to feel fulfilled, a place to feel safe or a place to just be. There are other places that can feel good, but these feelings come from satisfying the false self. These are the feeling that come from getting things, seeing that things get done, controlling others, satisfying sensual and power needs. For me these needs do not lead to a feeling of fit, or a sense of belonging. They lead to fulfillment of the false self.

July 14, 2003

This morning I went back to morning prayer before breakfast and complete solitude until noon. I remember now that when I was in the hospital I did pray, I prayed a lot. I remember those six lines from Merton's Journal entry of May 17, 1968. They kept running through my mind:

> When the mind is stirred and perceives things before it as objects of thought, it will find in itself something lacking. To find this 'something lacking' is already a beginning of wisdom. Ignorance seeks to make good the 'lacking' with better and more complete or more mysterious objects. The lack itself will be complete as void. Not to deny subject and object but to realize them as void.[1]

This is the feeling of being a part of something that is infinitely greater than the self.

July 15, 2003

The contemplative life is lived out each day waiting for the awareness of God's love. It is not an active search that ends in a discovery that once found can be described in detail to others, manufactured, packaged, marketed, and either sold or given to the world for its benefit. The process moves on many fronts because the human being is complex with many different needs that must be satisfied in order to sustain a healthy life. But the one constant in the lives of all of us who search is prayer, and by prayer I mean sensing and affirming God's presence.

I have learned that being one with God comes mostly through my willingness to let God claim a natural place in my life. This discovery was learned after a long period of time in which I realized that I could not become God's love in the world through self-determination. A shift in the locus of control from the false self to God's love would be required. It would only happen through the lifelong process of transformation.

I find it difficult enough to sustain the focus needed to live a contemplative life in a setting of solitude. But it was even more difficult to live a life with a contemplative focus in today's world with its constant barrage of competing demands. Yet, expressing love for others must ultimately take place in relationship with others. The contemplative must be sufficiently in touch with the world to allow the love that is shared with the world to be grounded in reality.

What I am learning is that for me a life composed of extended periods of solitude nurtures a healthier life, and that as a healthier person I am more disposed to give love away when the opportunity arises, than to protect it and hoard it for some future day.

July 16, 2003

Awareness comes in fits and starts even in solitude. A rush now, a long dry pause, and then another spark that catches and the flames burn again. I think that the past four months have been the most productive of my life in spiritual awareness, growth, and in gaining a sense of personal health and wholeness. I just seem to be more aware and open to change. And then there has also been filling in the empty spaces in my life that I have had for so long and never noticed.

In spite of my improved emotional health and feelings of wholeness, I need to face reality about my physical health. I am not really feeling that well. I feel tired and weak after almost any physical exertion. I think I need to get myself emotionally ready for by-pass surgery.

July 17, 2003

Yesterday was a low day for me physically and spiritually. Doubt kept poking its way in through the holes and made energy to fight despair difficult to find. The best thing that happened last night was when it was time to go to bed. When I awoke this morning some of that doubt was still there. I toyed with not facing today and going back to sleep, but I was afraid to do that, afraid that if I did I might not regain my sense of purpose, and so I got up. At morning meditation I was almost immediately washed over by the exciting awareness of what I had found here in solitude in the Alabama woods. I got up today and met the world eyeball to eyeball and the world blinked. I will not easily get lost again because I know where I came from and where I am going.

July 19, 2003

In the past I have said that I show love when I help another grow in life affirming ways. But there are other ways of relating to people that are also considered loving, such as taking delight in seeing others grow and in showing concern, empathy, compassion, trust, affection for others, being caring and showing respect unconditionally. It seems that all of these can be ways of expressing love when they help another grow in healthy ways.

July 24, 2003

The sun is now up. Beams of light stab through the trees and create a mosaic of greens. Birds moving through the woods, water dripping from the leaves—two heavy storms last night. The sound of a train coming in from the North West on the Norfolk and Southern line. I can hear forever. The cool air is fresh and clear after the storms. This is a day so filled with natural beauty I could sing. What an unbelievable day in east-central Alabama for the end of July. I am excited to be alive.

July 27, 2003

I don't know whether it is cloudy today or not. A fog hangs over the woods. The trees at the end of our lane that leads to the road to town are a gray-green mass, hardly distinguishable as individuals.

August 6, 2003

I took Olga out to a flower and gift shop today to do what she likes to do. She was like a chocoholic in a candy store; couldn't keep her hands off of pretty things. She delights in pretty things, got a red bowl and four small foliage plants for the living room. She is constantly thinking about rearranging the house. At the gift shop this afternoon I got impatient and agitated as I waited. All I wanted to do was get out of the store. But Olga just stood there looking and handling things seemingly unable to make a decision. My impatience began to seep out, and I became conscious of a growing anger. What started out to be a loving moment ended by being anything but. My false self won that round. My true self never even had a chance. Only later, while in meditation, was I able to see the incident for what it was. Transformation is a life-long process.

August 12, 2003

Lord, I think that I need some of your help with health issues and my life in general. This solitary life of mine needs some tinkering. I am not exactly satisfied with the way it has been going.

August 13, 2003

I said yesterday that I thought that my solitary life needed some tinkering and I still feel that way. I just want to be careful not to pull out the good stuff with the weeds. In working with my journals I have become very much aware of how much my contact with the Benedictine community at Three Rivers, Michigan influenced my life in the 1980's. But that influence was not always appropriate for the life I was trying to live. As a secular contemplative I lived a life that was constantly available and open to violation from the demands of the world. In the midst of all of this, I tried to carve out enough solitude for contemplation. The monk is different not so much because he does different things, but because he is a different person who lives in a different world. I think that I missed this distinction back in the eighties and it led to my doing some pretty silly things in an attempt to establish a spiritual discipline. I am still not a Benedictine monk and never will be. I need to sort this out again before I start tinkering with my solitary life. I don't want to start pruning and weeding the wrong plants and start planting the wrong things, a good topic for meditation.

August 18, 2003

Yesterday morning I slipped. My feet went out from under me and I fell into the ditch alongside of the road while I was trying to get closer to an interesting rock I wanted to see. At the time, and for several hours afterwards, I thought that I had hurt myself very badly, but apparently it was not as serious as I thought. Right now I am very thankful that it wasn't worse.

August 20, 2003

On Monday morning I felt better about my fall on Sunday, but today I am not so optimistic. My thinking is cloudy and slow and I still have a lot of pain in my back. Work at my desk this morning was very unproductive. I feel that something has happened that is going to take a long time to heal.

September 8, 2003

Always the periods of lukewarm faith, the apathy, a tendency to forget the direction of the path I am following and the Eden in which I live. And always the return to remembering the fidelity that God has shown, raising me up when I have fallen, bringing me to new faith, new insights. Always there when I turn to him.

September 15, 2003

I think I am beginning to notice some improvement in the back pain. I am now into my fourth week since the fall. Very slow progress. The morning still begins in fits and starts, and I don't get to work at my desk until 9:00 or 9:30, and even then the Darvaset and muscle relaxant that I am still taking dull the edge of my concentration. But I am feeling better, and I hope I have turned the corner.

September 17, 2003

Still not on the schedule that I was on back in April. It is as if someone has opened the drain in the room where all of my energy is stored and it keeps flowing out. Took a walk with Olga today. When I got back, I sat down to meditate on *Little Gidding* and I fell asleep several times. Later I worked for a while with Psalm 72. This is a royal psalm which celebrates a king of the Davidic Dynasty, clearly a theme that was central to the people of Israel. It was a part of their history and their culture written hundreds of years before the Christian era, and it really puts me off when I read a commentary that is laced with historical reconstructionism that co-opts and corrupts the original intent. It's a Psalm of the people of Israel, and their king, not a Psalm about Christ the King.

September 18, 2003

Autumn is the best time along the road for spider webs and ornamental grasses that have gone to seed. Weeds are so delicate yet so strong, so persistent, so well built for the days of the Alabama fall. Back lighted or front lighted they are there when I walk in the early morning as dew transforms them into fleeting, exquisite works of art. I say I am exercising my cardiovascular system when I walk, but in truth I am exercising my sensitivity to an ever-changing world just as much as my heart.

September 21, 2003

We planned to go to Church today but we overslept. Well, there's always next Sunday. I have not outgrown Church. For me it is still a tradition, a community, an institution that serves needs that I have carefully tucked away for a later time.

I could say that the Church is too symbolic for me to allow it to die in my life, but it needs to be more than a symbol for something and needs to be something more than a social or religious event. It needs to be a spiritual event.

September 23, 2003

I have finished listening to Psalm 81 sung by the Norwich Cathedral Choir while I followed along with a commentary. I was deeply moved by how much the Israelites gave up when they turned their backs on God, and yet how ready God remained to "feed them with the finest wheat" if they would only turn again to him.

September 26, 2003

A full and rich day—breakfast, walk, work at my desk, lunch and nap, drying weeds gathered for Olga from along the road, taking Olga to the doctor's for a checkup. All of this was mixed with Psalms and prayers before breakfast and again in the afternoon, and with meditation before supper. The meditation came seemingly out of nowhere.

September 28, 2003

Well, it is Sunday morning and it looks as if we will finally get to church this morning. Between my heart attack and my fall, I thought we would never get there. Another classic early autumn day. Not a cloud in the sky, and temperatures in the low sixties when I walked Buster before breakfast.

We did get to church, and any concerns that I might have had about finding a compatible Episcopal church near us have vanished. Olga and I agreed that we will have our letter transferred. I think we have found a church home.

September 29, 2003

Another clear, bright, chilly morning. Temperature down to 46°. I awoke without the alarm at 6:00, got up and did morning office before Olga and Buster got up. It feels good to be doing this.

September 30, 2003

Even though I have been living a life with a good deal of solitude I have been involved in three ventures in the past couple of weeks that have brought me into limited contact with the social world. Olga wanted to sign up for a class on Monday afternoons this fall given by the Lifetime Learning Program at the local university; I have decided to sign up as a volunteer for the Community Market, a part of the East Alabama Food Bank; we have decided to join the church here. These two steps plus the decision to join the church here should meet Olga's need to reach out into society and my limited need for enough social contact to see Christ in the world.

October 3, 2003

Another classic fall day in Alabama. I'm back to being productive in the morning. Each day I am feeling a little stronger. Took more food to the distribution center for the food bank today and turned in my application to volunteer. Also phoned our previous church in Florida and had our letter transferred up here. If I am to continue with any fidelity to my commitment of solitude that I made when we moved here, I must watch my tendency to over-commitment that I demonstrated in Florida. I came here to seek solitude and to redefine my life. So far I have been faithful, but I know how easily I say yes to society. So far I have never felt so fulfilled and so whole. I have never been so aware of an evolving spirituality that seems so right.

October 9, 2003

Very satisfying contemplative prayer time this afternoon. Meditated on the effects of the decisions that could lead to greater social involvement. My desire was to just be with God and find out what was on his mind, thus a mixture of listening and participating but not in the sense of bringing an agenda for him to deal with. I was surprised to find that among the issues that came up, the one that we spent the most time on had to do with getting a living will and dealing with death. Very little time was spent on my weakness for over-involvement. I feel free and satisfied, and I sense that something is going on that I am not fully aware of. Whatever it is, I am convinced that all shall be well.

October 17, 2003

This week has flown by, work at the desk has been productive and interestingly, not all straight line. Prayer time has been rich. I am using the *Four Quartets* again as a starting point for meditation in the afternoon and it has been very helpful.

Two health care appointments were canceled and rescheduled, Olga's dentist and my cardiologist. They will come up again soon, but for today I have two good solid blocks of time for solitude that I hadn't expected. It was a gift. Never in my memory have I had so many good days in a row with the persistent feeling that I am in the right place at the right time, doing the right thing. Olga is happier and more content than I have known her to be in years.

Took Buster to the veterinarian today. Dr. H. thinks that he may have lymphoma. At this point he is not showing serious signs of decline but they can be expected. We have had a wonderful life together, and I want to live each remaining day with him to the fullest. He is not in pain and I want to be with him as long as I can. It may be several months or a year. I will miss him dearly when the time comes.

October 28, 2003

Silence was starting to be violated in the mornings with talk that could be kept till later. Olga and I discussed this and agreed that we had let that drift a bit. For the last few days things have returned to something more like the original plan.

I just looked out of the window on a spectacular scene. All that was left of the setting sun was illuminating the tops of the trees on the ridge of the hill to the east. The leaves and branches were painted in scarlet and gold while the lower branches and trunk, now in the shadows, had turned a brown-gray and black. I never saw such a sight before. Who else has painted trees that look like that?

I took Buster to the vet again today. No real change in his swollen lymph glands, and I think Dr. H. is more and more convinced that it is lymphoma. Buster definitely is slowing down and has even started to break training occasionally. Olga and I both say we are ready for what will come if it is Lymphoma. At least we say we are. I went out into the woods yesterday to look for a place to bury his ashes when the time comes. Found a perfect spot that looks down on the valley and the stream below.

October 31, 2003

I flunked a follow-up stress test that my cardiologist had scheduled, and clearly he is interested in getting to the bottom of this. So, I have another angiogram scheduled for this Friday. Something further needs to be done before I have another heart attack.

November 10, 2003

Went into the hospital last Friday for an angiogram and came out with a third stent. I am O.K. with this, assuming that it works. Frankly, I was already for bypass surgery and would have said yes without hesitation, but the stent is a whole lot less fuss and muss and has a shorter recuperation time. I am satisfied, actually pleased. No trouble forgetting the thanksgiving this time. I am blessed and I know it.

November 12, 2003

Meditated today on what it is that I stand in awe of; I think I know but I don't want to take it for granted. If I can answer that question I will have clues that tell me where to look to find what it is that I really worship, and perhaps find out what my ultimate concern really is. What is it that I stand in awe of?

November 19, 2003

I was silenced and moved when I contemplated the beauty and complexity of a bird's foot violet last spring. I am thrilled by a thunderstorm. I am excited by the surf, or by rushing water, or the wind. I am intrigued by the process of birth in both the animal and plant kingdom. But, what do I stand in awe of?

November 25, 2003

Today I was listening to a number of the Psalms of Assent. They are simple straight forward, and honest. These people talked about their God with such fervor that I can hardly doubt their deep conviction and trust. The people who wrote these poems stood in awe of their God. For me it's God's creation and seeing his love at work in the world; that's awesome.

December 4, 2003

Buster continues to fail. His breathing is quite rapid and he eats very little. Yet, there is something to celebrate. Though he did not eat breakfast today, he did eat about half of his supper. He slept quietly last night. He shadowed me most of the morning. When he needs to go out he no longer barks, he sort of squeaks through his nose. This is something. He still desires to communicate. I don't know words to express how I feel right now other than love mixed with sadness. I will miss him a whole lot. We have had a friendship that is only known by those who experience quiet love, the love of just being with each other. This is a love that goes beyond facilitating the growth of another. It is one thing to say, "More than anything I want you to grow and become what God has created you to be," and its something else to say, "More than anything I want you to live. You don't have to be who you were several years or even several months ago, I just want to be with you as you are right now."

December 18, 2003
Buster died last night. It was a very peaceful death and I was with him when the spark went out. He raised his head, looked at me, and then he died. His body died and it will be cremated and the ashes buried here in the woods around us. As for his spirit of love, it lives in his dynamic energy released into the universe. This is the perpetual process, the cosmic dance. Sadness mixed with joy, in an infinite process. But I miss him.

Buster and I had been together for over twelve years. At times, as with anyone else, he was a bother and a chore like when our whole house was infested with fleas, and it took several months, and I forget how many pesticide bombs, to get the situation under control. There were three or four times that he ate things that were life threatening and had to be rushed to the vet to have his stomach pumped. There was the time when he ran into the cornfield next to our house and got lost. I found him wet and shivering forlornly by a stream about a mile away. What a reunion we had. In his final days he slowly lost control of his bowels and bladder. He went from being a bright, inquisitive, energetic puppy to being an incontinent old man. All through this time he constantly reminded me how much he loved me and that his love for me was not conditional on my being a perfect friend.

Then one day it occurred to me that Buster was as much of an incarnation of God's love as anyone else I knew. It dawned on me that all of my talk about attributes such as compassion, human decency and facilitating the growth of others didn't fully define love. These attributes had helped me to satisfy my need to conceptualize and define love, and to conceptualize the incarnate Christ as being a manifestation of God's love, but there was something about my love for Buster that was not cognitive. I loved Buster, and Buster loved me and there was nothing about our love that could ever have been enhanced by an intellectual understanding. I realized how few people I really have loved and how far humanity has to go before it will become an overwhelming expression of God's love in the world.

For the moment all thought of defining or conceptualizing God, or love, or the spiritual self disappeared from me. To know God, I had to experience love, and my spiritual self had to become love. I realized that my mind could not understand the complexity of God, or God's love, or the self, but I could be a part of the experience. I realized that I could not fathom love; it, like God, was ineffable.

December 24, 2003

It is Christmas Eve. The tree is trimmed, dinner is made and ready to be put into the oven. Soon Kate, Graham, Pam, Thomas and Austin will be arriving for dinner and gift exchange. For me, and for a lot of people, this is still the celebration of God coming into the world. How long will that myth continue to be a part of our active heritage I wonder?

Yes, the story of God coming into the world, born to humble parents, is a favorite story for many. But certainly, God has been in the world for a lot longer than two thousand years, at least the God that I feel so close to has been. But, I guess it's a good thing to stop at least once a year and remember the Nativity story.

I am really trying to get into the spirit of it, but I am not doing very well. Yesterday I was particularly aware of Buster's spirit as it interacted with countless other spirits that dance in these woods that have already become a sacred place for me.

December 25, 2003

Sadness burns within me, a sadness that goes nowhere. I don't understand it. It hangs like a dark cloud. I really miss Buster. God does not want me to deny my sadness. He does not expect me to be joyful today. He wants me to grieve, to come to him in prayer and tell him that in spite of the fact that it is Christmas I am sad, and a bit angry that he had to go so soon, and I miss him.

January 1, 2004

Despite my health problems and Buster's death 2003 was a good year. Solitude has become a reality. I have never had as much solitude as this for such a sustained time. Ten months have gone by as if they had never been. I have taken to solitude as if I were born to it. I think I was. The days, one after another, have been filled with little surprises to delight in, surprises that make no demands and that require no particular response, surprises that are just to be noticed and enjoyed. I feel at last that I have become who I was created to be. My take on the culture that I grew up in and still remember well is that few people are encouraged to be who they were created to be. They are not encouraged to find satisfaction in being their true self. The result has been a lot of unnecessary anxiety, despair and frustration. It seems that too frequently we want to make people into who they were never cut out to be, and then reward them for not being themselves. It seems that the prize comes, or so we are told, by riding on the main line of social recognition and success rather than taking the pathways and byways that were created for us to walk on.

January 7, 2004

Christmas lights are down and Epiphany is here. It's the season to celebrate bringing the Light into the world. For me the important thing to remember is that we didn't put all the lights out when we packed them away for another year, the Light is still here for those who can see it in the world.

January 20, 2004

This afternoon I worked with a good cross section of people of the community stocking the shelves at the Community Market. I got the feeling we were all there for one reason, to be a part of a volunteer process that feeds the hungry. There was minimal social interaction among us. We were there to get cans, boxes and bottles of food on the empty shelves for tomorrow morning when the needy will return. For me it was not a social time. It was feeding the hungry.

For some time I had been unable to accept graciously the conflict I sometimes felt between my idealized conception of the purposes of social institutions, and what I saw as being a corruption of those purposes by excessive attention to the institution's image, or preservation of the institutional status quo. This had happened to me with the Church. For some time, I had been too quick to see the maintenance of the Church and its attention to image as compromising its institutional purpose. I had confused what I considered a weaknesses of individuals within the Church with a weakness of the church as an institution. I see now that in many ways I had been too quick to judge, and too slow to tolerate human differences, human inconsistency and human failing.

Perhaps the reason for this insight lay in the fact that I had previously been deeply involved in the activities of the Church in almost all of the parishes that I had previously attended, and this close involvement with people coupled with a frenzy of activities had often led to an unhealthy familiarity. There was more than I realized in the old saying that familiarity breeds contempt rather than a realistic acceptance of human imperfection, or honest differences in the way others see the world. Now I was seeing the Church through the eyes of a marginal person standing on the edge looking at it, and it looked different, and I found myself using my journal as a confessional.

January 30, 2004

When I consider all of the outreach that our church is engaged in and their very open position about service to the needy, I realize that I have been unfairly hard on the Church in the past. Here is a church that believes that its parishioners have a responsibility to serve the needy. Here is a church that tells the story of our heritage in the context of a stirring liturgy. I don't know how much they celebrate the myth, but I feel comfortable when I attend. They seem to celebrate the sacraments in a context of community, and even though I stand on the edge of that community I feel comfortable. How much they would support my contemplative position, my personal relationship with God and my desire for solitude I don't know. I haven't tested that, and I feel no need to do so.

My detente with the Church was a further reminder that I had neither rejected nor left society. I had just moved to its margin. Social institutions of a culture, as imperfect as they may be, will always remain essential for cultural stability. They serve very important functions for those who daily live their lives in the active world. Most of the intentional ministry of the Church, since it's beginning, has been directed to the people of God as community, and this is appropriate from their perspective. My detente was based on a relationship in which I could find personal meaning in the liturgical, sacramental, and pastoral functions of the Church and still identify with the Church as a community without personal involvement in its organizational and social functions. I am aware that this is a theologically controversial position to take, and I must always be alert to the danger of drifting into a position in which God becomes my personal deity.

Suddenly I found myself marginally involved with three social institutions: education in the form of the Lifelong Learning Program at the nearby university, social service at the food bank, and religion as an institution that daily reminds people of the work of God in our everyday lives and in our cultural heritage. But in all three cases my involvement would be different than it had been in the past, and for the present that would be O.K. with me, if it was O.K. with them.

February 12, 2004

My journal, in part, is a record of the lamentations that I bring to God, the hope and thanksgiving that I feel, the praise that spontaneously flows from me, and the trust and faith that, in the long run, all shall be well.

As I read over recent entries, I become aware that the past month has been one of little conflict, and a period of peace. Now that I have gotten back on my feet from the last stent placement procedure, and I am feeling more like myself, I have returned to volunteering with the Community Market one afternoon a week. Olga and I seem almost totally at peace with each other, I have accepted Buster's death with a calmness that surprises even me. On balance, this has been a very good year.

February 14, 2004

Another in a series of cloudy, rainy days, a harbinger of spring. Yesterday the spring peepers started their chorus in the swamp down by the creek. The ground is saturated with water in preparation for the release of the spring of life that is wound tight and waiting for the signal to start.

February 18, 2004

The universal dance of spring has begun on planet Earth in East Central Alabama. The peepers are at it strong now. The yellow catkins of the aldars are blowing in the breeze. Their tiny swollen red stigma bask in the warm sun. The flowers of the quince have started to appear. Spring is dancing shyly with God. In just a few weeks there will be a botanical orgy as the rhythm of the universe strains to break its winter bonds.

Ahead of Olga and me was the matter of taking stock of what had happened during the year and making a decision about whether we would return to a central place in the social world we left, or remain on the edge in pursuit of a life of solitude. This was part of the agreement that Olga and I had made a year earlier when we came here, and this needed to be a joint decision. We needed to assess what worked and what didn't. We had already made some adjustments to accommodate to Olga's style and preferences and some to honor mine. Others could easily be introduced if we wanted to do so. All of this lay before us in the days and weeks ahead.

February 27, 2004

We have been here for a year. There is no place I would rather be. There is nothing I would rather be doing. I have found peace under the best conditions of solitude that I could expect.

All of this has been worked out in the context of an agreement with Olga, which I will continue to keep. I will continue to show a caring sensitivity to the family, people I meet in town, at stores, church, the doctor's office, and the clients and volunteers at the Community Market. I will continue to pay my taxes and vote. But, I will not be drawn back into the most frantic, materialistic, insensitive, ego enhancing culture that the world may have ever known.

I was a part of that culture for most of my life and for most of that time I thought that was all there was. Over the years I have met some very fine, loving, caring, creative people and I am fortunate to have counted them as friends, and neighbors and associates. They have given me hope. But most of my time was spent in hustling to make it in a frantic world. It's nice to know that there is something more in this amazing creation. I was beginning to wonder if I had been put on the wrong planet or at the wrong time. Now I know that this really is the right planet and the right time, and the scary part of it is that I almost missed it. Of course it's always been here. I was just looking in the wrong places and trying to convince myself that I was doing the right thing.

March 13, 2004

There's no doubt about it, the world has run its big circle around the sun. It's spring again. The flowering pear is out all over, and the redbud came out today in the mixed hardwood and pine woods surrounding us. The day before yesterday I saw sparkleberry along the road down by the creek.

March 16, 2004

A week without rain and the violets, Indian strawberry and blackberry leaves along the edge of the road are all covered with the dust raised by the few cars that pass. Now that hunting season is over, the deer are returning from the deep woods. Their tracks are all over again. No sign of the wild turkeys yet.

March 17, 2004

Another day volunteering at the Community Market. Week after week the food keeps pouring through the agency to feed hungry people. I am told that there are over 23,000 people living in poverty in this county.

The shelves that I stocked last week were empty today and ready for restocking. I am impressed with the variety of nutritious food that they get: meats, dairy products, fruit juice, cereals, pasta, canned vegetables, and produce in season. Over three hundred and seventy tons of food was distributed to people in the county last year. The volunteers are a dedicated bunch. Without them it would never work, without them hunger would be a lot worse.

It rained for about two hours this morning starting around daybreak, but we need more. Today the hog plumb was in bloom again. I remember it from last year. Between the volunteers and the clients at the food bank, and the dance of spring, there is no need to ask, "Where is God in all of this?"

March 20, 2004

After a year, it is becoming clearer each day that solitude is not a place; it is a state of mind. Solitude is not the only place where God lives, but it allows me to see him in ways that I missed so often in the middle of society. Solitude is not transformation, but it has made contemplation possible for me in ways that I never thought possible, and it is contemplation that continues to nourish my transformation. Solitude has nurtured freedom, caring and creativity in ways that I never expected. Solitude is not in short supply, as some may think who consider it to be a place. It is infinitely available to those who want it.

March 22, 2004

It has been a little over a year since we unpacked the boxes, moved furniture around one more time and declared ourselves to be moved in. Yesterday, Olga and I had a brief discussion that will ultimately lead to a decision about whether we will continue as we have for the past year, whether we will make some major adjustments to the way of life we have been living, or if we will declare our period of solitude to be ended. Olga's first year has been quite different from mine. First of all, mine was a year of self inflicted, partial solitude interrupted occasionally during the day by contacts with Olga, infrequent contacts with Pam and Graham, Thomas and Austin, and self initiated contacts with merchants in the stores and with health care people. Olga's year of solitude was initiated by me, agreed to by her, and lived out as an agreement, but it was nothing that she would have chosen for herself. I have not been as available to her for companionship as I might have been, or as she would have liked at times. She has had to be alone for hours on end, more than at any previous time in her life. Her lifeline to society has become Pam who takes her into town regularly on Fridays to shop and have lunch. The telephone is used to maintain contact with her family and people she had known on the Beach and in Ohio. The daily newspaper and mail order catalogs have largely become her substitute for stores in which to shop for things. All in all she has done amazingly well in adapting to a life that was not of her choosing.

I have already shed some of the self-inflicted limitations created by a schedule and a discipline that were initiated to protect my solitude from intrusion, but were really not necessary. For example it just didn't make sense any more to set an alarm to get up at 5:30 each morning to make time for contemplative prayer when I have all day for contemplation if I want it, and usually awaken by myself around 6:00 anyway. Most of the changes I have made in my life over the year have been influenced by learning that solitude is a state of mind that is nurtured and supported by a self directed life, lived out in a particular place and guided by a set of routines that give it direction and purpose. It is not a lonely place set off from the world. It is much more available than I ever imagined when I lived in society.

Soon Olga and I will have more conversations about what we want to do next year.

I expected that subsequent conversations would identify a number of personal needs that were being thwarted by our solitary life, but to my surprise and delight that did not happen. It took a year for Olga and for me to fully realize that our life on the edge of society was a lot more than tolerable. It was actually stimulating, growthful and enjoyable. Our lives slowed down, became less hectic. Time became a moment to savor both new and old things that were now done in a much more deliberate and usually enjoyable way. Time became a space defined by a moment in which to live. Time largely ceased to be a goad used by society to keep the machinery going. The moment became the space in which to do something that the true self needed to have done. The whole idea of "getting something done on time" which had previously meant a time set by someone else, vanished. It just ceased to be something that guided our life. Time ceased to be something to fill or spend. The future and the past became less demanding and less relevant.

Thoreau found that time was the stream he went a-fishing in. We rediscovered what he meant by that. We found that we liked the freedom that came with being self directed and responsible for our own lives. We cherished living in a world that largely didn't know that we existed. It was very different from living in a world that constantly told us what it wanted us to think and do, and what time to start and when to stop so that we would fit into its time.

After a year of solitude we decided to continue what we were doing, and to continue being who we were for as long as we were able. We resolved to be increasingly attentive to each other and our family and the few people that we might meet in town. And, we didn't feel the least bit guilty or disappointed about leaving the life that we had lived in the past. We knew we were being who we had been created to be. Things would change and so would we, but for now we were where we should be, doing what we should be doing. I no longer needed to define union with God, love, the true self or solitude. I was living with them daily.

## NOTE

1. Thomas Merton, *The Other Side of the Mountain: The End of the Journey*, ed. Patrick Hart (San Francisco: Harper San Francisco, 1998), 104–105.

# Epilogue

It was four years ago that Olga and I left the busy highways of society and struck out on our own down a solitary road that winds its way through woods where others seldom travel. We find that we enjoy the opportunity to be free from the societal intrusions of a materialistic culture that for years we so uncritically accepted as being commonplace. We enjoy this place of solitude that has become the destination of a quest for a compatible relationship with God and society. Having said that, I am aware that I could easily be misunderstood, and I want to avoid that if at all possible. I have not advocated that each of us should define our own private God in a way that separates us from others, but rather that we should seek a relationship with God and with humanity that is consistent with our true self. We are all part of the ongoing human experience of becoming who we were created to be. And yet we are all linked to each other by a common creation. We are a community—local, national and global—and being a member of that community brings with it a responsibility to all who are a part of it. I have never tried to escape that reality. Before me has always been the question "Can I live in solitude, in a congruent relationship with God, and at the same time honor my responsibility to love my neighbor?" Until I faced that question, understood what it meant, and answered it in the affirmative I would always have had doubts. But when it was finally answered, all that was left was to do it.

It is here in solitude that what had been happening to me for twenty years has found new meaning. Up to this time, I lived in a fragmented world of partial meaning that never quite made sense. The pieces never quite fit. But here they have formed a believable composite. Solitude has made spontaneous contemplation possible for me in unexpected ways that I never knew before. Solitude has made it possible for me to slow down and notice the world around me including the explosive beauty of creation as well as the hope, pain, desperation and love that can be radiated by people around me. My conception of contemplative prayer changed slowly over most of the years of my spiritual journey, but it changed dramatically when I moved to solitude. It became less and less something to be scheduled and increasingly it became a spontaneous part of living each day. Moments of the unity of God, love and the self have become an increasingly frequent experiential reality. As this has happened, the possibility of humanity evolving into God's love has become truly believable.

Julian of Norwich had it right a long time ago when she said, ". . . all shall be well and all shall be well, and all manner of things shall be well."[1] It took solitude for me to realize what she meant by this amazing statement of hope and faith.

## NOTE

1. Julian of Norwich, *A Lesson of Love: The Revelations of Julian of Norwich*, ed. and trans. John-Julian (New York: Walker and Company, 1988), 61.

# Sources Referenced

*Anglican Religious Communities Year Book 2002–2003*. Harrisburg, PA: Morehouse Publishing, 2002.

Brother Lawrence. *The Practice of the Presence of God*. White Plains, NY: Peter Pauper Press, 1963.

Buber, Martin. *The Eclipse of God*. New York: Harper, 1957.

Burns, David. *Feeling Good: The New Mood Therapy*. New York: HarperCollins, 1980.

Campbell, Joseph. *The Power of Myth*. With Bill Moyers. New York: Anchor Books, 1991.

Catherine of Siena. *The Dialogue*. Translated by Susan Noffke. New York: Paulist Press, 1980.

*The Cloud of Unknowing*. Edited by William Johnson. Garden City, NJ: Image Books, 1973.

de Chardin, Teilhard. *Christianity and Evolution*. Translated by Rene Hague. New York: Harper and Row, 1971.

———. *The Divine Milieu*. New York: Harper and Row, 1960.

———. *The Phenomenon of Man*. New York: Harper and Row, 1959.

de Mello, Anthony. *Sadhana A Way to God*. Garden City, NJ: Image Books, 1984.

Devers, Dorothy. *Christian Growth Through Faithful Friendship*. Cincinnati, OH: Forward Movement Publications, 1980.

Edwards, Tilden. *Living in the Presence*. San Francisco: Harper and Row, 1987.

———. *Living Simply Through the Day*. New York: Paulist Press, 1977.

Fromm, Erich. *The Art of Loving*. New York: Harper and Row, 1956.

Gallagher, Blanche. *Meditations With Teilhard de Chardin*. Santa Fe, NM: Bear and Company, 1988.

Glidden, Aelred. "Guessing At the Future." *Abbey Letter*, no. 178 (Summer, 1994).

Hall, Thelma. *Too Deep for Words: Rediscovering Lectio Divina*. New York: Paulist Press, 1988.

Hanh, Thich Nhat. *Living Buddha, Living Christ*. New York: Riverhead Books, 1995.

Hawkins, Peter. *The Language of Grace*. Cambridge, MA: Cowley Publications, 1983.
Higgins, John J. *Thomas Merton on Prayer*. Garden City, NJ: Image Books, 1975.
Huelsman, Richard J. *Intimacy With Jesus*. New York: Paulist Press, 1982.
*John of the Cross, Selected Writings*. Edited by Kieran Kavanaugh. New York: Paulist Press, 1987.
Julian of Norwich. *A Lesson of Love: The Revelations of Julian of Norwich*. Edited and translated by John-Julian. New York: Walker and Company, 1988.
Keating, Thomas. *Open Heart, Open Mind*. Amity, NY: Amity Press, 1986.
Kelly, Thomas. *A Testament of Devotion*. San Francisco: Harper and Brothers, 1969.
L'Engle, Madeline. *A Swiftly Tilting Planet*. New York: Farrar Straus and Giroux, 1978.
———. *The Irrational Season*. New York: The Seabury Press, 1979.
Lindbergh, Anne Morrow. *Gift From the Sea*. New York: Pantheon Books, 1955.
May, Gerald. *The Dark Night of the Soul*. New York: Harper and Row, 2004.
———. *Will and Spirit*. New York: Harper and Row, 1982.
McDermott, Mary Shideler. *In Search of the Spirit: A Primer*. New York: Ballantine Books, 1985.
McGann, Diarmuid. *Journing With Transcendence*. New York: Paulist Press, 1988.
Merton, Thomas. *The Asian Journal of Thomas Merton*. Edited by Naomi Burton, Patrick Hart, and James Laughlin. New York: New Directions, 1975.
———. *Bread in the Wilderness*. Collegeville, MN.: The Liturgical Press, 1986.
———. *Contemplative Prayer*. Garden City, NY: Image Books, 1971.
———. *Disputed Questions*. New York: Harcourt Brace Jovanovich, 1960.
———. *New Seeds of Contemplation*. New York: New Directions, 1961.
———. *The Other Side of the Mountain: The End of the Journey*. Edited by Patrick Hart. San Francisco: Harper, 1995.
———. *Seasons of Celebration*. New York: Farrar, Straus, Giroux, 1965.
———. *The Seven Story Mountain*. New York: Harcourt, Brace Jovanovich, 1948.
———. *The Silent Life*. New York: Farrar, Straus and Giroux, 1957.
———. *Turning Toward the World: The Pivotal Years*. Edited by Victor Kramer. Francisco: HarperCollins, 1997.
———. *Zen and the Birds of Appetite*. New York: New Directions, 1968.
Murdoch, Iris. *The Bell*. New York: Viking Press, 1958.
Nouwen, Henri. *Behold the Beauty of the Lord*. Notre Dame, IN: Ave Maria Press, 1987.
———. *The Genesee Diary*. Garden City, NJ: Image Books, 1981.
O'Connor, Flannary. *The Complete Stories*. New York: Farrar, Straus and Giroux, 1971.
Pennington, Basil. *Centering Prayer*. Garden City, NJ: Image Books, 1982.
Percy, Walker. *The Second Coming*. New York: Picador, 1980.
Progoff, Ira. *At a Journal Workshop*. New York: Dialogue House, 1975
Sanford, John. *The Kingdom Within*. San Francisco: Harper and Row, 1970.
Shaw, Thomas. "Asking The Question." in *Ways to Pray*. Cambridge, MA: Cowley Publications, 1984.

Sinetar, Marsha. *Ordinary People as Monks and Mystics*. New York: Paulist Press, 1986.
Smith, Martin, L. *The Word Is Very Near You*. Cambridge, MA: Cowley Publications, 1989.
Spong, John Shelby. *Why Christianity Must Change or Die*. San Francisco: Harper Collins Publishers, 1998.
Thoreau, Henry David. *Walden*. New York: Dodd, Mead and Co., 1946.
Tillich, Paul. *The Dynamics of Faith*. New York: Harper and Row, 1975.
Underhill, Evelyn. *Mysticism*. New York: New American Library, 1955.
*The Way of the Pilgrim*. Translated by R. M. French. San Francisco: Harper and Row, 1956.
Wuellner, Flora Slosson. *Prayer and Our Bodies*. Nashville, TN: The Upper Room, 1987.